The Crisis
of the
Working
Mother

Resolving the Conflict Between
Family and Work

by
BARBARA J. BERG

SUMMIT BOOKS
New York

This is a work of nonfiction. Interviews and questionnaires were among the sources used in writing this book. Although the comments volunteered by the participants have not been altered, in some instances the names, places and other details concerning the identity of these participants have been changed.

Permission granted: Free to Be Foundation;
"Housework" by Sheldon Harnick

Published by SUMMIT BOOKS
A Division of Simon & Schuster, Inc.
Simon & Schuster Building
1230 Avenue of the Americas
New York, New York 10020
SUMMIT BOOKS and colophon are trademarks of
Simon & Schuster, Inc.
Designed by Irving Perkins Associates
Manufactured in the United States of America
1 2 3 4 5 6 7 8 9 10

ISBN 0-671-49956-4

Acknowledgments

I AM INDEBTED to a great many people whose interest and encouragement made this book possible. To all the women who answered my questionnaires and to those who agreed to be interviewed my gratitude is immeasurable. Not only did these working mothers make time in their already overloaded schedules, they willingly shared their deepest feelings with me. Their stories were sometimes humorous, sometimes sad, but always affecting, and this book is theirs as much as mine.

I also want to thank Dr. Edward Speedling, of the Department of Community Medicine at Mount Sinai Hospital, for his invaluable help in designing the questionnaire; and Wendy Reid Crisp, editor of *Savvy*, Elizabeth Crow, editor of *Parents* and Donald Hipschman, publisher of *Homemaker*, for their willingness to help me distribute it.

The expertise and experience of many social scientists whom I interviewed enriched my study. They broadened my understanding of a variety of topics and urged me to explore new areas of inquiry.

Ileene Smith of Summit Books did a superb job of editing my manuscript; the book was greatly enhanced by her efforts. My agent, Anne Borchardt, is an on-going source of information, advice, and support. Her early enthusiasm for a book about working mothers launched this project.

Finally, I want to thank my family who sustained and inspired me through every phase of this work.

B.J.B.
New York City
November 1985

For
Laura, Alison, and Andrew

Contents

Prologue

I MADE A halfhearted attempt to clean some day-old jelly off my son's high chair and glanced up at the clock. Ten-fifteen. Yemi, my baby-sitter, was fifteen minutes late, I still wasn't dressed, and in exactly forty-five minutes I was supposed to be at a downtown meeting with an editor of a well-known magazine to discuss the proposals for some articles I'd submitted to her weeks before. Getting this interview was no easy task, and now to think that I might be late for it filled me with anxiety.

Lifting my son onto my lap, I punched out the telephone numbers of Yemi's apartment. While I held the receiver to my ear, ten-month-old Andrew struggled free of my grip and drunkenly toddled to the television set, where his sister Alison, less than one year his senior, was engrossed in the show "Mister Rogers' Neighborhood."

A voice thick and heavy with sleep, which I recognized as belonging to Yemi's roommate, answered the insistent ringing. At exactly that moment Andrew proudly turned up the volume of the television to a deafening pitch.

"Is Yemi there?" I asked, my fingers crossed in an instinctive ritual of hope.

"What? I can't hear you," came back the drowsy reply.

"This is Barbara. Is Yemi there?"

"Wait a minute, I'll check."

I could almost see Yemi's roommate surveying the tumble of sheets, blankets, books and backpacks that was their crowded student apartment for signs of life.

"Nope. She's gone."

"Any idea how long ago she left?" I asked.

"Nope, sorry."

I said my good-byes quickly and hastened to save our graceful dieffenbachia plant from my children's repotting efforts. Ten twenty-two. Bits of soil were scattered over my kitchen floor like so many chocolate sprinkles, and uncertain whether my mischievous duo would recognize these dots as inedibles, I shooed them out of the room and latched the door.

I willed myself calm but, in truth, I felt as incapable of quiescence as Mount St. Helens. Lifting a child under each arm, I put them in my bedroom so I could dress, with a chance that they would do no damage either to themselves, each other or the house. I dashed into the bathroom to brush my hair and put on some lip gloss. I was gone maybe one minute, two at the most, when I was summoned back to my room by the sounds of my children emptying the contents of my underwear drawer and throwing themselves onto it as if it were freshly fallen snow.

"Stop it, you two!" I snapped, my voice having a sharp metallic ring unfamiliar to us all. Immediately they paused to look at me. Alison's face dropped and seemed to dissolve like a wax mask set too close to flame, and Andrew regarded me mournfully, his eyes round and wide with hurt.

Immediately I regretted my tone, my anger, my lack of appropriate discipline, my lack of appropriate planning for the morning. It was 10:35. Still no Yemi. Tension rose like yeast.

Quickly gathering the children, who squirmed and complained vigorously, I deposited them in their cribs, lifted the sides with far more conviction than I felt and walked from their room. They cried; loud, large, damp sobs. Don't go back in, I told myself, struggling to resist all my instincts and habits.

If Yemi walked in the door right now, I could still make it, I reasoned. Maybe I'd be five minutes late, but that would be okay. I dressed in rapid, jerky movements, accelerating each action like a cartoon at fast speed. Ten forty-three. She hadn't come. I began to pace. I opened the door as if sheer force of will could make her appear, but the hallway was empty.

The hearty wails of protest from the children's room changed into faint, resigned mews. I tiptoed to the door. When they were babies, I used to love to watch them fall asleep. But today I allowed myself none of that, rushed and impatient as I was, and I felt a sense of deprivation mixed with everything else I was feeling.

At 10:52, heavy with disappointment, I picked up the telephone to postpone my appointment. "I'm terribly sorry, but something's come up. I can't get free now. Could I possibly come in some time this afternoon?" I asked the secretary. There was a pause, then a curt, maybe condescending—or was I imagining it—"Oh, I'm sorry, that's impossible. *Really.*"

"Well, could I make it for some time next week?" I asked hesitantly, in a tone more befitting a seven-year-old than the thirty-year-old I was.

"Just a moment, I'll check her calendar. No. She's out of town for the first two days next week and then has a really tight schedule for the rest of the week. I don't see how I can possibly squeeze you in. Why don't you give us a call in a few weeks?" she said routinely and clicked off, leaving me with the dead receiver in my hand. I stared at it as though it were an alien object. Tears of frustration welled in my eyes. I blinked them back, for at exactly that moment, with almost staged timing, Yemi rang the doorbell.

"Where were you?" I asked as I threw open the door.

"The train was stuck for forty minutes," she said, pulling off her backpack and setting it on the floor.

"But I had an important meeting that I had to cancel," I said helplessly.

"Oh, really, I'm sorry. But why didn't you tell me to come in an hour earlier to give yourself some leeway?" she asked, her face full of genuine concern.

Ah, yes. Why hadn't I? As so often happened, Yemi showed far more business sense than I. At that moment it would have been hard to tell which of us was the employer and which the employee.

"Well, at least I'm here now," Yemi said brightly, exhibiting that dauntless cheer that made her so good with the children. The problem was that "now" was exactly when I didn't need her. I had already canceled my appointment, and with the children sleeping, I could count on an hour or two of uninterrupted writing. Yet I couldn't tell Yemi to leave. I knew that she depended on the money I paid her to help with tuition. I thought about paying her and telling her she could go, but decided a walk might do me some good. It was a magnificent day. But I felt a dry, dull indifference to it all, my internal world as dreary as earth after Persephone's departure. I walked for a while, then entered a local coffee house, its predictable combination of cappuccino and quiet a balm for the most troubled of spirits.

Between frothy sips the scenario of my morning replayed in my mind. I'd been irritable with the children, unable to get into their world, too distracted to play with them or to discipline them properly. They'd cried themselves to sleep, and for what? The appointment that I'd looked forward to, prepared for, had been canceled, put off indefinitely. And worse, I'd presented myself as disorganized rather than as the cool, competent professional woman I hoped to be. Would an editor believe I could be trusted to get pieces in on time? Would I in her place?

Why *hadn't* I made sure to be there on time? Why *hadn't* I told Yemi to be in at nine so that I could dress without any pressure? I knew she relied on the trains, which were eminently unreliable. Why didn't my children know by now to stay out of the plants? My dresser drawers? Why hadn't I set limits for them? Oh, I was giving myself bad marks all around.

But why? I had everything that I wanted: two sweet babies whom I adored; a lovely stepdaughter, Laura, from my husband's first marriage, a wonderful husband, involved as I was with the children, both of us conversant with the latest parenting literature. Weren't we, after all, part of the new breed? Role sharers? Participatory parents? Dual careerists? In short, weren't we the cutting edge of American coupledom?

What was going wrong? Why was I failing at tasks that seemed so simple and obvious? Surely I knew the rules of good mothering *and* of being a professional. What was there about putting the two together that was so hard? Someone ought to write a book about it, I thought as I went off to relieve Yemi.

PART ONE

Understanding
Our Conflicts

CHAPTER 1

Some Hard Facts About Working Mothers

WOMEN ARE TOLD that a great deal has changed, that we've come a long way. And at first glance it seems as though a lot *has* changed. Take a restaurant during lunchtime in any business district and you can see the difference: neatly suited women taking out clients, meeting with associates. Clothing styles cater to the busy woman executive; magazine and television advertisements all try to woo the new woman. You won't see mom preparing breakfast for busy children and hubby these days. Now it's dad and the kids putting water in the instant oatmeal as mom dashes off to make the rounds at the hospital or negotiate that merger. And you can hear the difference. Even word grafts like *chairperson,* which sounded so odd just a few years back, sound almost natural now, and all but the most diehard of the establishment refers to he *or* she when gender is unknown.

But upon closer look, the scope of the change is not what it first seems. It is true that more than 52 percent of all women, married and unmarried, with preschool children are working (in 1960 that figure was only 19 percent) and a third of all women with babies under seven months old are working also.[1] But doctors, lawyers—women in what are sometimes referred to as the high-profile jobs—have attracted a disproportionate amount of attention. The plain and uncomfortable fact remains that 80 percent of all working women are still employed in such traditional woman's jobs as waitress, file clerk, hospital aide. "Pay for full time women clerical workers is extremely low," said Karen Nussbaum, executive director of 9 to 5, the National Association of Working Women. "It averages just over $11,000 a year for women as compared with male clerical workers who earn over $17,000."[2]

Twenty-eight-year-old Boston hospital worker Pamela Yore's salary of just over $10,000 a year is lower than that of her male co-workers who perform similar jobs. With an ailing husband and a young child, Ms. Yore suffers greatly from this inequity, but she says, "You learn not to make too many waves in the workplace; if you do, there will be ten people there waiting for your job."[3]

And the picture is not much brighter for other women, no matter what their profession. A recent study shows that for white women entering the labor force, wage discrimination is increasing during the 1980s as compared with the 1970s, in spite of the affirmative action programs and educational gains made by women during the decade. Even worse, as women remain in the labor force, the difference between their wages and that of their male counterparts appears to be widening.[4]

This disparity between women's and men's wages affects all women, but it falls with particular hardship on "female heads of households [who] are the disproportionate group of people in poverty."[5] Especially for these women—but for their wealthier counterparts as well—the issue of child care is crucial but not hopeful, given the combined effects of federal cutbacks and the scarcity of convenient low-cost high-quality day-care facilities. Only 1 percent of the 374 major companies polled in a survey by Catalyst, a nonprofit organization that helps working women, had on-site day care, and few of the others had any plans to inaugurate it.[6]

The corporate world's failure to respond more fully to the needs of working mothers is in keeping with the reemergence of conservative attitudes nationwide. Companies feel little incentive or pressure to initiate such programs as day care, job sharing and extended maternity leaves in a society that is reaffirming the values of individualism and of traditional family life and gender roles.

Children's television, perhaps as good an indicator as any of the thinking of the country, reflects this latter trend. The sixties and seventies witnessed the advent of "Sesame Street," with those lovable, furry, androgenous Muppets who captivated adults and children alike. Strength, courage, intelligence and skill were linked to neither race nor sex. Other stations followed suit, and when my children rose at six A.M., too early for public television, I had no difficulty finding nonsexist shows for them.

Watching with Andrew recently, I was struck by how much television had changed. On a typical afternoon the choice was such old favorites as "Batman and Robin," "The Incredible Hulk," "The Six Million Dollar Man" and the new "He-Man and Masters of the Universe," which is the most popular children's television show in America. These programs embrace the vision of a traditional male-dominated world, where male strength is so great and invincible, it is truly supernatural. In the beginning of "He-Man," when the muscular cartoon character reaches his spectacular sword high above his head and shouts "I have the power," the symbolism is too obvious to ignore.[7]

Amitai Etzioni, sociologist and professor at George Washington University, commenting on the conservative swing in society, said, "In earlier times, we had a social order. Now nothing is clear any more. Our present is miserable; our future is uncertain. So the idea of a powerful establishment, based on a solid set of rules, appeals to us."[8]

A solid set of rules determining behavior, and definition of sex roles—these augur poorly for women in general and for working mothers in particular. In a recent study published in the *American Psychologist,* Claire Etaugh reported that only seven out of the twenty-four most influential child care books published in the 1970s approve of women working while they have young children, a view supported by a survey conducted by *Working Woman* magazine. Of those questioned, 56 percent of the employed men and 43 percent of the employed women thought that working women should not be mothers, while 63 percent of the employed men and 52 percent of the employed women thought that having a mother who worked outside the home was bad for children, especially those under the age of six.[9]

Retrogressive proposals and laws, and unsupportive, even critical, public attitudes are particularly unsettling for working mothers, because we have so few role models to follow. In the generation of women before us, most were either mothers or, as they were pejoratively called, career women. It took a maverick spirit indeed to try to combine both roles, and she was hardly held up as someone to emulate. According to a psychiatrist writing for *Life* magazine in the mid-fifties, a young mother who worked did so because she rejected the role of wife and mother, and "while she may find satisfaction in her job, the chances are that she and her husband and children will suffer psychological damage and she will be basically an unhappy woman."[10]

The prevailing dictates that kept the women before us at home deprived today's working mothers of examples to emulate and of mentors to whom we could look for encouragement or instruction. Like pioneer women, we have been left to find our own way in an environment as bewildering as it is difficult.

My study of society had taught me a lot about why it was so hard to combine both roles, but I needed to know more. I needed to know about the women themselves: How did they feel about the complexities and problems of their lives? What did they feel were their greatest conflicts?

I began to think about it, read about it, I even talked about it with a few friends, in a casual way. One friend was having trouble holding on to a job, another to her baby-sitter, still another to her husband. For none was it easy, and even when everything looked as if it were in balance, the women were plagued by deep and persistent worry.

They worried that they were causing emotional damage to their children by being apart from them each day, that their professional lives were being shortcircuited by the time and energy they devoted to their children, that their marriages were suffering and that their own emotional and physical resiliency was being strained to the breaking point. One thirty-one-year-old nurse explained:

> It was my day off, but I had to get up at 7 A.M. with my son. I put him in the highchair. As I reached into the fridge to get him some juice, I knocked over a cup of milk on the shelf and it spilled over everything. It was the last straw. I threw the cup into the sink and slammed the refrigerator door. I started crying. I felt incredibly angry—my day off, and I had to clean the fridge! I picked up a chair and threw it. My husband came in to see what was going on. He'd never seen me that upset. By that time I was on my knees, taking everything off the bottom shelf and throwing it into the sink. My husband told me to get out of the room, that he'd take care of it. I went into the bedroom and just lay there and sobbed. It was just too much. I'd had it.[11]

Anne Garonzik had also had it. Anne had been working in the Humanities Division of the Rockefeller Foundation when, in her early thirties, her first son was born. Although she had never thought about giving up her career, she was shocked to discover how difficult it was to leave her son at the end of her six-month maternity leave. "I felt a tremendous sense of responsibility for this little life and I thought, no one else in the whole world will care about it this way. But it was very important for me to show that I could do everything," Anne explained of her decision to return to work. Yet the tugs and pulls of motherhood gave her less time than she had anticipated.

"After David was born, I could no longer stay late at work," she said. "I also felt that I never had any time for myself; it was hard enough with my husband's schedule to find time for us. My friendships with other mothers also seemed to dwindle."

Anne continued to pursue this hectic life even after the birth of her second child complicated her schedule further. But then when her younger son was two, she read in the newspaper about the tragic death of a young woman she had known professionally, and she suddenly realized that life doesn't go on forever. The shock of her colleague's death forced her to reexamine her own life. "I was perpetually tired and worn out, I felt as though the house was being run by an absentee landlady, that I was missing the most precious moments of my sons' lives, and I felt that I was becoming marginal in everything." After a lot of thought Anne handed in her resignation at work. "Who knows?" she quipped. "I may be in the vanguard." Then her face grew serious again and she shook her head sadly and said, "I think that it's very hard for women—I felt like I was a runner hitting the wall."

While some women undoubtedly will follow Anne's example and drop out of the race, others will, out of choice or necessity, continue to live lives that are grueling marathons of work, energy and detail, enduring great stress and fatigue and pain. But either way, the costs will be enormous—to society, to our families and to ourselves. Christine Melton, a thirty-one-year-old ophthalmologist and mother of three, eloquently expressed a feeling apparently ubiquitous among working mothers. "Some part of this is a loss of sense of self—sometimes I can see myself dissolving into bits, one part owned by my patients, one part owned by my children, one part by my husband. There is the loss of the ability to have something for yourself."

The irony of this is clear and painful when I think back on those exuberant days in 1969 when feminists stormed the Atlantic City beauty pageant or joined ranks, ten thousand strong, to march down Fifth Avenue in 1970. The goals were liberation, self-fulfillment. No longer would we be, in Simone de Beauvoir's phrase, "the other." We would be whole, ourselves, free to oversee our own destinies.

Why then did the women I spoke to feel an attenuation of self and talk about loss of identity, lack of autonomy, alienation from the very lives we were supposed to own? "I feel I'm on an endless race *against* my life," said Amy, a San Francisco attorney.

Why did we feel so deeply fragmented? Estranged? Why did one woman tell me that the better she does at work, the worse she feels? Why did another say she couldn't bear to hear about her son from her baby-sitter? Why did a third say she doesn't ask her husband to share in the household chores? Why did women use phrases like "torn apart," "ripped in two," to describe their lives?

What is there that makes combining a job and motherhood so terribly hard? I asked. But this time I didn't ask myself; I asked women across America.

The response to my questionnaires was overwhelming. I laughed, cried, rejoiced, felt saddened. The stories were those of courage, strength and hope: An over-the-road dispatcher from Indiana, whose second husband left her on Christmas Day with no support for her three sons, often taking on a second job "just to feed and clothe [her] family." A woman from Pittsburgh reported working all night in a garage so that she could use the dreary midnight hours to study for her doctorate, while one from the South told of taking her child with her to work in a sleeping bag when she had to stay late and no baby-sitter was available. And still another, a black college counselor from Texas, related struggling constantly for nine months with such severe morning sickness while she was pregnant with her son that she had to run out of meetings, all the while "needing to keep a professional appearance."

They were women married, women alone, women accustomed to sharing their feelings, women who were not; and I felt proud and revitalized by them all, connected to them by their humanity, their tenacity, their ingenuity, their pain and their struggles. "It's a struggle all the time," said Margaret, an associate director of a private corporation in California.

Yes. A struggle. But what kind of struggle? Not the struggle with schedules, the difficulty with the who-goes-where-when, not the struggle with household tasks, not even the struggle over finding quality child care. That was all there, of course, and important, too. But the women did not dwell on the practical, logistical struggles, tough and sinewy though they are.

No, it was the internal struggle, lodged deep within; elusive, imprecise, a battle waged for the ultimate stakes: a battle waged for who they are, and it affects every aspect of their being.

Now at last I began to find answers. For as I read, I felt as though these women's words were like a secret voice speaking from my very bones, and I began to understand not for the last time, but for the first, why it was so hard. I began to identify the corrosive ingredient in the mix of motherhood and job, the reason that made the combination so excruciatingly hard; the reason that explained better than any other why I never had my baby-sitter come an hour before I needed her, the reason I hadn't been able to set the right limits for my children's behavior, the reason we didn't always do as well at work as we were capable of doing, why we never took time for ourselves, why we so often developed symptoms of stress, why many of our marriages were tension filled. Guilt: the excoriating interface between our two roles; hidden, erupting, disguised, insidious, insistent guilt.

Here is Madeline Fay, a Boston endocrinologist who was a full-time mother and did not even start medical school until her boys were in school, feeling guilty that she will not be home to have dinner with them—now eighteen and nineteen—because she has to stay at the hospital with a young patient.

Rosalind Konigsberg, holding an important managerial position at Metropolitan Life Insurance, feels so guilty about "not having time to do the kinds of things other mothers do—playdates, museums"—with her four-year-old son that for years she and her husband didn't go out by themselves in the evening, even on weekends.

And there is Carol Ostroff, a West Coast CPA who built up her own highly successful accounting firm, saying that "the guilt feelings about leaving my two children are my greatest problem."

Because of that feeling, "I don't do much for myself. [Otherwise], if I . . . worked until 7, I might want to go for a long run or go to the gym and work out or a movie, but I don't do any of that kind of thing. I'm either working or with the children." And another woman, whom I'll call Wendy, on the editorial staff of a large daily newspaper in Washington, D.C., feels so guilty about the time she spends with her daughter that she developed skin rashes and back pains before she understood the problem.

Like a litany, it runs through the voices of working mothers. "I feel guilty about everything (and I feel guilty about feeling guilty)," said an assistant professor of chemistry from Indianapolis; "I was very excited to get back in the mainstream, but at the same time I had to (and still do) deal with *extreme* guilt," reported a manager with an automobile leasing firm in California: "Terribly guilty—because I am not raising my daughter except on weekends, days off and after work . . . and do not feel my husband's and my relationship is at all what it used to be," wrote an employment manager at a bank in Ohio. "Guilty and sad"; "Guilty but desperate to escape full-time mothering"; "The guilt was killing"; "The most painful experience of my life . . . I still have a hard time dealing with the guilt"; "I almost always feel guilty about something."

Surprised as I was by this outpouring of guilt, I was even more startled to see that it seemed to exist regardless of whether a woman was forced to work for financial reasons. "I returned to work for the financial security . . . but felt guilt about leaving my daughter in anyone's hands but my own"; "I felt guilty, but knew I had no choice," a divorced cashier from Pennsylvania; "Guilty, but compelled by the need to support family," said a social service administrator from Cincinnati who is a single mother; "Extreme guilt, sadness, anxiety, I was getting divorced and had to work."

Also unexpected was that the guilt was present even when the mother felt confident that her child was being well cared for. "Guilt and sadness—yet confidence in his caretakers," wrote a product manager from a San Francisco brokerage house; "I feel guilt every day that I leave them, even though I have made excellent arrangements for their care," explained an executive from Memphis. "I felt guilt—although my mother cared for them very well," a manager with a telephone company in Mississippi revealed.

Self-reproach runs high and wide: for going back to work, for taking a leave of absence, for staying at the office late, for leaving work early to attend a school play, for not getting a promotion, for being in a too-pressured position, for being irritable with our children, for not disciplining enough. Like a burr, our guilt attaches to the different facets of our lives, and it hurts us.

Ask men if they feel guilt about combining the roles of parent and wage earner, and you have the answer even before they can give one. So stunned are they at the suggestion that they are rendered momentarily speechless. For them being both father and breadwinner are positively synonymous with being *men*. Ossified in time and tradition, this double role merely comprises two components of a well-integrated whole. There is no sense of incompatibility, no discontinuity and certainly no guilt. "When I have to work several nights in a row or travel a lot, I miss the kids. I mean, I feel unhappy about it. But guilt? Why should I feel guilt?" was a typical response.

Why do women have such a heavy, burdensome sense of guilt? Where does it come from? How does it affect us? And how can we combat it?

CHAPTER 2

Understanding Guilt

GUILT IS AN intensely painful, personal emotion. It is the most internalized of all our feelings, as complex as it is insidious. "Like an iceberg, seven-eighths of which is hidden, the greater part of guilt lies submerged within our unconscious and there it exerts its pressure."[1]

Guilt becomes incorporated into the conscience, lodged in the superego, through a process called identification. Freud likened identification to a swallowing up of one person by another.[2] It is the incorporation, assimilation, internalization of an idealized image of the people who represent power and protection, especially our parents. It begins early—our ideal of the perfect mother has its source somewhere within our first year of life, according to eminent psychiatrist Gertrude Blanck.[3]

For both sexes, the mother is the first identification. But as little boys and girls go through the psychological process of separation and individuation (ages 1 to 3), important changes occur in their respective relationship to her. *Separation* means recognizing ourselves as distinct physical entities from our mothers, while *individuation* means acquiring a special personality by imitating and integrating bits and pieces first of our mother's personality traits and then those of others into our own.[4]

At best, separation is only partial for all children, but, in general, it is more complete for little boys than for little girls. The boy has a father, a man with whom he can identify and disidentify with his mother. For a little girl the process is more complex. She tends to turn back toward her mother, to demand from her, to be disappointed in her and to remain always ambivalently tied to her—this first, fiercest and most powerful attachment.[5]

26

Little girls transform and internalize their mothers' values, ideas and ethics, to develop a model of proper behavior and a standard of mothering: who a mother is, what a mother does, how a mother acts. Through an interaction between our mothers' unique personalities and the particular social, economic and historical milieu in which they found themselves, our mothers created standards of mothering that became part of us, as integral and vital as the blood in our veins.

Experts believe that there is probably no other role with less latitude than our idea of the perfect mother. Firmly fixed in our young minds, our mothers' ways became our ideal. They became our ego-ideal, as psychiatrists call it, the image that our egos, the "I" part of our personalities, is always striving to emulate.[6]

"No other model is more significant to a woman than her mother," according to psychiatrist Roy Grinkers, Jr. "There's no question at all," he stressed, "that in *all* women, the first and primary role model is the mother. [Even] twenty or thirty years or more after childhood . . . the mother is still her primary influence."[7]

Although we may be adults, although we may have moved far from our mothers physically, emotionally and intellectually, this model exists in our unconscious, *unknown* to our conscious self. It is an ideal against which we are forever measuring and judging ourselves.

When we find ourselves lacking or behaving in ways that are contrary to this model—even if we consciously choose to depart from it—the response is automatic and immediate: guilt. Paul Ricoeur, the philosopher, stated, "Guilt becomes a way of putting oneself before a sort of invisible tribunal which measures the offenses, pronounces the condemnation, and inflicts the punishment; at the extreme point of interiorization, moral consciousness is a look which watches, judges and condemns; the sentiment of guilt is therefore the consciousness of being inculcated and incriminated by this interior tribunal."[8]

By its very nature, then, guilt wants, indeed, demands punishment. Like a ruthless prosecutor seeking vengeance, guilt does not let up until it exacts restitution. As individuals, we respond to our guilt in different ways. Some of us may try to deny it and avoid its punishing ways by overcompensating behavior, which can actually bring about the very things we fear. In others of us, our guilty

feelings may lead to a host of self-defeating actions. All too frequently our guilt manifests itself in psychosomatic symptoms, Arnold Huschnecker, a psychiatrist and an expert in this field, told
me. "On a physical level, we may develop aches, pain and fatigue,
gastrointestinal or cardiovascular disturbances, dizziness, neuralgia,
numbness or tingling; on an emotional level a person may feel
anxious, depressed, angry, withdrawn."[9]

We are not, however, usually aware that the distress, the inner
turmoil, the *angst* we feel is caused by guilt. Neither are we aware
of what it is we really feel guilty about. When we are conscious of
the feeling, we tend to attribute it to something obvious, accessi-
ble: a thrown-together dinner, a missed school trip, a late report.
But the origin of guilt is unconscious. It is the feeling that we have
betrayed an inner sense of self. It is deep and devastating anguish
because we have departed from our own standards.

"The crisis for me was being a mother that came up to my own
standards. It was impossible,"[10] said one woman, giving voice to
the sentiments of working mothers across the country. Feeling unable to meet our own/our mothers' standards of mothering is all
but inevitable for the present generation of working mothers. For
it is a failure produced not by any lack on our part, or on our
mothers'. It has been brought about neither by rancor nor by ill
will but by the patterns of historic change from their world to
ours.

To understand why this is so we must, as it were, enter a time
capsule and go spinning back to the years after World War II, to
the 1950s and 1960s, to the world of our mothers—a constricted
world in which the standards of mothering were rigid and clear:
child raising and homemaking; homemaking and child raising.

CHAPTER 3

The World of Our Mothers

"[WOMEN] HAVE MINDS and should use them . . . so long as their primary interest and activity is the home," proclaimed *Life* magazine in 1956, summing up the prevailing philosophy of the time—a time when a college professor of thirty-five years questioned whether women were capable of producing such "masterpieces as great books, great music and great works of art," a time when aging and fat were labeled women's worst enemies.[1]

It was a time when a psychiatrist, writing in a leading women's magazine, identified "the primary feminine qualities as perceptivity, passivity and the desire to nurture." And it was a time when the actress Julie Harris told the readers of *McCall's* magazine that in motherhood she had found the creativity she'd wanted all her life. "Suddenly it didn't seem so important to have a career. I'd almost rather not have one." And to be sure, the overwhelming majority of mothers of the era did not.[2]

Six million women were recruited into the labor force to participate in our nation's efforts in World War II, 60 percent of whom were married and the majority of whom had preschool or school-age children. But they were hurried back home at war's end. Interestingly, at the beginning of the war 95 percent of the women workers said that they planned to quit when their men returned, but 80 percent later changed their minds. Their hopes to continue working won support among women professionals and women in government such as Helen Gahagan Douglas. Theresa Wolfson, the economist, wrote, "The war worker cannot be cast off like an old glove." But cast off they were.[3]

Two months after VJ Day 800,000 workers, most of them women, lost their jobs in the aircraft industry—a number matched by layoffs in the automotive and electrical industries. Major companies like IBM and Detroit Edison resurrected the prewar policy of not hiring married women. By the end of 1946 millions of women had been fired from heavy industry. Reporter Lucy Greenbaum of the *New York Times* declared "the courtship of women workers" at an end. The romance of home and the family had begun.[4]

Inflation of the postwar era was high, memories of the Great Depression still fresh. Experts believed that the economy could not support both the returning servicemen and the female workers. It was clear which should go; few protested the choice. With vivid memories of the horrors of war, Americans sought refuge in the family. And women, so recently wooed into the labor force, were now serenaded with a chorus of praise for their vocation as homemakers and mothers that made the roar of the nineteenth-century cult of domesticity sound like a whisper.

A writer in *Ladies' Home Journal* advised American women that "their most important postwar job . . . [was] to have three babies a piece." They were urged to "correct the mistakes of the 1920s and 1930s and supply the world with an exploding population of freedom-loving and patriotic Americans." Hollywood films and magazines were filled with images of sweet, cuddly babies. The Broadway cast of one musical sang and danced to the joyous tune, "We're Having a Baby," and Lucille Ball, whose television show, "I Love Lucy," was watched by two-thirds of all Americans, managed to have one baby on the air and another off in the same week in 1953.[5]

Everywhere American women turned, they were surrounded by the rites of motherhood that helped encourage the postwar baby boom. For the first time since the beginning of the century, women were having more children than their mothers had had. The American birth rate soared in the 1950s, surpassing that of Japan and almost equaling that of India. The number of women with three children doubled, those with four tripled, and all the while commentators urged them to be even more prolific.[6] Psychiatrist Helene Deutsch thought women should have many children to protect them against the damage to the psyche when the last one left home, while her colleagues Ferdinand Lundberg and Marynia Farnham urged the federal government to award prizes to women for the birth of every child beyond the first.[7]

The pressure to have large families meant that women had to

wed earlier and spend less time on their education; in 1950 the average age at which American women married was lower than at any other time in the twentieth century; by the mid-fifties 60 percent of women were dropping out of college to marry before they had their degrees.[8] But while our mothers' generation may not have completed their formal education, they received abundant information on performing their main roles in life—that of homemaker and mother. The late forties and early fifties saw a change in the prevailing philosophy of child rearing from the rigid behavioral to the more humanistic developmental approach. While behaviorists favored early separation from the mother, exposing the baby to the harshness of the world by strict and early toilet training and bottle-feeding on schedule, the developmentalists believed that the human personality requires warmth, intimacy and trust in order to thrive. But while the baby was given more latitude for its needs and emotions, the mother's role became fixed.

Breast-feeding was no longer a matter of choice but the sign of devoted mothering, and it had to be breast-feeding on demand. The mother, of course, could not work or even be away from home for more than a few hours at a time. She had to be ready, able and willing to be always "on call." If not, if the mother showed the "slightest gesture of impatience [or a] furtive glance at the clock . . . [babies] react as if she were as wicked as a she-wolf."[9]

The developmental approach, which had its origins with Dr. Arnold Gesell and was popularized by Dr. Benjamin Spock, forged a standard of mothering in which the mother was intimately and inexorably involved with every aspect of the child's life. According to Gesell, the ideal mother, "instead of striving for efficiency . . . aims, first of all, to be perceptive of and sensitive to the child's behavior. Thus, she becomes a true complement to him, alertly responsive to his needs." If the mother found the stresses of this total immersion in the baby too difficult, Spock advised her to "go to a movie, or to the beauty parlor or to get a new dress or hat." As for finding work that might prove more fulfilling, he wrote, "If a mother realized how vital [her love and care] is to a small child, it may make it easier to decide that the extra money she might earn, or the satisfaction she might receive from an outside job, *is not so important after all* [emphasis added]."[10]

The essential responsibility of the mother for producing an

emotionally healthy child won additional support from Freudian psychology, so much in vogue in the fifties. Freud handed his disciples a formidable scaffolding for doctrines stipulating woman's practical inferiority as well as her role in producing disturbances in her offspring. As *sibling rivalry* and *oedipal complex* became household words and the family was scrutinized under the Freudian microscope, mothers could now be blamed for difficulties ranging from schizophrenia to asthma. Behind every homosexual, every frigid woman, every alcoholic, behind aggressiveness, assertiveness, ambitionlessness, was a mother—overbearing, oppressive, selfish, selfless.[11]

The centrality of the mother in the child's life was made even more acute by the virtual absence of the father. In her study of Chicago neighborhoods, sociologist Helena Lopata observed, "The responsibility for health, welfare, the behavior and ability of the child is basically unshared. The father is not held accountable for what happens to the children because he is not home much of the time." "I'm home so little," one man told a researcher, "I only see the kids for an hour in the evening, that is if I'm not going off to a meeting."[12]

The reason behind the father's separation from his family was the explosive postwar movement to the suburbs—developments outside the burgeoning cities in what used to be rural areas. One city planner called this trend the greatest migration in the history of man. Tucked away in the suburbs, away from their families and friends in their old neighborhoods, women spent their days dividing their energies totally between child care and homemaking.[13]

But not any old homemaking would do. Women were encouraged to make housekeeping their life work, to glory in it, to lavish in it. Women's magazines, which only a decade before had encouraged women to take jobs to help the war effort, now wholeheartedly supported the reappearance of the old-fashioned large family with mom at home. *Life* magazine applauded the "increasing emphasis on the nurturing and homemaking values among women who might have at one time pursued careers," while *Look* magazine agreed that the woman who saves her money to buy "a new home freezer" deserves far more praise than the "emancipated girls of the 1920's or even '30's."[14]

Under the banner of creativity, authorities set forth standards of homemaking that were rigid, traditional and time consuming.

Lynn White, president of Mills College, told college women that instead of studying abstract science and philosophy, they should study the "theory and preparation of a basque paella, of a well-marinated shish-kabab, lamb kidney sautéed in sherry, an authoritative curry."[15] Proudly women sewed their own clothes, baked their own breads, scrubbed, washed, cleaned and ironed, mended and waxed floors. Experts discovered that in spite of the development of laborsaving devices, our mothers' generation actually spent more time doing housework than did our grandmothers'—99.6-hour weeks, according to one study—and it is no wonder.[16]

Motivated by a need to find a sense of purpose in household chores that were essentially repetitive and often meaningless, women fell prey to the new advertising blitz aimed at giving their work a "professional status and add to their feelings of economic security." The idea was, as one report from an advertising agency said, "to make housework a matter of knowledge and skill, rather than a matter of brawn and dull unremitting effort." Surveys taken during the decade revealed that when a woman "uses one product for washing clothes, a second for dishes, a third for walls, a fourth for floors, a fifth for venetian blinds, etc. rather than an all purpose cleaner, she feels less like an unskilled laborer and more like an engineer and expert."[17] So women were exhorted to add their own bleaches to the laundry, to put pieces of clothing in the machine one at a time, to add ingredients to cake mixes, to put their own decoration even on ready-made clothing—all in the name of self-esteem and sales.

And it worked! So well that when 250 housewives were asked to choose from among four imaginary methods of cleaning, ranging from one so automatic that it was part of the heating system to one they would have to operate and push, the overwhelming majority chose the latter. As for the easier methods, a young woman remarked, "Well, what would happen to my exercise, my feelings of accomplishment, and what would I do with my mornings?"[18]

What did these women, those of our mothers' generation, do with their mornings *and* afternoons *and* evenings? The answer, for many of them, was driving: husbands to the station, children to school, then to the supermarket, then back home to unload the groceries, then back to school to pick up the children and to transport them to the cub scouts, dentist or a playdate. After the children were brought home, there might be another trip to the station before the car was finally put into the garage for the night. Many women spent up to twenty hours a week behind the wheel, half the number of most salaried employees.[19] And as for the rest of their time:

> Ye Gods, what do I do with my time? asked one young mother, repeating the question. Well, I get up at six. I get my son dressed and then give him breakfast. After that I wash the dishes and bathe and feed the baby. Then I get lunch and while the children nap I sew or mend or iron and do all the other things I can't get done before noon. Then I cook supper for the family and my husband watches TV while I do the dishes. After I get the children to bed, I set my hair and then I go to bed.[20]

Accounts like these go on and on:

> I get up at eight. I make breakfast so I do the dishes, have lunch and some more dishes, and some laundry and cleaning in the afternoon. Then it's supper and dishes and I get to sit down a few minutes before the children have to be sent to bed . . . That's all there is to my day. It's just like any other wife's day. Humdrum. The biggest time, I am chasing kids.[21]

This was a typical day for millions of women who called themselves housewives; American women who married and became mothers during and after World War II. Their days consumed by children and housework, housework and children, the brightest stars in the constellation of our mothers' lives shone with particular intensity when we were infants.

As little girls, then, we learned that the good mommy was home all the time taking care of us, catering to our needs. But—especially as we got older—we learned other things, too. We learned that many of our mothers chafed against their restricted sphere; we learned that underneath the busy daily-ness of their lives, there was a deep and stagnant well of frustration and sorrow.

Many of the women of our mothers' generation were bright and well educated. They had done well in school and had been encouraged by their middle-class upbringing to achieve. Now, cut off from meaningful outlets for self-expression, their creative energies turned inward and plagued them. As one put it, "When you are married and with small children, you have a lot of things you would like to do, but can't—you don't have the time and facilities. If I could, if I had peace one [or] two hours a day, I would continue voice lessons, buy a piano, study. . . . My greatest satisfaction does not come from 'terrific dinner' as much as from 'she sings well.' "[22]

Another woman said, "I've tried everything women are supposed to do—hobbies, gardening, pickling, canning, being very social with my neighbors, joining committees, running PTA teas. I can do it all . . . but it doesn't leave you anything to think about. . . . All I wanted was to get married and have four children. I love the kids and Bob and my home. There's no problem you can put a name to. But I'm desperate."[23]

In the *Feminine Mystique* Betty Friedan documented the universality of the problem without a name, but our mothers, the women suffering from this undiagnosed ill, thought they were alone. Writing of the 1950s, sociologist Lopata said, "This is one of the few times in recorded history that the mother-child unit has been so isolated from adult assistance." Only 2 to 4 percent of the women she interviewed listed friendship as an important part of their lives; only 16 percent of the housewives reported seeing a friend in their homes during the typical day.[24] As Nancy Chodorow wrote in her book *The Reproduction of Mothering,* these women had emotional needs that weren't being met.[25]

It is difficult, almost impossible, today in this time of self-disclosure, when women write about and share their most intimate experiences—miscarriage, divorce, widowhood—to appreciate the conspiracy of silence that stifled our mothers' generation. Recalling her own unhappiness as a young mother, one woman, now a grandmother, said, "You didn't admit these feelings, not even to your best friend."[26]

While many women of our mothers' generation still find it hard—threatening, even—to disclose the depths of their unhappiness, some are willing to talk about it. My own mother, a magnificently intelligent woman who earned a master's degree in history before my older sister was born, had always maintained that her greatest joy in life was raising the two of us. Only once—and that was just a few years ago—did she confide how difficult and confining that life was, how my father, a clinical psychologist, was away working so many evenings, how much she was home alone with two infants, how difficult it was dealing with my persistent early food allergies. "My greatest wish was that I'd see the day that you were old enough to sit in a high chair," she remembered.

I do not know how much of that frustration I perceived as a little girl, but I do know that as far back as I can remember, my mother was busy taking courses. When I picture her, I see her sitting, head bent over books piled up on our pink dining room tablecloth, preparing for the long-awaited day when my sister and I would be old enough for her to go to work.

Five years ago, when my father's deteriorating health forced my mother into an early retirement from her position as a supervisor in the New York City Board of Education, her sense of loss was palpable. "I loved working," she told me in a whisper, as though it were a secret. "I'd walk into my office and I'd feel exhilarated and renewed. It was all mine."

"It was *very* pressing that I wanted to be doing something that was entirely my own," Sally Carpenter told me, looking back on the years she spent raising her three sons in Ohio. I met Sally four years ago, as she drove and escorted and supported me through one of those hectic publicity tours that authors do to promote their books. Blond, stately and well spoken, Sally was thoroughly enjoying her first "real" job since her now-grown children were born. "Oh, I'd done all the volunteer work imaginable," Sally recalled. "The museum, the garden club, the hospital [where her husband is a doctor], but it doesn't give you much self-esteem," she said somewhat wistfully. "It didn't matter how much I enjoyed the children. . . . I had to do something to get out of that world I was in."

Helen Perlman of New York City had recently become a grandmother, but her vivacious spirit and the sparkle in her eyes make her look impossibly young for the role. "I feel better now than I ever did, now that I'm working again." A designer for a New York–based textile company, Helen is doing the kind of work she did before becoming a mother; she's good at it and is happy with it. "I stayed home with my daughter because that's what I was supposed to do, but when my daughter was about ten years old I realized that I was walking around crying all the time."

And Betty Schlein, assistant to former New York Governor Hugh Carey, recalled her unhappiness with the "classic route" she had taken after college. She taught for one year, got married and had her children before she was thirty. "There was no way to combine a family and career. [Twenty] years ago, I wanted to put my head in the oven every day."[27]

The unfulfilled lives of these women did not seem worth living. "Day-time sleeping is a form of suicide, yet amazing numbers of women resort to it," wrote a woman from Maryland who admitted that she, like most of her friends, used to sleep "inordinate amounts." It was very demoralizing to her, but for eight years, when her children were small, she slept during the day, took adult education courses and shopped. "Few people knew of my discontent. It was not something I could articulate well, and I was ashamed that I felt it. There was only one recurring thought," she recalled. "There's got to be more than this."[28]

Our mothers escaped—into sleeping, into reading: "I was an avid reader, I was addicted to books"; "I read everything"; woman after woman told me. Some escaped into daytime television or sometimes into their own fantasy world. "Portnoy's Mother's Complaint," a study of depression in middle-aged women, was the result of sociologist Pauline Bart's efforts to understand her own mother's drift into insanity. Bart quoted one woman in her study as saying, "I'm glad that God gave me the privilege of being a mother. . . . [My children] were my whole life, but it never worked out."[29]

In a class discussing mothers and daughters in literature, one woman said, "Most of us, we just bought the house and had kids. We didn't really think about it. When I think about the self-hatred I've bequeathed to my daughter . . ."[30]

Initially, when we were youngest and most impressionable, our mothers communicated to us that the good mother was someone who did not work outside the house, who stayed home taking care of us, whose life was a footnote to our own. But our mothers also, and perhaps unknowingly, communicated their intense unhappiness with the very role we were to emulate, the role for which they were to prepare us. What a harsh cultural bind for mother and daughter alike!

Therapist Doris Bernstein told me that women today want to reject the masochism inherent in the servant image of their mothers. "They simply want no part of it." And Dr. Esther Menaker, a leading psychoanalyst who was once an analysand of Anna Freud's, noted that "clinical experience with young women in recent years has indicated that a major factor in the repudiation or rejection of the traditional feminine role lived by the mother is the little girl's experience of her mother's unhappiness, her lack of fulfillment, her bitter feelings that life has cheated her, and above all her low opinion of herself."[31]

Terry Blake, a sociologist and consultant and mother of a four-year-old girl, recalled that her "mother had had the most negative self-image. She'd always say, 'Don't look at me. I don't look good.' "

"I never looked at my mother in any kind of admiring way," said Susan, a producer with CBS, remembering her childhood in Detroit and noting that her mother had dropped out of college to marry her father.

"I grew up outside Philadelphia in a small town of about five thousand," another woman told me. "My mom worked for about eleven years before my older brother was born, but not after that. . . . When she was in her forties she joined a garden club, so I think that that was an attempt to find some kind of involvement—I didn't realize this about my mother at the time—that she would have been a happier person if she had worked."

Carly Walker's mother had an opportunity to work, but only for a few years before her recent death, and "she simply adored it. When I was young, my mother stayed home and she was bored to death," said Carly, the mother of two girls, who owns and operates a bookstore in Massachusetts. "When I picture my mother, I see her sitting on the sofa reading. She catered very much to my father. But he told her all the time that she had no brains. Her image of herself was the one who couldn't spell, who couldn't add, all that she was good for was being a wife and mother. I think that my father felt threatened by my mother and I wonder if he put her in that role unconsciously."

As we grew older, we saw our mothers—our role models, the women we were to become—thwarted in their efforts toward self-realization and expression. A deep and bitter lesson, this one—and one we couldn't take lightly. It reverberated through the core of our being, and we resolved not to let it happen to us; we resolved to be different.

CHAPTER 4

The Cost of Difference

"MY GREATEST TERROR," confided a woman I'll call Naomi, a successful screenplay writer on the West Coast, "was that I'd grow up like my mother. She dropped out of college in her junior year to marry my father, a doctor, and then proceeded to have three children. You know," she said with a sad smile, "when I was graduating from high school, my boyfriend was the valedictorian, and I was the salutatorian. I used to have a nightmare, a real nightmare, that we'd get married and I'd sacrifice my career to his."

"My mother did not work, nor could she drive, write a check or do anything on her own," noted Judith of Houston. "I vowed early on that I would not be dependent."

"I used to hate it when people told me I looked like my mother, or that we had the same expressions," Marilyn, a friend from childhood, told me recently. Since I remembered Marilyn's mother as a woman of uncommon beauty, I was surprised. "Well, you know my mother was what they used to call petite," Marilyn explained. "I remember going with her to the butcher shop and Frank would say, 'Now what can I do for the little lady today?' And I used to feel embarrassed for her—it was everything I didn't like about being a girl."

"All my life, I consciously differentiated myself from my mother," said Terry, the consultant. "My mother is this, so I'll be like that."

This was no childish defiance or teenage rebellion, this vow to be different. It grew inside us and burned with intensity. We wanted, *needed* to free ourselves from the nexus of imposed inferiority. We would struggle against that early identification. We would not lead our mothers' lives.

So we made a creed of being different. I remember when I was in graduate school how proudly we carried our copies of *Ms* magazine along with our history notes. We let our hair grow long, sported aviator glasses. Robin Morgan was our inspiration, Gloria Steinem our role model. We would work, study, pursue opportunities that our mothers could never have dreamed of. Many of us swore we would never have children. We felt a clarity of purpose that was pure and unquestioned. At least not yet.

But with our exams behind us and only the dissertation ahead, we began to feel a nagging uncertainty about remaining childless. However wonderful and compelling our work, some of us began to question if our zeal to be different hadn't blinded us to another fulfilling experience—that of motherhood. "Are we missing out on part of life?" we'd ask ourselves, or sometimes hesitantly each other. The whisper of uncertainty slowly became a shout too strong to stifle, and from somewhere deep within the inchoate wish for a child struggled to the surface. So we would have our children, love them, care for them; but we would not be mothers as our mothers were.

Surely this was not the first time in American history that daughters yearned to live lives different from their mothers, to forge new paths, to go in new directions. What was unique to us— the generation coming of age in the sixties and seventies—however, was that we had the *opportunity* to act on these dreams and inspirations and to make them reality.

The economic and political climate gave us impetus; the women's movement (whether or not we subscribed to its tenets) gave us the possibility, the ideology, the rhetoric, the support. Experts agree that at no other time in America's past have the lives of so many daughters been so different—educationally, professionally, financially, sexually—from the lives of their mothers.[1]

Changes in attitudes, values, ideals, goals, which usually occur slowly, almost imperceptibly over several eras, were all accelerated between our mothers' lives and our own. Sharp, intense, concentrated. And, it is this difference, this actue separation at once so desirable and impossible, that is the cause of our inordinate guilt.

Dr. Menaker, who has studied the inner conflicts of women in changing social situations, explained why this is so. Our opportunities for self-fulfillment and for work away from the home represent the realization of a valued ego-ideal of liberation. But as we pursue these new goals, we are losing part of our past, and a very personal part at that. We have seen how the traditional ego-ideal is embodied in our mothers and became, in the course of our maturation, incorporated into our own personalities. It is, therefore, a psychological reality, an actual part of us, explained Menaker, even though we are not always aware of it in our daily lives.[2]

As our generation of women created a new and independent ego-ideal out of the social influences that have impinged upon us, we have separated not only from our mothers but also from part of ourselves. It is painful and difficult, this separation, for it implies rejecting the ideals, values and standards of that primal identification. And for this, the psychiatrists tell us, *"there is always guilt."*[3]

Dr. Martin Cohen, a clinical psychologist in Manhattan who treats many dual-career couples, has found that whatever notions women have about the importance of combining a career and family, if they themselves were raised by their own mothers, they feel guilty about it. Doris Bernstein also found "intense guilt" in working mothers regardless of how well they were actually attending to the needs of their families. "[Women even] tend to feel guilt about the wish to work," Bernstein observed, because they feel like they are violating an internal command from the idealized mother of infancy.[4]

It is important to be absolutely clear about this—the guilt does *not* originate in the dual pursuit of career and motherhood. The specific tasks of coordinating both roles—the logistics of it—provide our unconscious guilt with a perfect opportunity to attach itself. With magnetic tenacity, guilt adheres to the issues surrounding the combination of work and mothering. But it arises from the decision to be different from our mother, to choose a different lifestyle, to challenge her values, attitudes, child-rearing practices—this appears to conflict with what we have learned from our mother, with her standards of mothering, which are also our own.[5]

"My mother didn't work," said Rosemary Jennings, "and I think that that has a lot to do with the [guilt]. You know, doing the reverse of what your mother did. My mother once wanted to work," Rosemary said, recalling her childhood in Utah. "She had a background in social work, but my father, an attorney, said no. I never hear her complain about it, but when I was a little girl it seemed so dreary to me. . . . No one in my family ever talked about my doing anything but getting married. In my early days I was a secretary, now it's absolutely turned around," declares Rosemary, the mother of three young daughters who was responsible for many innovative programs in the Boston school system before coming to New York to pursue a doctorate in clinical psychology.

"Underneath all of [my achievements] I have an image of the perfect mother. I see people who fit into the picture momentarily. I see an interchange between a parent and a child and I think that that's the way I'm supposed to be operating." Only certain things conform to this image. *"Work doesn't.* I think that I have some standard, some inner standard, that I haven't articulated that I keep following around."

Like the proverbial carrot dangled before the burro, the standard of mothering beckons us to follow it in endless and futile pursuit. "The guilt is . . . I'm espousing something different from my mother . . . I'm not fulfilling what I should be doing as a mother, and it sets off a tremendous inner conflict in women," said Dr. Alan Roland, a psychologist and co-editor of the book *Career and Motherhood.* "I don't think one woman in our culture is untouched by this today."

As daughters, we not only have to deal with our conflicted emotions but also with our mothers' ambivalence about our careers. New York psychotherapist Marcia Rabinowitz explained that our mothers' feelings or what we believe they would have been about our work have an important effect on us. If we believe our mothers regard our work negatively, it's going to take an emotional toll on us.

In a recent interview Dr. Irene Stiver, director of the department of psychology at Boston's McLean Hospital, told me that "while some mothers may be vicariously very identified with the daughter's successes, others may feel quite competitive." Ideally, the mother who has led an unfulfilled life should rejoice to see her daughter pursue a different path, but the very real pride she may feel in her daughter's achievement may in fact be tainted with envy and disapproval. When these feelings are communicated to us—rivalry, criticism, misgivings—either implicitly or explicitly, we feel guiltier still about living differently from our mothers.

Ella Foshay, an art historian who teaches at Vassar College, rejected her mother's role. "I felt that you ought to give yourself up to be a good mother and that was part of the reason I put the decision off for so long." Busy getting her doctorate in art, Ella steadfastly avoided discussing her work with her mother. "She wouldn't be interested . . . She wouldn't tune in the way you wanted her to, so it was better not to bring it up because you would have been disappointed. I've learned not to put in front of my mother things that would make her feel competitive with me. I've learned to play these down, to pooh-pooh them so as not to stir up the competition."

When I asked Wendy, the editor from Washington, D.C., if her very intelligent mother who had never worked ever acted competitive with her, she smiled sardonically. "I'd just finished working on a piece that was very close to my heart. I'd really pushed to get it accepted in the magazine and had worked closely with the writer. My mother knew how terribly special it was to me. It appeared on a Sunday. I kept expecting my mother to call to congratulate me on it. Finally after about three days—I think it was Wednesday—she called. 'You know your piece? Well, it had three grammatical errors in it.'

"That's all she said. Three grammatical errors. I was livid with rage."

Another woman, a radiologist practicing in a small midwestern town, who did not want her name used, who did not even want to be interviewed because the topic was so painful, said, "I'll simply tell you this. My mother was strictly working class. No one in my family even went to college. When I announced that I wanted to be a doctor, she threw me out of the house. I haven't spoken to her since. Do you need any more?"

While this is an extreme example, almost all the women I spoke with recounted ways in which their mothers conveyed their ambivalence toward them.

When she was in the midst of a very challenging but time-consuming assignment, Terry's mother said, "I think it's wonderful that you're doing something. I should have done that when I was younger!" But then in the very next breath she remarked, "Nobody is like a mother to her child, no one can really substitute. I think Emily looks a little sad today, she misses you."

"Do you know how awful that makes me feel?" Terry asked rhetorically. "Like no direction is the right one."

"Women come into my office who are anxious and often frantic," reported psychotherapist Doris Bernstein. "What they say is, 'I want a place in the world, but my mother won't let me go,' rather than 'I don't feel capable of functioning outside the maternal orbit.' "[6]

The anguish that these women feel is vivid and familiar. We are torn between our needs for intellectual and financial satisfaction, and our equally strong needs to maintain continuity with our mothers' lives.

When we first began to leave the home and join the work force, we tried to avoid confronting this dilemma. We would be both the *compleat mother* and the *compleat professional*. We would be mighty and strong—so strong, we were superhuman.

CHAPTER 5

So Long, Superwoman

IT'S A MOTHER! It's a doctor! . . . It's Superwoman! Remember her—that high-flying creature from the 1970s hovering over our heads, urging us onward. Everywhere her accomplishments shone down on us mortals: mother, wife, career woman, gourmet cook, hostess par excellence.

In *Newsweek's* investigation of the life-style of working women with children, we find Patricia Schroeder, congresswoman, wife of lawyer, Jim, who at thirty-five had skillfully combined career, marriage and family. There was also Carla Hills, secretary of Housing and Urban Development, wife of Roderick, chairman of the Securities Exchange Commission and mother of four, pictured serving her lovely family an elaborate dinner.[1]

Susan Davis, featured in *Working Woman,* was a vice president at "Chicago's rapidly growing South Shore Bank. Since working on a business magazine at Harvard Business School in 1965, Davis, herself, has pioneered several business ventures of minorities and women from grass roots beginnings into successful enterprises." Davis reflected, "Looking back, I feel great about who I've become." Although Davis is now in the "intense family stage" with two preschool children, she is not yet forty years old and is already in the top 1 percent of Chicago women in banking.[2]

Now I, too, had a career and became a mother during the 1970s, but when I compare myself to these women, it's possible to note a slight difference in our life-styles.

I did not preside over my family at an elegant dinner table; in fact, I don't remember that we ever all sat down to a meal at the same time. Certainly *I* never managed to sit. Either I grabbed something from the fridge and ate standing up while negotiating spoonfuls of cereal to my children's mouths, or I ate at my desk as I wrote. I did, however, buy the requisite "Dress for Success" books, but my appearance never quite succeeded. In fact, I recall once giving a paper in an ivory linen suit, the single item of clothing that I had to wear on such occasions, with Andrew's jelly prints on the skirt. I wonder if that ever happened to Sandra Day O'Connor.

As for my career, well, I hardly had that relaxed intensity so essential to writing. The only time I relaxed was when I fell exhausted into bed, and as for the intensity, I had plenty of that, dealing with the children's temper tantrums, cleaning crayon designs off the walls and picking up toys. In fact, that was the problem. There was too much intensity in my life and it always came at the wrong time.

But still I clung to the conviction that it was important—no, not important, vital—to show that I could do it all: that I could be both mother and professional and that nothing would suffer, that I would work at a job and still be the eminently available, giving, nurturing mother. In short, that I could be a woman of the seventies—a working mother devoting time and energy to a career—but that my children would still have a fifties-style mom.

Madelon Bedell had been a researcher, a reporter, a writer and a publicist, but in her mind she said, "I was first and foremost a mom. A mom with a job." So she cooked and cleaned and cared for her children and worked and made sumptuous and complicated meals for dinner parties that prompted a guest to give her the ultimate compliment: "Oh, Madelon. Just look at everything you do . . . you're really a superwoman, do you know that?" She beamed, because she, like the rest of us, had imbibed the message: If you really feel that you have to work, it's all right as long as you do not neglect children, husband and home.[3]

If the superwoman syndrome entailed constant organization and attention to the domestic front—if it meant that work could not interfere with our home lives—the myth also stipulated the reverse. Children, family problems, pregnancy and childbirth were not allowed to conflict with our jobs. Never mind that men have heart attacks, skiing accidents, dental problems that cause them to be out of work. We denied the physical. Biology was not only not destiny, it was not excusable.

Anne Woodard, from North Carolina, who is with the First

Union National Bank, worked right up to the time she went into labor and was taken from her desk to the hospital in a wheelchair. Another woman deliberately dressed in bulky clothing so that her pregnancy wouldn't show when she interviewed for a medical internship. When asked about what she was planning to do about having children, she lied about the fact that she was already four months pregnant. And still another woman, from the West Coast, brought her infant with her to her clients' offices so that she could nurse him while she was working.

Amanda Bell, an associate at a prestigious Wall Street firm, experienced unforeseen complications with her pregnancy—high blood pressure, a cesarean section and a long-undiagnosed ulcer— but she forced herself to return to work still in a weakened condition. "I was determined to show [the partners] that a woman with a child could be the kind of lawyer they wanted," she told me. "The more they pushed one way, the more I pushed the other," Amanda said, recalling that it was an extraordinarily difficult period for her whole family. "But," she explained, "I always said that after the baby was born, I would go back to work. . . ."

When Marjorie Madigan, a college professor at Marymount Manhattan College, returned to work after her son's birth, it was with the same fiery determination. "Here was this baby that I loved so much . . . but I remember when I first started teaching at Marymount, I had a colleague who took a maternity leave and did not come back, and I remember thinking, that's not going to happen to me. A child is never going to change my career," she said, her voice filled with the conviction she had felt. "It was very important for me to be able to do both. And yet"—she paused for a moment—"I remember once feeling totally exhausted while I was wheeling Sean in his carriage and thinking, 'No one can do it all.' "

And probably no one can. Not the way that we were trying to. Not that incredible juggling act, leaping up the ladder of success with one foot planted securely on the nursery floor, a smile on our faces, clarity in our minds and unlimited affection in our hearts.

Whatever impelled us into such emotional, physical acrobatics? Whoever made us think we could accomplish such an impossible feat?

To some extent the early leaders of the women's movement did. The National Organization of Women (NOW), the largest of all the feminist groups, sought to gain equal rights for women and equal access to traditional male jobs. As these early feminists worked tirelessly and bravely to pierce such bastions of male supremacy as the corporate establishment [during the 1970s women constituted only 2 percent of the corporate executive elite], many of them either overlooked or underestimated the real difficulties and conflicts that mothers would face in dedicating themselves to demanding careers. Inadvertently they helped perpetuate the myth that the battle could be waged for professional success while the home front remained unaffected.

In her groundbreaking essay, "Equality of the Sexes: An Immodest Proposal," sociologist Alice Rossi, an early supporter of and activist in the women's movement, argued that a woman could indeed have both a home and a career. While Rossi accepted that there were some obstacles, she stated, "We should be wary of the assumption that home and work combinations are *necessarily difficult* [emphasis added]."[4]

Caroline Bird, author of *Born Female: The High Cost of Keeping Women Down,* downplayed a woman's conflicts about leaving her baby to return to the labor force, implying they could be resolved by a salary increase. Trying to allay the concerns of employers, whom Ms. Bird said "believe that you can't compete with a baby," she writes, "The fact is, of course, that you can. With money."[5]

As for how the children would manage when the mother went back to work, another theorist urged that they should be "systematically taught, as early as possible, how to fix simple meals for themselves, shop, use the phone, use public transportation, read a map, and pay attention to written messages directed at them as well as to record messages for other members of the family."[6]

Perhaps in some way the superwoman myth was a necessary stage of the women's movement. It gave women, so long told of their inabilities and inferiorities, a feeling of confidence and courage. Perhaps also there was a sense that the best way to get into the male domain was to assert that having women in the workplace did not necessarily mean a concomitant abandonment of domestic concerns. After all, most of the men doing the hiring were married and on some level identified female applicants with their own wives, who might attempt the same kind of role combining. Far better to convince them that things would go on as before—that beds would be made, dinner served and house and spouse basically unchanged. Perhaps it was conscious, perhaps it was unconscious, but during the seventies our feminist godmothers played down some of the problems we would face.

Betty Friedan, looking back at the movement's early days, reflected, "My own feminism began in outrage at the either/or choice that the feminine mystique imposed on my generation. I was fired from my job as a reporter when I became pregnant. Most of us let ourselves be seduced into giving up our careers in order to embrace motherhood and it wasn't easy to resume them. We told our daughters that they could—and should—have it all. Why not?"[7]

Indeed, why not have it all—a creed quickly taken up by advertising and the media, both of which did their best to foster the myth. The ensuing blitz at once appealed to the newly liberated woman, who was still the main consumer, while it attempted to assure the man that his woman would keep the traditional female attributes.

One popular perfume advertisement showed a glamorous woman coming home and swapping her briefcase for a fancy apron and then for a lovely cocktail dress as she sang, "I can bring home the bacon and fry it up in a pan . . . and never, never let you forget you're a man . . . cuz I'm a woman, W-O-M-A-N. . . ."

Another, trying to impress women with the long-staying effectiveness of a particular deodorant brand, showed how well it worked during all the stresses of the day: getting an active family off in the morning, at an important business meeting, rushing home on the bus and finally making dinner.

"Your hair can stand up even when you can't," proclaimed still another product: a hair spray that held while a woman rushed out in the rain to give her son boots as he got on the bus, dashed about at her job and finally went home to cook.

Years ago the effectiveness of hair sprays and deodorants was proved by women stranded on deserts or caught in hurricanes. It is telling that during the seventies an average day in the life of a working mother was considered comparable to a major disaster.

The New Woman's extraordinary prowess also found its place in many popular novels, which revolved around the theme of successful business women who also had complete personal lives.[8] How-to books gave working mothers the impression that if they just organized their time better, they could have it all. "Success-ful working mothers learn the arts of the efficiency expert," said one book. "It would be bedlam if I hadn't learned to manage our household in one-third the time I used to spend just thinking about the living room color scheme," said one working mother.[9] A guide to combining career and mothering acknowledged that while people can't "manufacture more time," they can make bet-ter use of the time they have. As it is often said, "managing time does not mean working harder, it just means working smarter."[10]

But "working smarter" did not seem to be the answer, and six-teen years after the *Feminine Mystique* was published, Betty Frie-dan acknowledged that many of the problems are not traceable to management and organization. Friedan wrote that the " 'super-women' who are trying to 'have it all,' combining full-time careers and stretch-time motherhood, are enduring such relentless pres-sure that their younger sisters may not even dare to think about having children."[11]

I sat and talked over dinner with the women medical students who take an elective course I teach on Literature and Medicine at the Mount Sinai School of Medicine. They are bright, earnest and savvy. Their eyes shine with dedication; they are yearning to be good physicians. Any one of them I would have taken for my daughter or for my doctor. But they are troubled, these young women. They have asked me to dinner to help them with a ques-tion as pressing as one on the next day's anatomy exam: How will we combine our demanding careers with the equally demanding job of mothering? They ask, and wait expectantly for my answer. Only one of the six thinks she might not have children; the rest are determined to, but how will they manage it?

Joanna: "There's not one person we know, male or female, who seems to be doing it well. Not one person we can emulate, learn from."

Margaret, whose parents are in the midst of a divorce: "I'm not going to give up my career the way my mother did and be miser-able my entire life, but how can I have a decent practice and still raise a child?"

Sherry, from a small town in the West, who wants to have a country practice: "Everyone says that we can have it all, but I have no idea how to go about it . . . I don't think that I can be a superwoman."

And neither can most women, if we are honest about it, as scientist and author Elizabeth Whelan was. In her article "Confessions of a Superwoman," appearing in *Working Woman* in 1981, Ms. Whelan is described as a woman who had it all—Yale, Harvard, wonderful career, wonderful husband with a wonderful career, wonderful baby, wonderful apartment and wonderful house—but somehow her life wasn't so wonderful. Between her exceedingly exciting but demanding career and that of her husband, and the needs of her baby and of their multiple dwellings, she could never seem to keep track of anything. She seemed to lose that necessary center of existence without which life becomes a chaotic mélange of events. In fact, at one point things became so disorganized that she needed her secretary to type a daily schedule. Looking back on it, she realized that "unconsciously I had tried to fulfill the traditional aims while keeping a firm grip on my career. I was intent upon having it all and doing it all well."[12]

Another successful woman, writing in *Good Housekeeping*, made a similar admission, saying that "for years mothers pointed me out to their daughters: 'See. She's the one who did it all.' What no one ever understood was that I knew that I wasn't doing it all. Underneath the good haircut, my head was spinning. But I was true to the myth, true to the deception."[13]

Susan, a vice president of marketing from Maryland, also tried to remain true to the deception. She revealed her life as a superwoman to me in the following way:

> There should be two Susans answering your questions. Susan # 1 and Susan # 2—Susan # 2 is the superwoman that astounded family and friends through her 20's—balancing school, business, child, volunteer work, government appointment and a husband. Number 2 never had time for herself. She was always giving, doing the "right thing," stretched like a rubber band between two retreating hands. She was just wonderful, but oh so miserable. Number 2 made husband unhappy because she was so unhappy. But she couldn't stop . . . I think she was trying to be everything in the world to everybody—Earth Mother, problem solver, corporate executive. I don't know what happened to her. Perhaps one morning at two A.M. after typing her thesis when she started scrubbing the kitchen floor while the third grade's triple-layer Christmas cake baked in

the oven, she slipped on the sudsy floor and knocked some
sense into her head. More likely it was the very real threat
of husband leaving and only son wanting to stay with his
dad . . . that caused a complete reassessment of values,
priorities and life . . .

Judith Coburn, writing in *Mademoiselle,* asked the question of
the decade: "Do superwomen really exist?"[14] Of course the superwoman was a myth and, like all myths, served a purpose. As long
as we believed in her, she provided us with security, a way of understanding and integrating the unfamiliar, the threatening, into
what was known and comfortable. But mostly—and this is where
her real appeal lay—she allowed us to deny our guilt.

If we could be our mothers and then some, who could be critical? Certainly not our husbands. Not even Benjamin Spock or
Sigmund Freud. The superwoman syndrome enabled us to be
without guilt, but also, alas, without growth. For her fantasy
blinded us to the reality of our lives, a reality with special joys,
problems and imperatives that require adjustments in our personal lives and in society.

In one sense the superwoman syndrome was as detrimental to
women as the feminine mystique, because it perpetuated a false-
hood about ourselves. It kept us from the truth and ultimately
from growth, for only children believe that they can have everything. Real maturity means making choices, understanding the
guilt that these may bring, *and going beyond it* to a fuller existence. For although women can, indeed, do everything, they cannot, as no one can, do it all at the same time.

It was with a mixture of relief and regret, then, that we said
"So long, Superwoman"—relief because we could finally take the
next step to liberation and look at what our lives are really about;
and regret because we would now have to face the guilt that her
demise implies. But as that fabulous creation, the superwoman,
faded from view, nothing arose to take her place—no new role
model, no legend, no way of understanding our tangle of emotion.
The void spread before us like a yawning chasm, and into it
flowed our guilt, our self-reproach, our apology. Whether we
wanted to go back to work, hated to go back to work or needed
to go back to work, we felt guilty about it.

"I was so unhappy being home, I knew that working had to have
a positive effect. But I still felt guilt," confided a middle manager

from Staten Island. "I felt very torn about returning to work. I always thought I'd be home to raise them [children] until they went to school. I felt very guilty but had to work after the divorce for financial reasons," related a technical writer from Tampa. "Since I own my own business I was very torn, but I felt I had no options . . . Guilt ran very high," recalled the president of a West Coast toy company. "I feel guilt. But my job is a great joy to me," wrote a cosmetician. "I feel really guilty, especially because I'm unhappy with the job I have," explained a postal clerk.

"Guilt feelings with regard to children is one of the biggest problems facing working mothers," Alvin Eden, pediatrician and author of the book *Positive Parenting,* told me. "A prime requisite for success of the professional mother . . . is mastering the feelings of guilt with regard to the children," noted famed sociologist Jessie Bernard.[15] "Guilt might make a woman do things subconsciously to sabotage her career," said Dr. Irene P. Stiver. "The guiltier you feel, the less sexy you feel," according to Dr. Merle S. Kroop, clinical associate professor of psychiatry at New York Hospital. Guilt feelings appear to be responsible for many of the stress symptoms we're seeing in working mothers, reported Morton Leibowitz, an internist.

Guilt seems to affect working mothers in four significant areas of our lives: in connection to our children, our jobs, our marital relationships and our sense of self. Within each category I decided to trace the impact of guilt on our feelings, our thoughts, our behavior, our actions; to identify it, understand it and find ways of getting past it.

I looked first at guilt and our children, because the issues around child raising are the focus of most of our guilt.

PART TWO

In the Nursery

CHAPTER 6

Why It's So Hard to Leave

"I HAD ALWAYS thought that I would go right back to work after I had a baby," confided Donna, a banker from Boston. "But once I was pregnant, I became increasingly unsure of that decision. I don't know why, but I started to feel guilty about leaving Josh before he even was born."

Like so many of us, Donna's guilt over rejecting her mother's model became intensified during her pregnancy. Typically, whatever our relationship with our mother was before, we tend to become much closer to her now. In *The Psychology of Pregnancy*, Judith Ballou writes that during pregnancy, women's attitudes toward their mothers shift in a positive direction, with the resolution of ambivalent feelings being one of the major tasks of pregnancy. "The developmental task," says Ballou, "is to feel and function like a mother." And not just any mother—*"like one's own mother."*[1]

One woman in her second trimester of pregnancy, who admitted that she and her mother had never gotten along, marveled at the change. "My relationship with my mother is much better . . . just that we're a lot closer."[2]

I, too, remember being drawn back to my mother during my pregnancies. The sense of a shared experience, and the special language that it imparted, gave us a commonality and closeness that had been dormant in our relationship. Suddenly she became my adviser, my mentor. And it felt very good.

This reattachment or rapprochement with our mothers is an important part of pregnancy, enabling us to see ourselves as competent adults capable of fulfilling the responsibilities of motherhood. But it can pose a heavy burden for those of us who plan to work after giving birth. We are striving valiantly toward autonomy, planning and thinking about how we are going to integrate our new baby into our working lives, while at the same time we are driven back into our pasts, fused to the image of our mothers.

As Dr. Roland explained, "When a girl becomes a mother herself, the identification with her own mother becomes very much activated. She thinks my mother was a good mother, she was home all the time. I should be a good mother like that and be home all the time also." When she does return to work, it is with the feeling—not usually conscious—that 'I'm not fulfilling my role as a mother . . . I'm pulled in a whole other direction by what I want,' and it produces a lot of guilt," according to Roland.

"I feel so guilty because my baby is so little, and I am at work eight hours a day, plus you have to add on a forty-minute drive each way," wrote a computer programmer from Michigan. "I'm guilty because I don't feel like I'm a good mother," said a New York executive. From all over the country I heard variations on the same theme: I feel guilty because I am at work instead of at home.

From Memphis a woman wrote poignantly, "[I feel] much guilt and sadness. Every morning I watch as my five-month-old gazes at my face and my two-year-old clings to me and I wonder [if they are suffering] because I work."

This seemed a crucial question. Does maternal employment outside the home actually harm our children, or is this just an illusion created by our guilt? In other words, is our guilt justified?

There are those who are concerned about the impact our working has on our offspring, particularly when they are very young. Dr. John Munder Ross, a clinical psychologist and co-author of *Father and Child: Developmental and Clinical Perspectives,* is among those who warn that a mother who returns to work too early can lose empathetic contact with her child. "If bonding hasn't happened, a woman has no sense of her baby's needs and no sense of maternal constance." The late psychologist Selma Fraiberg summarized this point of view when she worried about babies "who are delivered like packages to neighbors, to strangers, in storage houses like Merry Mites" and about what she believed would be the resulting increase in the "diseases of nonattachment."[3]

Attachment and *bonding* are provocative terms, because there is no agreement in psychological circles regarding when bonding occurs or how long it takes to develop. Does it happen immediately at birth? Or does it develop slowly over time? If so, how much time is needed? Ten hours a day with the mother? Two hours a day? No one seems to know for sure.

But even those doctors who believe, as Alvin Eden does, "that it is optimal for the child to have a mother who *wants* to stay home and raise him for the first few years," admit that there is nothing in the psychological literature—no study, no evidence—to support that view.

Dr. Jerome Kagan, a noted Harvard psychologist, has recently completed a comprehensive study of children who entered day care as early as age three and a half months, in which he found that day-care children are no more or less attached to their mothers than are young children raised exclusively at home.[4] A recent edition of the *American Psychologist* agreed with this finding. The journal noted that empirical studies have not produced any evidence that infant day care in itself disrupts parent-child attachment or impedes the infant's cognitive development.[5]

"The continuing relationship of the child to its need for care by human beings is being hopelessly confused in the growing insistence that child and biological mother or surrogate mother must never be separated, that all separation even for a few days, is inevitably damaging. . . ." wrote anthropologist Margaret Mead. "On the contrary, cross-cultural studies suggest that adjustment is most facilitated if the child is cared for by many warm, friendly people."[6]

Mary Howell, a pediatrician and psychologist, has made a thorough study of the effects of mothers employed outside the home on older children. In a ten-year review of the literature, Dr. Howell concluded that when such factors as widowhood and poverty were eliminated, "the more closely children of working mothers are studied, the more they appear just like the children of mothers who are not employed." Actually the main differences between the two populations appear to be positive ones. Children with two employed parents are less likely than children who have only an employed father to make sex-stereotyped assumptions about appropriate male/female roles and are likely to be more independent.[7]

The testimonies of children of working mothers seem to bear

this out. "I was raised knowing that what counted was my intelligence, creativity and talent, not whether I was male or female," said twenty-year-old Bonnie Smith of Massachusetts, whose mother is a full professor at Simmons College. "My mother's independence helped to produce an equally independent daughter and it's a wonderful feeling."[8]

Working, then, does not make you a bad mother or an inadequate mother. "The only kind of really bad mother," says world-famous pediatrician T. Berry Brazelton, "the only kind who can harm her children's development, is not the mother who spends time away from her child, but the one who doesn't care about her baby."[9]

Unfortunately the studies supporting maternal employment do not allay the guilt of working mothers one iota. Even those women who knew of them and referred to them and accepted them *still felt guilty.*

Of course, these reports should not be taken to imply that all women should rush back to work after having babies or that they will find it easy when they do. The decision to leave a child, particularly a young one, and go back to a job is one of the most difficult and complex issues facing the current generation of women. It should be made with careful consideration of the family's goals, finances, priorities and values; your own needs, professional as well as maternal; and your baby's emotional and physical needs. It should be made with a careful assessment of the kinds of child care services available and your family's ability to provide the kind of care with which everyone is most comfortable. And it should also be made with the awareness that your decision may be different from your friends' or colleagues', as two Chicago lawyers from the same firm discovered.

When Jane McTee, thirty-two, an associate, started to work part-time after the birth of her son, Galen, she believed that within the year she would be resuming the hectic role of a full-time litigator. But the more she thought about those tight deadlines, those unpredictable midnight-to-six-A.M. night shifts, the extreme pressure, the more she realized that this schedule would not fulfill her maternal needs. "I want to be home for dinner. I don't want a baby-sitter putting him to bed," she said—a desire that prompted her to leave the partnership track and become assistant director of medical and legal affairs for the University of Chicago, where she will manage medical malpractice suits and teach malpractice prevention to the university's hospital staff.[10]

Joan Hall, forty-four, a partner in McTee's former firm, thrives on the nonstop pace of managing her career and two sons. Ms. Hall, a blond woman with a broad smile who was the firm's first pregnant associate, admits that a large chunk of her salary now goes to employ a cleaning woman and a housekeeper, who often shops for her children's clothing and sometimes goes to school meetings. But it is the exchange she makes for the time to devote to her works-in-progress, which cover the tops of four desks in her Chicago lakefront office.[11]

Finally, the decision to return to work should be made with a deep understanding that there are choices, sacrifices and risks in everything in life. The one thing, however, that should not be part of the decision is *guilt*. Giving advice to the working mother, Dr. Brazelton declared, "First and foremost, *don't feel guilty* [emphasis added]."[12] As for other feelings? There will be lots of those: sadness about leaving; a yearning, desperate, at times to stay home; worry, deep and absorbing, when your child is sick or troubled; excitement when you reach home, so great that one woman reported running, high heels, attaché case and all, from the subway station to her apartment every evening. These are all positive and appropriate feelings. They show that we are lovingly connected to our children in the best ways.

Guilt is something quite different. Although it sometimes masquerades as concern, worry or love, it is not. Stubborn and oppressive, it is the feeling that we have violated our ideal standard of mothering. This sense of self-betrayal leads us into modes of thinking that are counterproductive and punitive. And—here is where the real danger is—*it may result in exactly the kinds of things that we fear.*

Indeed, while talking to working mothers, experts, professionals across the country, it has become abundantly clear that our guilt produces certain identifiable patterns of behavior in our relationships with our children. These include overcompensating for our absences and insisting on quality time; it affects the way we discipline our youngsters, the expectations we have for them, our willingness to admit that they are having problems and the ways in which we interact with those who are caring for them in our absences.

We have to try to understand these patterns and attempt to control them, for while working in itself does not seem to bring harm to our children, the guilt that we feel over it certainly does.

CHAPTER 7

Good Transitions
in Group Child Care

THE TINY TOTS Nursery in West Palm Beach, Florida, is a series of low, flat buildings perched around a small play area, with swings and a pretend spaceship in the middle. It is early morning but the sun is already hot, explaining the burnt shrubbery that borders the playground and the dry patches of earth that make its floor. Cars and pickup trucks stop in front of the buildings, and parents get out either carrying very young children—youngsters six months and up are accepted at the center—or holding hands with older ones. Some are men, but most are women, all ready for work, many dressed in uniforms. They are waitresses, hospital aides, beauticians, bank tellers, clerks. Some are nurses, a few are storekeepers, and there are teachers, too. Mostly they are white, but with a mixture of blacks and Cubans, they fill this center to its 118-child capacity almost every day for the entire day.

They are what one of the directors, Ben Smiley, described as low-middle class, many of whom married young, with little education and little preparation for parenthood. Divorce is rampant. So are hard times. These are women to whom the idea of work for self-fulfillment or self-realization is alien. They work because they have to; for survival, not to put a down payment on a beach house. For many of them, as for the woman I'll call Mary-Jo, the $40 or $45 a week rate at the center is a lot to pay.

"But what could I do without it?" Mary-Jo asked rhetorically. "For me, there are no ifs, ands or buts about it. I gotta work," she said, taking her hand out of her daughter's so that she could light a cigarette. Although only twenty-four, Mary-Jo had the worldly wise look of someone much older. Constantly reaching for cigarettes with hands ending in bitten fingernails, she seemed at once tough and vulnerable. A checker at Winn-Dixie, a large Southern supermarket chain, Mary-Jo had the job for three years, taking little time off from work when her daughter, now eleven months old, was born. "Sure, I thought about stopping for a while, but then my husband, he got laid off, and now that he's back at work . . ." She paused and looked down. "We're . . . we're thinking about another. I don't know. I always wanted lots of kids, so I gotta keep workin'. We still got those bills comin' in." The closer we came to the building, the more reluctant her daughter, Suzy, seemed to enter, holding on to her mother's legs as we walked. Mary-Jo kept peeling her off, an activity that proved useless. "It's not like she doesn't know it here, I mean she's been comin' since she's seven months," she said as she pulled her now-whimpering daughter across the threshold. I waited outside while Mary-Jo quickly deposited her.

"How do you feel about the center?" I ventured when she returned.

"What do you mean?" she asked.

"Well, are you pleased with it and the care they give your daughter?"

"Sure, I mean, it's a very good place and the staff are all real nice."

"But do you ever feel guilty about leaving her here?"

Looking straight at me, Mary-Jo shot back, "Sure I feel guilty. Wouldn't you? I feel as guilty as hell!"

Across the country on a very quiet block of small stucco houses in Los Angeles is another child care center. The Magic Years Program. Like Tiny Tots, it, too, has an infant center, a toddler center and a preschool center. But unlike the West Palm Beach facility, its fees, which start at $500 a month, make it one of the most expensive day care facilities in the country. Its staff-to-child ratio is one to three, not the one to six of Tiny Tots, and its parents, according to Director Bill Roberson, are professionals— doctors, lawyers, researchers at UCLA—and almost all are intact families. The facilities are cheerful, certainly adequate to care for the fifty-two youngsters, and Roberson is articulate and compassionate and clearly has an intuitive feeling for children and their parents.

When parents leave their children at this facility, they can feel assured that they have the best that money can buy. They should feel good, reassured, guilt-free. But do they?

Not according to Bill Roberson. "On a basic level, our whole American mythology says that women should stay home with their children and take care of them, and I think that however enlightened a woman may be that that kind of mythology plays on a person's psyche and it does produce guilt. They can rationalize it and say, but I need to work, and my child is in a good place, but still I think that guilt will play on them . . . If a parent drops a child off too easily during the day, I worry about that child."

In another part of the country at a different kind of center, another expert in child care voiced the same concern. Professor Annette Axtman and I sat behind the one-way mirror at the Center of Infants and Parents of Columbia University, which provides a place for students, staff and faculty to leave their children. As we watched the care providers, who are themselves working toward degrees in child development, interacting with their charges, Professor Axtman, director of the program, noted that some mothers are in and out in a matter of seconds, dropping their children off, saying something like, "Oh, he'll be just fine by himself."

Over and over again I heard similar complaints: parents too rushed in the morning to give instructions, parents too busy in the evening to learn what happened during the day. Beatrice Marden Glickman and Nesha Bass Springer in their extensive study of child care reported similarly that child-care personnel across the country complain that mothers are too eager to pick up the child and leave and do not spend any time waiting to talk to the people who have been with their child all day.[1] Of course, some of the rush may be due to fatigue and time pressure, but the prevalence of this pattern suggests a deeper meaning.

"Some mothers feel so guilty that they really can't cope with the idea that they are leaving their child—they leave abruptly, the leave is jagged. They don't provide any sense of continuity," explained Professor Axtman. If we could have a printout of what was going on in their minds, it might be something like this: I am putting my child in a child care center and I am raising my child in a very different way from the way my mother raised me and that makes me feel guilty. When I hear about my child from others, when I have to face the fact that others spend more time with my child than I do or that others know my child better than I do, it is like rubbing salt into a wound: it exacerbates my guilt. So I try to avoid that uncomfortable situation as often as I can.

Sure, it's hard to learn at the end of the day that your child really missed you or cried for you or was fighting a lot with his peers, and it's equally hard to hear the pride in a child care worker's voice when she tells you how your daughter took her first step. Sure, it's hard to hear those things from strangers, but it's better to hear than not. For if you don't know what is happening with your child during your absence, you won't know what's happening during the time you are together, as a friend of mine whom I'll call Jane discovered.

Hard-driving, successful and always a little behind schedule, Jane gave birth to her own literary agency and her son within six weeks of each other. When her son was an infant, she kept him at home and worked out of her apartment, but as he grew, so did her profession, and when he was fifteen months old, she began bringing him to a warm, supportive child care center on a lovely tree-lined street on Manhattan's Upper West Side, while she rented an office.

She was pleased with the care at the center and, aside from scheduled conferences, spent little time there. When her son began having trouble falling asleep at night, she assumed that they were letting him nap for too long during the day. At first it wasn't a problem; as long as he's getting enough sleep, it's all right, she reasoned. But when it began to turn into real insomnia, Jane decided it was time to talk to the child care workers. She got to the center a little early one morning so she could tell the child care workers not to let Brenden nap. And she was more than a little surprised when she learned that he had not been napping at all.

The center thought he was giving up his nap because he was getting lots of sleep at home; Jane, of course, had thought the reverse. As seen from either side, there was no problem. Only when both experiences were compared did it become apparent that there was something going on with Brenden, some fear, perhaps, that was interfering with his normal sleeping pattern. Jane made an appointment to speak to the care worker that evening, and they pinpointed Brenden's anxiety to their joint pressure on him to give up his bottle and drink from a cup. Together they decided to ease up a bit and hope that Brenden would become interested in the cup on his own.

Not a big problem and easily resolved once it was understood—in fact, it is fairly typical of the countless developmental disturbances that children go through. That is why communication with child care workers is so important. Child care experts, whatever their particular view of maternal employment, agree that children do best when there is consistency of care. When routines are predictable, children develop security and learn trust.

While an integrated flow of time and care seems best for the child, Bill Roberson of The Magic Years pointed out that much of a young child's normal day does not flow but is made up of transitions: snacks, diapering, dramatic play, quiet play, outdoor play, rest. Often these transitions are bumpy and disruptive. Add to this the transition of going to and from a caretaker and you've got a lot of segmentation, which has the potential of being unsettling and anxiety producing for a child.

If your child is being fussy because he is teething, you should tell the center how you comfort him. If your child is showing an interest in toilet training, you should tell the center how to proceed. Imagine how confusing it is for a child whose parents are putting no pressure on him to toilet train to spend eight hours a day with a worker who does. And it isn't only bad for the child, it's bad for you. Unless you communicate how you do things at home and how you would like your child cared for, you may be assuaging your guilt in the short run, but you are really relinquishing control over your baby's care to someone else, and that, in the long run, will make you feel much guiltier.

If you find that you are getting into the habit of dropping off your child quickly and picking him or her up without waiting around to talk to those who have been with him all day, here are a few things you can do. The first is to schedule that time into your day—an extra five or maybe ten minutes at the most on either side. Just enough to say—Bill's had a tough time getting up this morning, or Nancy dressed herself, or What kind of day did Jake have? It might even be a good idea to mention this new plan to the care worker, so that even if you're too hassled to remember, she or he may.

Some centers, such as the one at the Demonstration Nursery

Center, University of North Carolina, use cue cards that contain information you might want to give about your baby. These can be very helpful, even if you just fill in a few important phrases, like refused supper last night, slept well, or didn't have time to read her a story last night—please try to do it today.[2]

A good center should be an extension of a warm, loving home; your child's day in it, more predictable than unpredictable, more affirmative than negative. To this end we should try as much as possible to have harmonious transitions back and forth. Facing up to our guilt will help achieve this.

Understanding and dealing with our guilt may also help us secure better group child care not only for our own children but for other families. While so many women of all classes laud the benefits—intellectual and emotional stimulation—of good infant day care, we also know how scarce "quality" centers are. According to data collected by the Pre-School Association, mothers of 223,500 New York City children younger than six work outside the home, but only 77,450 places are available in public and private child care programs. Other cities have similar shortages.[3]

The problem has been highlighted by the changing and enlarging population who use day care. Once the "housekeeper" of the poor, group child care is now seen as a desirable alternative to the baby-sitter long used by many middle-class families. Speaking on this topic, Sheila Kamerman, professor of social policy and planning at Columbia University's School of Social Work, emphasized, "[Group care] is not just for other people's children. It is for all our children."[4]

But all our children will not be able to find spots in good group care programs unless we are willing to fight for them. At present 80 percent of the women in the work force are of childbearing age, and approximately 93 percent of them will become pregnant during their work careers. Despite some celebrated examples of employer-sponsored day care—Stride-Rite Corporation, Hoffmann–La Roche and Corning Glass Works—only 120 corporations—a fraction of the country's 6 million total employers—provide on- or near-site child care services.

Investigating the current nationwide shortage of employer-sponsored day care for the Carnegie Foundation, Dana Friedman found that few employees made management aware of their needs.[5] Since management theorists agree that "organizations do change when they are under pressure and rarely when they are not," Friedman sought to understand the employees' reticence.[6]

Job insecurity in a time of high unemployment must surely inhibit some from speaking out. But, as Friedman points out, group letters, petitions and union spokespersons can all lessen the risk of individual advocacy and have in many cases accomplished their goals. Many organizations are providing some form of financial assistance to help offset costs of away-from-home care, which can range from $1,500 to 10,000 a year per child.[7]

Friedman suggests that beneath all the obstacles is the inhibiting power of our own ambivalence about working mothers. Guiltily bound by a particular "memory of motherhood," we do not feel free to press for the changes our present lives demand.[8]

CHAPTER 8

The Other Woman in Your Child's Life

WE WERE SITTING eating dinner and Andrew asked, "How come you never make spinach? My mommy says spinach is good for you," I put down my spoon and looked at him, somewhat surprised, for I couldn't recall ever having said that. "Which mommy?" I asked jokingly.

But to him it was no joke. "My mommy Vilna," he replied with all the solemnity that a four-year-old can muster.

"Vilna isn't your mommy, she's your baby-sitter," I corrected.

"Oh no," he said with certainty. "She told me I have two mommies. A Mommy Barbara and a Mommy Vilna."

Suddenly I lost my appetite.

In explaining why they choose a baby-sitter or "surrogate mother" over group care, most women emphasized that they preferred the one-to-one interaction. "My children receive the care and attention of an individual rather than an institution," explained Pamela, a computer operator from Oklahoma. Another woman put it this way: "There are too many different people at the center. I want my son to be able to attach." But here is the catch: Attachment to a baby-sitter is the best of all possible worlds, but it is also the worst of all possible worlds.

"I felt insecure as a mother and yet deeply guilty because I wanted to go back to work. Nothing worked out. I wasn't happy at work. And I wasn't happy at home. I always felt as though I was doing the wrong thing. I wasn't the mother—the English nanny was the mother. I suffered," said Maggie Simmons, a forty-year-old magazine editor and mother of two young children, expressing the common fear of being supplanted by a baby-sitter.[1]

One woman confessed to bursting into tears when her son cried out for the housekeeper during the night, while another said, "I abdicated motherhood to a baby nurse and nanny."[2] And therapist Alan Roland, speaking from his personal experience, recalled that his wife Jackie's guilt always seemed alleviated if he, not the housekeeper, was taking care of the children. "It's not that the quality of the care was very different but [Jackie] felt less guilty if I was around even though the housekeeper was someone the kids like very much."

"I was afraid my son would love his caregiver more than me," confided Judy, an accountant from Tennessee, while Connie, a secretary from Iowa, felt envious that her sitter was the first to get the children's news at the end of the school day. And Julia, a banker from New Jersey, confessed to feeling troubled because "I want my son to remember *me* as his mommy—not the caregiver," she said.

"There's a real fear of being displaced by their child's caregiver," said Stephen Segal, president of Resources for Parents at Work, a Philadelphia-based company that holds seminars for working parents. Sometimes this fear is so great that mothers stop working, as did Brenda Shenck. "I never want Michael to come home and yell 'Ma,' and have someone else answer," said Brenda, a former model and actress who ran her own clothing boutique in Chicago before deciding to stay home full-time. Other women for whom work remains a compelling need handle this concern differently.

"My baby-sitter was tops," wrote a market researcher from Detroit. "But my kids got so attached to her. I kept hearing, 'Joella said this,' 'Joella said that'; it was too much. After a while, I let her go." Segal reported that one mother told a story that immediately struck a sympathetic chord in the other mothers at the seminar. The mother of a preschooler asked her daughter: "Whom do you love more, me or Charlene?" To which the daughter responded: "I love you a million times, I love Charlene a trillion times." The mother fired Charlene—a response that met with nods of approval from the audience.

I, too, would have nodded, for I felt like doing nothing more that night of the "two mommies" than firing Vilna. But why? She was wonderful, the perfect baby-sitter. I liked her, the children liked her, and on the two or three days a week she came, I knew that I could work free from worry. So why in the world did I want to fire her?

"Women often feel very guilty when the child becomes too close to the housekeeper," explained Dr. Roland. Rationally it should be the other way around. We should feel upset if our child doesn't like the baby-sitter, dreads being left with her. But when that person is obviously important and loving to the child, why feel guilty?

Could it be because a housekeeper, totally involved with our children and our home, is uncomfortably like our own mothers? Doesn't she become identified in our minds with our image of the good mommy, while we, busy rushing and working, seem by comparison the bad mommy? Doesn't this heighten our sense of pain and guilt over separating from our first and most important role model, and ultimately make us feel competitive with our caretaker?

"It's awfully easy to get into a situation where the surrogate and mother become competitive about . . . a baby," noted Dr. Brazelton in a recent interview.[3] And this competition isn't only over love, it's over care, too.

Many of us choose baby-sitters who have grown children of their own. As Robin, a software engineer from New Hampshire, explained, "The sitter is a more experienced mother than I am." Our sitters have been through the various stages—the teething, the temper tantrums—that are mystifying and new to us. It's to be expected that they have their own ideas on how to deal with difficult behavior, to feel that they are the experts, while we mothers are the novices. It is also to be expected that our baby-sitters, whom we *want* to be warm and caring toward our children, should want some of that affection returned. What employee doesn't hope her or his work will be personally rewarding?

What, then, can we do when we find our children clinging to their sitters or housekeepers or following their advice rather than our own? Should we, as many of us do—as I was about to do—fire them?

I would have thought so if I hadn't had the chance to discuss this with the noted child psychiatrist Eleanor Galenson. According to Dr. Galenson, unless the housekeeper or sitter is deficient, it's more important to maintain consistency of care.

Of course it's hard to hear endless remarks like "Joella combs my hair this way," or "Vilna is more fun to play with than you," but something Stephen Segal told me makes it easier: "Just as you can't feel the same way about another person's child as you do about your own, your child can't feel the same way about a caretaker as he or she feels toward you." If we can hold on to this thought, we won't feel as vulnerable to our children's declarations that they love their baby-sitters more than they love us, and we won't feel hurt or undermined if our baby-sitter puts a dress on our daughter rather than the overalls we picked out.

Once we free ourselves from guilty competition over these issues, we will be able to focus on the significant ones: communicating to our baby-sitters how we want our children cared for.

It is important that we feel comfortable about being able to give them directions. To do this, it's good to remember that they are really our *assistants* rather than our substitutes or surrogates, as they are commonly called.

It also helps to be clear and direct about our views on those things that mean a lot to us: sharing toys with friends or siblings, responsibility for personal belongings, resolving differences of opinion, amount of television, appropriate snacks, discipline style, when and if you want your child to nap, what is the customary bedtime ritual, when and where homework is done, for example. Instead of saying, "If Johnny messes up his room, it's okay to punish him," it is better to say, "When Johnny messes up his room, I tell him that he must clean it up before he watches television. I'd like you to do the same thing."

Since you are not home, it's hard to know how your directives are being followed. Hard, but not impossible. There's nothing wrong with asking in a pleasant way, "How much television did the children watch?" "Did they have milk after school?" Of course, you don't have to do this every day; just often enough to keep tabs on your family and make sure that the lines of authority are clear.

As well, many women I know, including myself, have from time to time resorted to spying when they are uncertain about how their children are being cared for. Kathleen, an administrator from Connecticut, advised women to take the time to pop in unexpectedly on their sitters. "You'll learn a lot." If you're worried that your housekeeper who is always a little late coming to work is also late picking your toddler up at the Y, ask another mother in the group or the teacher to check. When I wondered about how well Vilna was able to watch my two whirling dervishes at the playground, I decided to drop by one day, and never again would I worry.

Knowing that you are in control—that your values and standards are being transmitted to the child even in your absence—will reinforce the feeling that *you* are the mother even if you are away at work.

When you discover problems or a breakdown in communication, try to solve them at once. Talk to the caregiver calmly and privately. It's not easy, because few issues seem to evoke greater feelings than the quality of child care. Sometimes the results are good, sometimes not.

I tried to be very sensitive to Vilna's feelings when I spoke to her because I knew that she was very much attached to my children and proud of how much they cared for her. I told her that I was really glad that she and the children were so close, that it showed how wonderful a job she was doing, but that it was better for them not to be told that she was their other mother. "It's confusing to them and will make them feel that they can play one of us off against the other, and this will ultimately make your job harder," I said. I didn't need to mention it again.

Sometimes, however, the problem is recalcitrant. Christine Melton, the ophthalmologist mentioned earlier, experienced this with her live-in housekeeper, who was creating what Christine called the dumb-mommy syndrome. It goes something like this: " 'Oh, poor Catherine, you have a cold. I guess that mommy forgot to put on your gloves.' It was a whole undermining thing," Christine said. When it didn't end with repeated talks, she did the only sensible thing and dismissed her. For while child psychologists such as Dr. Stella Chess warn against a "constantly changing array of caregivers," Dr. Chess also stressed that children are more resilient than we think and that "part of what [they] have to learn in this world is that people are different and that you behave in one way in one situation and another way in another."[4]

When you do have to fire a housekeeper or baby-sitter, it's best not to go into too many details with your child. Experts advise saying something simple and matter-of-fact, like, "It didn't work out," or "We didn't fit one another's needs." Most children will accept this and take the departure in stride. Occasionally a child will have some difficulty when a favorite nanny or baby-sitter leaves. This happened to Gary, the three-year-old son of my friend Sara. When Sara fired Lucy, who had taken care of Gary since his birth, he became unusually irritable and stubborn. Sara immediately reassured him that he wasn't to blame for Lucy's leaving and tried to get him to express his feelings about it. She helped him realize that it was perfectly normal to miss someone whom he had known for so long. Sara recalled that the hardest part had been trying to maintain some continuity for Gary by sticking close to his usual schedule. This is no easy accomplishment, because the transition between baby-sitters can be fairly disruptive of family routines.

The time of upheaval can be shortened, however, when you know the traits that you are looking for in the new person. Many women try, as Sara did, to find those qualities that they felt were lacking in the last sitter. Lucy, for example, had been wonderful with Gary when he was a baby. She was warm, nurturing, honest, neat and willing to follow directions. But she was not really interested in engaging Gary in intellectual or creative activities, and Sara felt these to be increasingly important as Gary grew older. Within a few weeks Sara was able to hire a woman who embodied the qualities that she was looking for. Gary liked her immediately and was soon back to his good-natured self.

So while you should not fire a housekeeper because you feel she is getting too close to your children, you should if she is no longer fulfilling your or your child's needs or is creating any kind of dissension within your family. It helps to remember that they can be replaced in your child's affection, but you can never be.

CHAPTER 9

Quality Time

"DO YOU REMEMBER feeling guilty?" I asked.

"Ah, constantly; total torment. I was in total conflict every single day. I'd leave in the morning and he would cry. I'd get to the elevator and press the button and say, 'I'll never get through this . . . ,' " answered Harriet Whitelaw, an international art dealer and the mother of two sons and one stepson.

The beautiful antique earrings and necklace that she was wearing connected Harriet to the world of art that is both her passion and her profession. It hasn't always been this way. Combining her personal interests with her career was a long and difficult journey of marriage, divorce and single parenting, a story that Harriet tells with a blend of humor and sadness.

A bright, articulate woman in her early forties, Harriet was raised in the typical traditional home of European immigrants to America. "My mother did not work," she said emphatically. "Women in Warsaw did not work. She came from such a culturally different environment that it was hard for her to understand that there was another way." But Harriet knew early on that for her there would be another way. "I always did extremely well in school," she admitted cautiously, "so I always felt that I would be able to do something well professionally." But, following the conventional path for middle-class girls during the fifties, Harriet prepared to become a teacher. "I graduated from college at nineteen, I was put in a New York high school with kids who were eighteen; it was a miracle that I lasted as long as I did: three and a half years. But at twenty-three I decided that I wanted to do something with antiques, and because I was twenty-three and I thought that anything was possible, I went to Parke-Bernet Galleries to a very distinguished Englishman and told him that I wanted a job. At first he laughed. But the next morning he called me and told me that if I wanted it, the job was mine."

For the next two and a half years this man was her mentor. "I went through college all over again. Every night I came home laden with books on everything from Chinese art to French furniture. At work I would wander over to the painting section on the other side of the floor and try to learn a little on my own.

"I remember thinking, I'll never know a Max Ernst from a Picasso, but suddenly it all came wonderfully alive." Realizing that she wanted to work with painting, Harriet, now thirty-one, seven months pregnant and unhappily married, agreed to take over a well-known art gallery on Madison Avenue in Manhattan. "In a way, it was totally insane," she said, reflecting on that decision, "but I knew that things weren't going well with my husband, and I was anticipating that I might need a way to support myself and the baby." As her marriage continued to deteriorate, Harriet found herself managing a full-scale business that was extremely demanding and taking care of her new baby, David, often with inadequate baby-sitting help. "It was really hellish, but I decided I had no alternative."

But even the realization that she had to work and the knowledge that her salary was crucial to their well-being did not mitigate her sense of guilt.

"The guilt I had was the worst feeling in the world," she said, her face suddenly sad and serious. "I could take anything, but not that—it was just too painful."

"Did your guilt affect the way you related to your son?" I asked.

"Yes. I did try to compensate. When I came home from work at six-thirty at night I just tried to cram everything in. I tried to be super perfect. Everything that he wasn't getting all day had to happen in the hour and a half before he went to bed."

Harriet's response—to pack it all in—is typical of women trying to assuage their guilt.

"When I feel guilty," said Anne Simon, therapist and mother of three-month-old Zachery, "I've observed myself maybe trying too hard when I'm with him, feeling like there has to be a lot of interaction, a lot going on, and I've observed that maybe because of this, I haven't allowed the quiet time."

Experts in child development have pointed out some negative

implications for the child and the parent-child relationship when children are not allowed enough time to relax. By evening most babies, even if they are physically rested from an afternoon nap, are "psychologically frayed." Anna Freud saw this process as the "deterioration of a child's ego." According to Dr. Brazelton, by the end of the day a child needs his ego boundaries defined by less rather than more stimulation. He or she looks to the parents to provide a peaceful resolution to the day.[1] Working mothers, however, are just getting home at six or seven o'clock and our sense of apology often makes us overload our children with activity beyond their ability to cope. Unfortunately, this kind of intense end-of-day interaction can make children uneasy and insecure.

Alvin Eden, who, as a pediatrician, talks to countless working mothers, told me that because of guilt at not being home, "some [mothers] try too hard and in the time that they spend they have to make every minute count. It becomes kind of frantic." Young children are sensitive to their mothers' tension and become increasingly anxious themselves. Dr. Eden gave me a good example: A mother may feel guilt because she hasn't seen her baby all day. When she does get home, she rushes in to pick up her infant, who may be tired and begin to cry. The mother will then go in each time the baby cries to cuddle and sing to her. But, as Dr. Eden points out, the baby will then expect to be held whenever she cries and will begin to learn that crying is a way of getting attention. "It becomes a vicious cycle," he explained, "and it's not very healthy."

Children have to learn constructive methods of engaging adult attention and of tolerating some frustration. Mothers can help babies develop these qualities by first allowing them some quiet time, and then, if they do begin to cry, by waiting a few minutes before going in to comfort them.

Why do we have this need to compress everything into the available time? *Quality time.* Few phrases are more common among working mothers. It began as a concept presumably meant to reassure us, but it has actually come to increase the pressure. For whatever quality time means—and no one seems to know for sure— it has become another hook for us to hang our guilt on.

The concept of quality time is relatively new. Books on child rearing and child development ten, or fifteen years ago didn't even mention it. Time with a child was time with a child, good, bad or indifferent. If our mother spent the afternoon volunteering at a local hospital or out shopping all day, and yelled at us when she came home, she didn't worry that we weren't having quality time. But today's working mother does worry. She worries a lot.

When large numbers of women first began seeking employment outside the home, research psychologists told us that the quantity of the time that we spent with our children was not as important as the quality of the time. Immediately we latched on to the idea. We all knew mothers who were home all day talking on the telephone or visiting with neighbors; mothers who were there but not there. How you spent your time with your children, obviously, was more important than how much time you spent. Of course, we understood that without sufficient quantity, the quality was bound to suffer, but in general we accepted the axiom.

Over the last few years, however, the idea of quality time has become transformed into a rigid code with specific dos and don'ts. Quality time has come to mean that the time we spend with our children after work must be consistently superior and free from strife. Alison Clarke-Stewart of the University of Chicago, one of the first to address the notion of quality time, stipulated that it should be "not only warm, loving, non-rejecting, but . . . stimulating and enriching."[2] Professor Bettye M. Caldwell of the University of Arkansas urged that quality time be "one to one" and should "involve something the child wants to do." Not allowed as part of quality time, said Caldwell, is listening with one ear, losing your temper several times or having your quality time interrupted. Suppose you have just begun a quality-time session with your child and the phone rings, hypothesized Caldwell. "If possible, have someone else answer it, if not speak briefly."[3]

While it is unclear exactly how the supportive concept of quality time became changed into a fixed set of rules, a goal to be achieved on a daily basis, what is clear is that working mothers are the very ones who are espousing it. Quality time is "when I give my child my individual attention and do something he wants to do," wrote one woman; "Doing positive activities together, being able to be patient and really enjoy them," was how another woman expressed it. Working mothers typically urge others to "spend as much quality time as possible with your children," and the recent crop of handbooks offer advice on how to do this.

One popular guide for working mothers defines quality time as "simply one parent, one child, and no distractions."[4] Another gives suggestions for achieving this. "Pushing dinner back an hour later and devoting your first hour home to playing and talking to your children." "Moving closer to your place of work" was another suggestion. "Instead of spending an hour or two on the highway or railroad you can be spending it on the road to family closeness, or playing games at the dinner table so that your family will find the meal more interesting and want to linger." Or, "play hooky with your child. Stay home from work and keep the child out of school to work on a special project, go shopping, sneak off to a matinee or take in a ball game. (Of course, do not do this too often)," the author added.[5]

However women try to achieve quality time, most would agree with Ann, a speech pathologist from Oregon to whom the concept means giving "the best of me" to her children, ages six and one, when she gets home from work.

This insistence on always giving the best of ourselves to our children after a whole day at work puts yet another demand on us.

Most of us are faced with numerous chores when we come home from work. But we find ourselves postponing these until later in the evening to spend quality time with our children. Since the formula requires a one-to-one interaction, those of us with two or more children have the difficult and often impossible task of finding something to occupy the others while we have quality time with one.

Because we have been advised that the time should be "enriching," most women I interviewed engaged in numerous activities with their children on any given day. Play-Doh, sewing, arts and crafts, doing a puzzle and coloring are all squeezed in between dinner and bedtime. Diana Hymphries, an interior designer from Dallas, told me about a friend to whom quality time meant "doing about four hundred things each time she and her daughter were together."

The requirement that quality time be "stimulating" is difficult for us as well as for our children. We have already seen how overloading a baby with stimuli can have negative consequences. It can also be harmful to an older child, because it discourages real concentration and involvement in any one project. Children develop skills of concentration when they learn to become absorbed in a large task rather than breeze through many small ones. And how can we comply with the stipulation that quality time "always be happy and warm" if our children misbehave during it? Countless women confessed to feeling terribly guilty if they scolded rather than played during a period they had set aside for quality time.

Quality time as it is now defined "has turned out to be for [working mothers] another opportunity to fail," said Stephen Segal. Many mothers rush home all set to give quality time to their children, only to discover that quality time is not on their youngster's agenda. A woman I met at a conference in Minneapolis told me that she had left work early to spend some quality time with her four-year-old. "I was going to take her out to dinner. Just the two of us. My husband was working late, and my son was at scouts. The only problem was that when I got home she was glued to the tube and didn't want to go. I insisted, she put up a fuss. By the time we left, she was in tears and I was on the verge of them."

Many times I have turned off my typewriter early and gone home, filled with anticipation at seeing my children. Sometimes I might pick up a craft project for us to work on together, only to find that Andrew preferred to play garage alone in his room and Alison wanted to visit her friend Janie down the hall. "But I rushed home to be with you . . ." I find myself saying, the disappointment clearly mine, not theirs.

As long as we rate how good or worthwhile our days are by whether we've had "quality time" with our children, we are setting ourselves up for difficulties. First of all, we're making unrealistic demands on ourselves as well as on our children, for it's as hard or harder for them to deliver quality behavior on schedule as it is for us. Second, we are conveying a sense of apology to them, which inevitably undermines us. As Elaine Dwyer, a nurse from the Pacific Northwest, said, "I try to spend quality time with Timmy. I think that he wraps me around his finger because he knows when we are together he has my attention."[6]

Finally, in spite of all of our good intentions, we are distorting the real meaning of a parent-child relationship by insisting that quality time is its ultimate goal. If we really think about what we want for our children, most of us would answer that we want them to feel cared for and connected to us. Certainly playing with them, working on a hobby or project, snuggling and reading are all ways to create that bond. It's important for children to know that their mother *wants* to spend and *enjoys* spending time with them. But limit setting and dealing with unhappy behavior are also parts of a relationship, and the time we spend with our children can and should include these kinds of interactions also.

Quality time, as it is now being used, is a fiction. It is what we want our children to want and need as a way for us to discharge our guilt. We should try to be more relaxed about the time we spend with our children rather than seeing it as a session, or as something prescribed. Sometimes the evenings or weekends with our children will be wonderful and sometimes disappointing. But we will all do better if we accept good times *and* bad times as natural times in a family.

Interestingly, researchers in the Harvard University Pre-School Project found that youngsters who were most competent came from homes in which parents acted in the role of "designers" and "consultants." Many of these mothers worked outside the home and spent less than 10 percent of their time interacting with their babies. While they accomplished household tasks or talked on the telephone, they were available to answer a question, put a piece in a puzzle or help a toddler up from a fall. Dr. Burton L. White, the director of the project, explained, "I think some parents do a disservice to their children by being around them too much and paying too much attention to them."[7]

When the mother stays in the background, a child learns the valuable skill of getting and holding her attention when he needs it. And he also learns that he doesn't always need it just because she is there. Most mothers who work outside the home would probably not want to stay in the background too long. But it's encouraging to know that your child won't be harmed and might even be helped if you do so sometimes.

While mothers seem to have taken the idea of quality time to be their very own responsibility, fathers, even if they are not living with the family, can and should be involved in the time spent with children, be it play, limit setting or being on call. When I've had to work and Arnie was with the children, I was always amazed at how well he managed *and* how happy the children were. It was just as important that he spend time with them as I. Of course, I had always known it, but now I knew it in a different way, and it made a lasting impression.

It isn't just that the children need to know that both parents love them, although the importance of that is inestimable. It's that Arnie and I, as most people would, bring our different styles and interests to our interactions with the children. I tend to be the reader, the storyteller and board-game player, while Arnie is more apt to construct a city out of cartons with them or to take them on a one-day trip. Not terribly interested in bedtime, schedules or square meals, he's the perfect balance to my ways.

We stopped worrying about whether we have "quality time" with Alison and Andrew when we finally realized that the time with our children, no matter how it is spent, is equally valuable to us all. It is very difficult to reenter our children's lives at the end of the workday, but if we are able to get the support of our husbands or boyfriends, it surely helps. So does divesting ourselves of the spurious notion of quality time.

CHAPTER 10

Overcompensating

OVERCOMPENSATING, LIKE QUALITY time, comes from a deep sense of apology, a feeling that we have done something wrong and must make amends. "I found it very hard to control my purchasing when I was Christmas shopping for my eighteen-month-old. I almost brought the entire toy store home with me! When I really think about it, I know that my son would never know the difference if I bought less. My gift-giving was really overcompensation for having to leave him with a sitter all day,"[1] wrote Andrea T. Just of New Jersey.

"Jennifer has so many clothes she could never wear them all. There are outfits that I put away with the labels still on. . . . Mark has a color television and a stereo in his bedroom. I indulged him with the video for his birthday. I do enough for three birthdays [each year]. I really go nuts at Christmas and their birthdays, I really overdo it," confessed Alice, an executive with a large accounting firm.

"I buy love a lot," admitted a New York stock analyst. "I'm really into bribes. I have a box of treats in the closet, under-five-dollar items, some are fifty cents. My surprise box. I buy love a lot," she repeated.

Sherry, a public relations expert from Ann Arbor, said that each time she worked late she'd bring home a little gift. "Then one day I looked at his room, and it was literally overflowing with toys, and I thought, why in the world am I doing this?"

It's a good question. Why do we load up our children with gifts? Why this excessive consumption? "[It's] a sop for guilt," says Boston's Dr. Mary Howell. "Because employment out of the home still seems tradition-breaking for women, working mothers are particularly prone to this sense of guilt."[2]

"[Because I work], I give in more, overcompensate with toys," explained Pamela, a realtor from Ohio; while Susan, a vice president of a Maryland wine importing firm, wrote, "I cover guilt when traveling with presents."

"The working parent wants to give, and the giving feels like giving, but it doesn't quite work that way," cautioned Ellen Galinsky of Bank Street College of Education, who designs seminars for working parents. The unrestrained giving of toys and presents can confuse our children about what is of importance in life. Sitting on the floor of our local Y, I listened as a teacher discussed the concept of freedom with a group of children whose ages ranged from five years old to nine. We had just watched a film about Abraham Lincoln and slavery, and the children had been asked what freedom meant to them. Immediately the faces grew thoughtful. Then one little girl eagerly waved her hand. "I would like to be free to have my ears pierced and buy earrings but my mother won't let me." "I want to be free to get a Walkman," called out a seven-year-old boy. "Another Cabbage Patch doll"; "A computer game." These children could only conceive of freedom as acquisition. Buying becomes equated with the highest good.

While we all have to decide for ourselves what we want to convey to our children about the significance of ownership and property, when we guiltily overbuy presents, objects take on an exaggerated and distorted meaning. Through our responding to a child's endless requests with an endless stream of gifts, the child comes to measure his or her self-esteem by the number of things you buy, according to Dr. Howell. A toy or game is "proof" that Mommy loves me, that I am a good person.[3]

In young children particularly, this belief takes on an almost magical intensity. Unlike our love or affection, however, the presents we heap upon our children cannot comfort them or provide any lasting security; this causes them constantly to long for more, a longing that is perpetuated by its very insatiability.

Once this pattern is established it can lead our children into ways of behaving that are paralyzing. We all know people who respond to any kind of depression by heading for the stores; people who reach for the cookie jar whenever they are upset. None of us would purposely pursue such a path for our children, but over-buying may be setting them on exactly this course.[4]

When we peek into our children's rooms and realize that they are indistinguishable from a toy store, it's time to stop and ask ourselves, as did the public relations officer, Why in the world am I doing this? Is it for us or for them?

Are we buying our children what they *need* or what they *want?* There's a world of difference between the two. Children's wants are unending. They want what they see on television, they want what their friends have—no matter if they have six other varieties of it—they want what their siblings have. And, if my experiences are typical, they want 92 percent of what they see in any particular store.

"I want that," Alison will say, pointing to some Day Glo–colored object.

"What is it?"

"I don't know, but I want it."

Many times, particularly if I've been hassled or pressured to get an article in, or I haven't been around as much as usual, I'm tempted to give in to this illogicality. Many times I *have* given in. Now I try to say something like, "I know that you want it, but we can't have everything we want."

Sometimes this leads us into a discussion about the value of objects and about learning to love and take care of what they do have. Other times, however, the unbought toy remains a source of tension between us, an enduring disappointment and frustration. But frustration, as we have noted before, is something a child must learn to deal with. It can't and shouldn't be washed away by our needs to give.[5]

Often the disappointment isn't over how many toys as much as what kind of toys your child wants. Some families, for example, don't like Barbie dolls; in other households toy guns are not allowed. If you have strong feelings about the kinds of things you want your child to have, stay with them.

Two years ago, when all the children were wearing those sparkly antennae on their heads that made them look like so many creatures from outer space, I refused to buy one for Alison. My list of objections was long. "Uncomfortable," "expensive," "silly," I told her. This one caused us many squabbles, but I was determined to stick to my decision. That is, until the day of our block's annual street fair, when all the little girls were buying them from one of the vendors.

"Please, Mommy, can I have one?" Alison asked, as she had one hundred times before, fully expecting me to say no again. But it was one of those damp, heavy September days, and I had been working hard, available to the children, but unavailable to them too. It seemed like such a small thing, and it would make her so happy. "Okay, honey, you can have it," I said.

Yet strangely and significantly, my yes did not really please her at all. Oh sure, she rushed off to buy one—a glittery extraterrestrial affair that she quickly put on. But she was troubled. "How come you let me buy one when all along you kept saying I couldn't get it?" she asked repeatedly. Whatever happiness she got was diminished by her confusion about my change of mind. I really learned something that day.

Another thing I've learned, particularly as the children have gotten older, is how important it is for them to use the money they've earned doing extra chores around the house for their own purchases. Gleefully extravagant when mommy and daddy were doing the buying, they've become spartan when some of the money comes from their Snoopy banks.

Of course, there are still times for presents: birthdays, holidays, special occasions. And even times for spontaneous, fun gifts. But those times shouldn't be when you are feeling guilty about working late and you sense that your child is missing you. At those times your child would benefit more from some extra attention from you, your husband, an older sibling or, if that's not possible, from another adult with whom your child is close. It may not have flashing lights and fly around the bedroom, but it is ultimately of much greater value.

"Smother love," that's what Dr. Lois Hoffman, a pioneer in the study of working mothers and their children, calls it and there are many smother-loving mothers among us. These are "guilt-motivated" women, according to Dr. Hoffman, who tend to overprotect or overindulge their children as a way of expiating their guilt at spending part of their time in a personally gratifying activity.[6]

This kind of overcompensating can take a number of forms; one is excessive worrying about children's physical well-being. "My guilt trip is that something terrible will happen to one of my children," said Gwen, an editor at a major publishing house. "I'm absolutely paranoid about it. I don't even let my twelve-year-old walk down a different aisle in the supermarket."

Another woman I know keeps her child indoors for days on end when she has a cold, certain each time that it's going to turn into pneumonia. And a New Jersey executive and mother of three related the following story:

> I was rushing out to a meeting and making Christie a chicken salad sandwich. But as I drove to the office, I began to think: was there a chicken bone in the sandwich? Was there? Was there? Yes, I was sure of it. I had been so preoccupied with my work, so busy thinking about my meeting, that I had left a bone in my daughter's sandwich and now she was going to choke. Immediately I stopped the car and called the school. "Don't let Christie eat her sandwich," I pleaded. And then, because I didn't trust the school to take the lunch away, I postponed my meeting and went to the school myself.

And I, a smother-loving mother if ever there was one, used to be so frightened that Andrew would fall off the ladder to a slide that I would stand ready to catch him. One day, when he was eighteen months old, he turned to me as he was going up, pointed to a nearby park bench and said, "Sit right there."

"What?" I asked, utterly stunned.

"Sit right there," he repeated, and only when I left my post did he march forward, a triumphant smile on his face at his newfound freedom.

According to psychoanalyst Karen Horney, an overprotective mother may believe she is acting in the child's best interest, but is actually disregarding her child's need for independent development.[7] Eminent child psychologists find that when we overprotect our children we inevitably project our own fears onto them. Often this leads to anxious, clinging, regressive behavior, or it can encourage the reverse: defensively exaggerated recklessness. At six Andrew is a daredevil who can give Evel Knievel some competition with his daredevil stunts.

Hand in hand with guilt-motivated overprotection goes overindulgence at home. As one expert in child development stated,

"To reduce the guilt . . . women tend to demand less from [their children] and to provide few opportunities for the child to learn through doing or meeting challenges unaided. They tend, in other words, to supply the child's needs too readily and completely through their own activity."[8] Psychologist Alan Roland agreed that the guilt over working "gives women an impulse to do as much as possible for the children." Reflecting on his personal experience, Roland said, "Our son will be twelve in February and he still wants us to get his cereal for him."

A similar situation occurs in the Allen household. Ten-year-old Jeffrey's mother, Jill, works hard and is often harassed at the end of the day in spite of the help her husband, David, gives her. Jeffrey's main responsibility is to feed the cats—certainly he's capable of doing more, but Jill asks little from him. "It doesn't seem fair," she said, "to deprive him of his afterschool time. I think that he needs the time to himself, to relax and daydream—to just fiddle around."

But what really happens after school is a different story. Jeffrey usually sits in the kitchen enjoying time with his mom, while she does all the work. She doesn't ask him to pitch in, and he doesn't volunteer. He doesn't even feed the cats, who purr and rub against Jill's legs begging for food. When she reminds him of his chores, he doesn't respond. Finally she washes out their dishes and feeds them herself.[9]

"Here, I'll do it," or "Let me do it," or "Don't bother, I'm nearly finished," are expressions we use liberally. Carolyn, an insurance executive, wrote, "[I] find myself picking up after them more often—when I should be teaching them—just because it's quicker." Eileen, a private school director, admitted, "I tend to be lax in making them participate [in household chores]," while Jan, a social service administrator, wrote, "My children do very little in the way of chores, much to my dismay."

"Our daughter is having trouble pouring the milk, immediately we reach for the container; our son needs reminding to make his bed, we go in and do it. We tell ourselves it's easier, it's faster, it's neater. But it is also "guilt motivated," according to Caroline Zinsser, an educational consultant who writes about children.[10]

Because of this guilt, we don't feel we can make any demands on our children. We don't feel that sense of entitlement that would enable us to say, "Look, I've really had a rough day, I could use some help." Instead we overcompensate by doing too much. "I had a terrible nagging guilt that my family would develop . . . some dreadful disease if I didn't prepare inviting, nutritious meals every night," confessed Maxine, a personnel manager in a large corporation. "I equated meal preparation with the proper execution of my motherhood responsibilities. I continued to keep the responsibilities to myself, not because I wanted to do everything, but because I felt [they] were mine, not my children's."[11]

Maxine also felt that she had to do everything, particularly before she went on business trips. She planned and organized every detail for her sons and husband so that they would survive while she was gone—until, as she said, "I realized that it was to compensate for my own guilt at being away. I had to convince myself that my mothering continued even in my absence." Once Maxine came to grips with [the] guilt, she understood how she could cope with it. She began to talk with her sons about her being away and found out they weren't bothered by it. They knew that she had to leave and they knew that she was coming back. She realized she had been "depriving them of planning for themselves. I was the one who felt like staying near them, but it was my need, not theirs." Now Maxine lets them plan things like housecleaning and marketing and they've learned a great deal.[12]

Our tendency to do everything for our children deprives them of more than learning specific household chores. Children who are overindulged don't learn what it feels like to participate in a family, to work together for a common goal. They retain an infantile belief in their own importance and power. What's more, they are not getting an opportunity to understand our needs, as one mother discovered.

She and her son, David, returned home late one night, and as soon as they got inside, he asked her to make him some soup for dinner. Ordinarily she would have, even if she was too tired. But on that night she said, "David, no soup. I feel pressured." She asked him for help, which he gave gladly. The following evening he came into the kitchen and gently asked, "Mom, are you in a good mood tonight? Do you think you'd mind making soup?"[13]

While few of us can expect to meet with this kind of success the first time we shift gears with our children, it's worth riding out the rough spots until we reach a more equitable distribution of responsibilities. Most of us feel as resistant to assuming this new role as our children may. Many women told me that they feel "demanding" or "selfish" when they ask their children to help. I think it's important to remember that we are actually giving to our children more than we are asking when we encourage them to become sharing and responsible human beings.

When we attempt to cater to all of our children's needs, we are of course depriving them of learning how to work things out for themselves. A child psychologist, the late Haim G. Ginott, discussed this point with a group of mothers. One of them related how she had forgotten to put the previous night's laundry into the dryer, with the unfortunate result that her son did not have a pair of dry socks to wear to school. She rushed about trying to find a solution, but he rejected all of them. She felt guilty and communicated her guilt to her son. The day began with both of them upset and angry.

Dr. Ginott described a better way of dealing with this sort of situation. It is important to acknowledge that there is a problem, in this case by saying something like, "There isn't a dry pair of socks in the house. This is a real dilemma. What can we do about it?" That way the child knows that you appreciate the difficulty, but that you are giving him room to work it out his own way, like borrowing a pair from his father.[14]

But most important, explained Ginott, *is not to let your child see your guilt feelings.* "When a child is given the power to activate our guilt, it is like handing him an atomic bomb . . . the child who stirs up his parents' guilt feels guilty about what he has done." And Ginott stressed that we feel anger, sometimes even hatred, at the people who make us feel guilty.[15]

When we overbuy or overprotect or overindulge, we are letting our children see our guilt as clearly as if we had a scarlet *G* emblazoned across our attaché cases. So the next time we find ourselves purchasing still another stuffed animal or feeding our son's goldfish or making spaghetti for our daughter when the whole family is having chicken, we ought to stop and think about what we are doing and why. The best way to get over our guilt-motivated overcompensating is to follow Dr. Ginott's advice: "Don't just do something, stand there."[16]

CHAPTER 11

Mea Culpa

I COUNTED. SHE had said no six times before finally giving in. My friend Lois, who owns a small clothing store, had told her whimpering three-year-old six times that he could not have another cookie before she finally handed him one. What happened involved more than just another sweet.

Her son now realized that if he nagged and complained long enough, he'd get what he wanted, and I saw that Lois, precise and tough in business, was having as much difficulty setting limits as the rest of us.

Limit setting means deciding what is and isn't acceptable behavior in your child, deciding when to say yes and no and, above all, sticking to these decisions. It sounds easy but it isn't, particularly for working mothers. "Guilt makes women reluctant to set limits that are reasonable," said Stephen Segal, the consultant, while T. Berry Brazelton provided a graphic example of this.

Mrs. Tucker, a medical secretary, was having a lot of trouble putting fifteen-month-old Kara to bed. After a lovely ritual of stories, hugging and cuddling, Mrs. Tucker put Kara into bed and joined her husband at the dinner table. Immediately she was called back into the room by Kara's cries. "Water," "another story"— all kinds of attention-seeking devices. Back and forth, back and forth the Tuckers went, not having a moment to eat and all the while becoming more and more frustrated. This miserable situation prevailed for an hour and a half, with parents and child equally out of control, until Kara, totally exhausted, fell asleep.[1]

According to Dr. Brazelton, this situation is common when the mother and father are both employed. No amount of reassurance can relieve the fear that the child has been neglected or mistreated during the day. Nothing seems to take away the guilt. "But these guilty feelings do not help Kara," said Brazelton. In fact, they incapacitate the parents to play an important role for her—that of helping her learn limits. Actually this kind of behavior will do children more harm than being separated from their mothers during the day. For the child will soon learn that the mother feels inadequate as a parent and is trying to make up for her other life by giving in too much.[2]

An accountant supervising a staff of eight in what is usually a ten-hour day wrote, "I probably spoil [my son] more to make up for the time I am not with him." "I am more lenient with them because I feel guilty about being gone all day," confided a banker from Maine.

However much child psychologists may disagree on other points, they are absolutely in accord that children need to have limits spelled out for them clearly and consistently. It makes them feel secure and loved to know what is and what isn't acceptable behavior.

As working mothers, we explain our difficulties in defining boundaries and insisting on them because we are eager to avoid confrontation. We say that we feel guilty because we have so little time with our children and that we want that time to be pleasant and harmonious. One woman expressed it this way: "I tend to overlook misbehavior in favor of constant peace, tranquillity and love." But the problem is that when we do overlook misbehavior, the result is usually not tranquillity but more misbehavior.

A certain amount of misbehavior is normal; some of it, however, may in fact be due to improper discipline. But regardless of the cause, we blame it on our working, and this inhibits our ability to deal with it effectively. The expression *mea culpa* did not originate with working mothers, but it may as well have, we have made it so completely our own.

In discussing how they viewed normal developmental stages— the sleep problems, the temper tantrums, the terrible twos—here is what working mothers, regardless of educational and professional background, had to say: "I tend to blame myself for behavior problems." "First—I blame myself." "I blamed myself when [my child] was going through separation anxiety." "Deep down I feel guilty—maybe if I were always available they would be different."

"I do feel guilty. It's my fault entirely." "Tantrums—felt it was my fault."

Remembering the subconscious nature of guilt and remembering also that it always seeks punishment, we can begin to appreciate its malignant orbit. We blame our children's problems on our work; this not only blinds us to the real cause, but it has a strong punitive component because it makes us feel sad, depressed and inadequate. The more we feel this way, the more negative our interaction with our children, the worse they are likely to behave and the more guilt we feel. Here is a self-fulfilling prophecy if ever there was one.

Marsha, a data processing expert, felt what she called "a tremendous tendency toward self-blame." Having recently received a report from school that her five-year-old daughter Lindsay "wasn't as self-confident as she might be, that she didn't always try new things," Marsha immediately faulted herself. "I thought that maybe I should have been home doing things with her, and I thought that she was in one day care center that wasn't as good as she should have had. She had kids to play with, but the adults, although they took good care of her, weren't as involved, and retrospectively, I feel very guilty about that. I took it on myself, and my husband didn't."

Nadine, who works in a large advertising firm, had a similar response to learning about her three-year-old Alicia's behavior at the day-care center. "Guilt comes in. I'm not spending enough time with her. She had biting problems and I completely blamed myself. Everyone said when a child bites, she's angry. She's angry at me and I felt miserable and depressed. And when your child is in day care and your child bites, suddenly this close relationship that you have with the [other] children's parents dissolves. . . . It seems that every time she did it there was a direct relationship to my being away, and that caused a lot of guilt."

As with Marcia, this guilt made itself felt. "At first I deny my guilt," said Nadine. "Then I get real angry, depressed, miserable and then irritable."

This kind of self-punishment is common among working mothers, according to Stephen Segal. "When kids are having problems, mothers see it as a direct consequence of their working." But by doing this, we are missing the probable cause of the disturbance. Lindsay's lack of confidence and anxiety could have been due to an overbearing teacher or classmates, or the imminent arrival of a new sibling. As for Alicia's biting, it could have come from an overly controlled atmosphere at the center, or she may have felt frightened and threatened by some of the other children.

Dr. Gail Reed, a New York psychoanalyst who sees many working mothers, said she frequently hears, "Something is wrong with the kid—it's my fault because I'm a bad mother," which, Dr. Reed noted, "makes them less effective as parents." Child psychologists agree that when you are feeling guilty about the job you are doing as a mother, your interaction with your children tends to be marked by many flare-ups; it is likely to be less even tempered and consistent.

If you begin to see these qualities dominating your relationship with your child, it is important to get back on the track of effective discipline as soon as possible. The problem is that for some people, the idea of *discipline* immediately conjures images of the rod, of punishment; it is rarely seen as a way of building sound behavior patterns.

In order to discipline effectively and consistently, you have to have some understanding of what kinds of behavior are acceptable to you and what kinds are not. Sometimes this is simple. For example, hurting another person, destroying or taking someone else's property are not acceptable under any circumstances. These are rules that are easiest to establish, because they encompass the common principles of our society.

But what about those more subtle and ambiguous principles that relate to what goes on in your family? Should your children be allowed to dominate the dinner discussion? Should they be able to watch MTV? Should they be allowed to trade their toys, clothes, books with friends? How should they respond if one of their siblings hits them? Do they have to clean up their rooms? These are for you and your husband, and possibly your children, to decide.

Then, of course, there are the intangibles—the whole question of values, cooperation, generosity, honesty. In these, as in all the rest, decide what's important to you and stick to it. But don't be upset if there are some surprises along the way. We have always tried to instill sharing and compassion in our children, but when Alison gave her Freeky Freezie mittens—the rage of the under-six set—to a friend whose mother wouldn't buy her a pair, I wondered if we had gone too far.

Once you are clear about the kinds of behavior you hope to encourage in your children, it's easier to achieve it, but only to a point. The number of books giving conflicting advice on this topic are truly mind boggling. Some experts believe that spanking is acceptable; others urge, instead, behavior modification, such as a system of rewards like gold stars for good behavior. Many suggest a time-out period of five or ten minutes in the child's room when he or she is misbehaving, while still others endorse withholding certain privileges, such as television, a treat, a chance to stay up late.[3]

From this haze of information it is possible, however, to glean a few salient points of agreement: Never tell a child he or she is naughty or bad, always say that the behavior is bad or unacceptable; don't make threats or use bribes or sarcasm; don't punish in any way that is really traumatic to the child and do try to make it fit the misbehavior. If your child comes into your room at six-thirty in the morning and this isn't allowed in your family, you may just be "too tired" to take her to a movie that afternoon. If the child willfully throws a toy, you may decide to take it away for a time; if your children have come to blows over which television show to watch, maybe the TV is best turned off. And—here is where so many of us fall down—once you prescribe a punishment, carry through on it. The key is consistency. The same rules of behavior should apply to children who live with you and those from former marriages who visit.

While we all must find the method of discipline that is most effective in our families, the one that works best in mine was suggested to me by author and educator Ellen Galinsky. Galinsky advises providing a structure that gives "children a choice and gives them a sense of their growing autonomy." Following this advice, I tried to get the children to stop fighting over who was going to play with a particular toy by saying, "We have a problem. You can't both have the game in your rooms at the same time. How can you work it out?" Miraculously, incredibly, they did not rip the Shoots and Ladders board in two, as I had expected. They stopped, thought about it and decided to take turns. On another occasion I pulled to the side of the road and turned off the ignition because they were fighting while I was driving. I told them it was too distracting for me to drive with so much noise and bouncing around in the back. How could they stop it? They decided to "separate" by putting down the armrest between them. And we were able to continue on our way.

But sometimes, even with the best advice, your child's behavior is troubling, your son wets his bed, your daughter has a school-related anxiety. Usually it is just a developmental stage, part of the typical difficulties of childhood that will disappear in time. But when these pieces of behavior linger longer than parents feel is reasonable, many begin to wonder if their child is experiencing some deeper problems.

Dr. Martin Cohen offered a few ways of figuring this out: "Does the child have friends? The child should not always be in the same role with other kids—scapegoat, bully, attention getter, loner. Does the child have some passion, something that really excites him or her, something that the child can really become absorbed in? Does the child take care of herself physically? Is she always having accidents, not eating, not sleeping? By the time the child reaches the latency period (around eight years) the child should be able to delay gratification, shouldn't always be demanding, *but* the child should feel secure enough to show anger and to make demands. Usually parents will know when their child is having some trouble," said Dr. Cohen. "There will be some cry for help."

But this cry for help resonates with a special intensity in working mothers. For here, again, guilt rears its Hydra head and prevents us from getting the appropriate advice. Every child psychologist with whom I spoke was struck by the inordinate guilt felt by mothers who have to bring their children for counseling, tutoring or psychotherapy. They see themselves as failures in a global way. The guilt is excruciating; "it feels deep and physical," was the way one mother expressed it. The idea of bringing a child to treatment is so painful that we first try to deny the problem, ignore it, hope against hope that it will go away.

Jane is an accountant with a large firm in Connecticut. Her son, Douglas, now nine, is a happy, well-adjusted child, but it hasn't always been this way. When he was about three years old he began to exhibit some disturbing signs. "He was pounding his head on the wall . . . terrible behavior," Jane said, but she always felt that in "the long term it would work out." Admittedly feeling guilty toward Douglas, particularly after her divorce, Jane was prepared to overlook a lot of things. She remembered one time when they were getting out of the car in the midst of a downpour, and Douglas, instead of hurrying into the house as Jane had urged, sat down on the soaking sidewalk and howled for fifteen minutes before she was able to drag him inside. "Other times I would put him in the car, put his seat belt on and by the time I got over to my side he would be gone—running down the street."

But then came the day when Douglas tried to get out of the car while it was in motion. It was a horrible, jagged moment, when Jane felt all her coping resources dissolve. "I pulled over and got hysterical screaming and crying and I said, 'We're not making it. We cannot handle this by ourselves. We have to go to a counselor.' " Looking back on all this, Jane, a woman full of intelligence and insight, finds it hard to understand why she waited so long to seek professional assistance; yet many of us ignore escalating problems.

It's the sense of stigma attached to taking a child to a therapist that makes mothers feel so guilty, explained Beth Israel's Dr. Stanley Turecki, who specializes in treating difficult children. Children usually do not share this sense of shame. As long as they are assured that this kind of doctor will not give them an injection but is someone who will play with them, talk to them and help them with a problem, they generally look forward to going.

Often the counseling or therapy for a child is of short duration, and it is encouraging to know that new research has shown that "one bad year at an early age will not necessarily produce later problems in children"—provided, of course, that we do not let our guilt prevent us from seeking appropriate help.[4]

CHAPTER 12

What's the Hurry?

THEY'VE BEEN CALLED children without childhood, hurried children, miniature adults; but however they are labeled, most of us would agree with Dr. Herbert Zimiles, a senior research psychologist at the Bank Street College of Education, that "kids today pass through the formative states more quickly. There is a loss of childhood as we know it." In their everyday demeanor, the language they use, the things they know, their activities with peers and particularly their relations with the adult world, children today are decidedly different from those of a generation ago.[1]

Marie Winn, author of *Children Without Childhood* and an authority on this subject, attributes these changes to the social upheavals of the late 1960s and the early 1970s, the availability of drugs, the so-called sexual revolution, the popularity of television, the frequency of divorce and the number of women employed outside the home.[2] While all these factors are to some extent responsible, what has yet to be analyzed and understood is the way in which the guilt we feel has become an additional force, thrusting our children into premature adulthood.

It starts when they are young; infants, in fact. It is no longer acceptable just to have a baby—we must have a superbaby who does everything ahead of schedule. At Eeyore's, a popular children's bookstore in Manhattan, the number of books and learning packets promising to promote infants' early development has skyrocketed over the last few years as a result of parent demand. On a recent afternoon at Eeyore's I watched a tall, well-dressed woman, smart leather attaché case in hand, looking through the books methodically. "Which of these is the best to get him reading?" she asked one of the saleswomen.

"How old is he?"

"Seventeen months," she answered, then asked agitatedly, "That's not too late to start, is it?"

Well, some experts might say that it is. Dr. Bernice Cullinan, president of the International Reading Association, believes that parents should begin teaching children how to read the moment they bring them home from the hospital, while Dr. Bettye M. Caldwell, who heads the National Association for Education, thinks that you could begin with a six-month-old.[3]

Other specialists in child development, however, disagree—and strongly, too. Dr. Edward Zigler, Sterling Professor of psychology at Yale University, deplored parental overinvolvement in children's early learning. "We should appreciate children for what they are," he said. "Parents should let their children enjoy their childhood." He urged parents to remember that they can't stop a child from learning.[4]

"If you try to push children to read too early, they may just turn off," said Dr. John H. Flavell, professor of psychology at Stanford University; and Tufts psychologist and author Dr. David Elkind cites several studies in support.[5]

"I'm absolutely horrified by this superbaby stuff," Diane Kissner, a learning specialist with a private practice in New York City, told me recently. "I've heard of parents holding up flash cards to their three-month-olds. These are the children who won't learn to read. The pressure that we put on our children is absolutely incredible. I think that a lot has to do with the guilt that women feel. I'm working full-time, but it's okay because my baby is already reading." Dr. Mary Howell, the pediatrician and psychologist, summed it up this way: "Guilt sells a lot of superbaby training books."[6]

Using our children's achievements to expiate our guilt is all too common, and typically it builds in momentum, so that by the time our children are preschoolers they are feeling the kinds of pressure and anxieties once reserved for high school seniors. "It's become a little more difficult to get into a private kindergarten than to enroll in college," said Helen La Croix, director of admissions at Chicago's Frances W. Parker School, a private grade school. Peggy Bradt, executive director of the Parents League of New York, agrees that the panic to get children into good schools is beginning earlier and earlier, because of the increase in the number of working mothers.[7]

The feelings Amy Hest, a children's book author, had when she took three-year-old Sam to an interview at the nursery school of her choice reveal the level of tension that can be shared by mother and child alike. "Sam tore his name tag off, and the teacher gave me one of these and-you-think-your-child-is-our-kind-of-material looks and wrote something down. When we left, Sam and I were both in tears," Amy recalled. "I was furious with Sam and even more furious with myself for having subjected him to the experience."[8]

For working mothers, getting children into good schools has become, as one from Oregon, said, a top priority. So much so that parents will undergo herculean efforts to ensure admission.

"Jim didn't test well," Margaret, one of my friends, admitted with obvious distress. A bright, verbal five-year-old, Jim, whose parents are both college teachers, seemed to freeze when questioned directly. This was a deep and persistent worry for Margaret, who was concerned that he would not be admitted to a top private school. "I had already checked which of the grade schools were good when he was still in nursery school, but the problem was that the nursery school he was attending wasn't doing much with puzzles and with letters and numbers, even for a four-year-old. I feel guilt about his difficulty testing, and I wanted to have him coached before he took the ERBs [Educational Records Bureau examination, the College Boards of the New York City nursery school set]."

Margaret was able to arrange a tutor for Jim. Surprisingly enough, there *are* several services available to prep three- and four-year-olds, but even with intensive work twice a week, he was turned down at the school of her choice. When I spoke with Margaret, Jim had just successfully completed kindergarten at a fine coeducational school on Manhattan's Upper East Side, but Margaret is afraid to stop the tutoring. Although none of his teachers has advised it, she plans on continuing it into first grade, "at least until they determine which reading group to put him in," she said.

Like the great rush of a wave, our guilt hurls our children forward into pseudo-adulthood: skills, clothing, concerns—all the trappings of the adult world. For some of us it's a way of making sure that they are missing nothing by our absence; for others it's a justification of our working by demonstrating all the "extras" that our income provides. And for still others it's a way of hastening our children along, of making them grow up faster so that we can avoid the guilt we will have over leaving them. Or it can be a combination of these motivations.

David Elkind, who has written a book called *The Hurried Child,* explained to me that working mothers tend to compensate for the time they are not with their children by overprogramming them with all kinds of extracurricular activities. Elizabeth Bailey, a Los Angeles reporter, was struck by this when she returned home from a one-year assignment in London with her eighteen-month-old daughter. Guilt makes working mothers assume the role of childhood coordinator, noted Ms. Bailey. "Because they feel guilty, they [see] to it that their children [are] enlightened and/or entertained by a variety of classes and programs on a nearly daily basis."[9]

Some mothers are known to have separate calendars to keep track of their preschoolers' activities. Few of us are immune to the appeal of these classes. Who would not want our child to become an expert on the balance beam or the violin, and who among us would miss a chance to have our six-year-old become computer literate?

While we feel compelled to provide all this stimulation and education for our children, many of us are finding it terribly expensive and difficult to arrange. And, in fact, new studies are showing that accelerated children may well end up unexcelling adults.

One, conducted by clinical and experimental psychologist Dr. Martin Seligman of the University of Pennsylvania and his associates, deals with the pattern of helplessness—the feeling of not being able to control events, of not being able to help oneself or others. When children are consistently thrown into activities that are beyond their level, when their responses do not bring solutions, they begin to feel helpless. They may become withdrawn, apathetic and lose their motivation to learn other new things. Dr. Seligman found that helplessness can be learned or acquired and that it can carry over from one situation to another if children are not able to develop higher-order cognitive strategies for attacking problems that are necessary for academic success.[10]

Other research focuses on premature structuring. David Elkind cites many examples of children, trained from an early age to perform well in sports or the arts, who never fully developed the other parts of their personalities. They became constricted and socially inept, noted Elkind, who is concerned that this pattern of structuring will become common as more children are pushed to unreasonable early achievement.[11]

It's hard to strike the right balance between over- and underinvolving youngsters in extracurricular activities and educational programs, but it is important to give them some control; to be guided by their energy levels, tempos and interests. When seven-year-old Alison, whose typical school day is from 8:30 to 3:30, rebelled against ice skating on Tuesday afternoons and ballet on Fridays, I tried to change her mind but finally stopped the classes. Art was what she wanted to do, she explained, and I soon realized why. She's very good at it, it's a quiet activity, and since the classes were held in her school building, she did not have to travel when she was already tired from a long day.

David Elkind suggests that we can draw up a balance sheet, with achievements and responsibilities expected on one side and supports and freedoms provided on the other. If the two sides are equal, we are probably engaging our children in an appropriate amount of activity.[12]

Children, particularly those who are young, need long periods of unstructured time to experiment, explore, indulge their curiosity. They need to have a sense of abandon, of delight in just *being*. Dr. Nina Lief, director of the Early Childhood Center at New York Medical College, said that "not enough time for themselves results in children who show a lack of drive, less creativity and few inner resources." Dr. Martin Cohen also worries that children who are overprogrammed will turn into less imaginative and independent adults.

Urging children out of childhood is also evident in the way we dress them. A recent visit to an uptown kindergarten showed several children in designer clothing. All were in up-to-the-minute fashions—miniskirts, sequins, shocking pinks, oranges, neon colors. Not a pair of sturdy overalls to be found, not a peaches 'n' cream little dress among them. Here were four- and five-year-olds dressed smart, sassy and seductive.

When I commented on this and asked one of the mothers whatever happened to Carter's (the traditional maker of children's clothes that looked like they were meant for little ones, not rock singers), she didn't even know what I was talking about. She thought I meant Cartier. "Oh, I know their jewelry," she said. "Have they gone into children's clothing also?"

Dressing our children in grown-up styles not only encourages them to act in more grown-up ways but is also an outward expression of the inner maturity we expect them to have. All too often we treat our children as though they were adults, expecting them to have the understanding and emotional ability to deal with events far above their level. We reason with our children, bargain with them, take them into our confidence as though they were our psychological equals.

When I asked women how they explained leaving to go to work, business trips and missed school plays to their youngsters, they said they talked about money worries, job pressures and insecurities, promotions, deadlines and the like. Typically they embarked on lengthy explanations that admitted their own ambivalence and guilt.

One mother justified her need to work late to her son by telling him that she was in danger of being fired (which actually was not so). Now her six-year-old constantly asks her if she is going to "fire him" when he misbehaves. Her explanation had the unfortunate results of increasing her son's anxiety and also of violating his trust, for sooner or later he will realize the dishonesty of her explanation.

Rather than make up some excuse to our children in a misguided attempt to expiate our guilt or to win them over, it's best to give them a simple, matter-of-fact explanation: "Mommy had a lot of work to do and had to stay at the office late. I know that you miss me when I'm not home to see you before you go to bed. I miss you too." If you have mentioned the particular project you are working on to your child, it's fine to bring it into the explanation. One real estate agent, who makes a point of showing her children some of the houses she's trying to sell, told her five-year-old, "A very nice family wants to buy the white house with the blue shutters on Walnut Drive. I am going to work on the papers at the office tonight, so that the sale will go through quickly."

With young children especially, the more neutral and concrete you can be, the better. If you have to go out of town, it might be a good idea to tell your child how you are traveling and show him or her on a map where you are going. One mother reported telling her three-year-old that she was "going down South," and her daughter spent the next three days worrying about how her mommy was going to get back up through the ground. Because young children often have difficulty with the concept of time, some mothers make large calendars and encourage the child to check off the days until they come back. Stephen Segal suggested that mothers might want to leave little notes or short taped messages for each day they are gone. These approaches will help your child deal with your absences a lot better than unfairly burdening him or her with your conflicts about them. Marie Winn and other experts caution against our need to explain ourselves to our children and to plead with them to agree with us, understand us and forgive us.[13]

The craving so many of us have for our children's approval may cause us to expose them to situations and information that they are not equipped to deal with. Dr. Stephen D. Fabrick, a clinical psychologist in the Detroit area, thought that "the guilt over leaving children during the working day can convince [mothers] to tote their tots with them the rest of the time, even to the most inappropriate places."[14] Children are taken to adult gatherings where they are sometimes allowed to hear conversations and participate in discussions that are inadvisable for them. One eight-year-old reported to her teacher that she had heard her mother tell a friend that when she and her husband were at a company party she had become very attracted to one of his business associates.

For all their savvy and presumed sophistication, children simply are not able to handle the complications and confusion of our adult lives. Dr. Elkind has observed an increase in stress-related ailments in children—migraine headaches, stomach problems, insomnia—which he attribtes to our failure to differentiate children's needs from those of adults. For while our children may, indeed, look older and seem more independent, may sound more independent and may even act more independent, it is not the same as real maturity. In fact, the ultraindependent kids are often the ones who have unmet dependency needs that become evident during their adult years. Real maturity and autonomy, the ability to love and to share, to give unselfishly—the attributes that we value as adults—develop slowly in a childhood sheltered from the tensions and harshness of our grown-up world.

When we begin to see the role our guilt plays in our child rearing, we will be able to enjoy our children's childhood. We will have a far easier time disciplining them, dealing with those who care for them and interacting with them. We will be able to realize that by working, we are giving them so much more than we are taking away. As working mothers, we are helping our children to appreciate individual differences among people—their caregivers, the other youngsters in their day-care centers; to assume responsibility for themselves and, as they mature, for others; to become resourceful and adaptable; to understand the importance of sharing and of working together for a common goal. And we are giving them models of women who are energetic, courageous, capable and confident, and of families thriving through everyone's efforts; families held together not by traditional patterns of domination and subordination but by the mutual respect and trust of all its members.

PART THREE

In Our Jobs

CHAPTER 13

Obstacles at Work

"THE WOMEN AREN'T making it," said the chief executive officer of a Fortune 500 company, an observation that is amply supported. Although women have made impressive gains at the entry levels and in middle management, after "eight or ten years, they hit a barrier," said Janet Jones-Parker, executive director of the Association of Executive Search Consultants. "There's an invisible ceiling for women at that level."[1]

With the exception of Katharine Graham of the *Washington Post,* who readily admits that she got the job because her family owns a controlling share of the corporation, there isn't a single woman chief executive on *Fortune*'s list of the five hundred largest American industrial companies, and 64 percent of these have no women on their boards.[2]

In 1984 women had only 4 of the 154 spots at Harvard's Business School Advanced Management Program—a prestigious thirteen-week course to which companies send those executives with a crack at the top—and the figures aren't much better at comparable programs at Stanford and Dartmouth's Tuck School.[3]

In a major study of women in banking, law and architecture, West Coast psychologist Beth Milwid found that for all their hard work and drive, the frustrations are many and the progress excruciatingly slow.[4] Similarly, a study of academic women found them to be less likely to advance as far or as rapidly as men who are their peers.[5] And for women in the pink-collar ghetto—clerical workers, nurses, teachers—lack of status and opportunity for promotion are still the reality in a job market in which women's wages are only 64 percent that of men's.

The crucial question is why women aren't progressing faster. Of

300 executives polled recently by UCLA's Graduate School of Management and by Korn/Ferry International, an executive firm, 117 felt that being a woman was the greatest obstacle to their success. Many women note that the best assignments often seem to go to men. "Some departments like sales and trading or mergers and acquisitions are considered more macho, hence more prestigious," said a woman at a New York investment banking firm. "It's nothing explicit. But if women can't get the assignments that allow them to shine, how can they advance?"[6]

Women also find that they do not get the same kind of constructive criticism that their male colleagues get, and men agree. There are a vast number of men who can't critique a female's performance the way they would a male's, according to Eugene Jennings, professor of business administration at Michigan State University. It doesn't seem gentlemanly, men explain. Women aren't comfortable with the coach-team approach.[7]

Old stereotypes about roles die hard; every one of the subjects of Milwid's study felt that women had not only "to prove themselves, but to disprove negative stereotypes about women," such as that women are "less assertive," "less ambitious," "less flexible." *All women have to deal with these entrenched notions, but none more so than those with children.*[8]

"A woman can be Anna Freud, Einstein and Schweitzer rolled into one, and God forbid if she has small children," said Florence R. Skelly, president of the polling organization Yankelovich, Skelly and White. Skelly was surprised at the results of a recent study showing the "really negative carry-over effect that small children can still have on a woman's career."[9]

Gene Kofke, director of human resources at AT & T, believed that men make too many assumptions about the professional limitations of women with children—a belief well substantiated by working mothers.[10] "I was overlooked for a promotion and was told 'you probably wouldn't want to travel,' even though I insisted that travel was not a problem," complained Kathlene, a Connecticut contract administrator and mother of two. Cathy, a postal clerk raising her six-year-old son alone, felt "stereotyped as a mother" at work; Barbara, a medical student from New York, reported that an anatomy professor had informed her that "she had no business trying to combine motherhood with medicine," while Karen, a management consultant, was told, "You can't expect to move ahead as fast as [you] had been" after the birth of her daughter.[11] A Minnesota journalist put it this way: being a mother "lessens my status with my supervisor, it makes me appear to be less serious about my career. *Real career women are unmarried and childless—they think.*"

Increasingly, experts are voicing concerns about the impact children may have on a woman's career. Sociologist Andrew Hacker found statistically that a woman's earnings reach their peak in her late twenties. After that age, he theorized, marriage and motherhood intervene to keep her income on a plateau for the rest of her working life. Anne Jardim, dean of Simmons School of Management, worried that concerns about professional advancement will keep some of the brightest women in this country from having children.[12]

Peggy L. Kerr, the first female partner in the history of the New York law firm Skadden, Arps, asserts "it is no accident that the three most senior women in my firm have never married or were divorced long ago and all are childless. I have no doubt that if I had the wonderful husband and two adorable children I thought I wanted years ago, I would not be a partner today." In the UCLA study of executive women, 61 percent had no children.[13]

The corporate climate is doing little to encourage and keep women who want to have children, noted Dean Jardim, who, along with Margaret Hennig, wrote *The Managerial Woman.* Extended maternity leaves and benefits, on-site day care, flexitime arrangements and supportive attitudes would go a long way toward easing the constant conflicts that working mothers feel—conflicts that transcend education, economics and marital status.

"Dividing my attention is a major problem. Always making decisions about whether I will focus on work, children or husband. And whatever I choose, I feel guilty about the others," wrote the director of a national organization for business women. Ann, a banking marketing officer from Maine, said, "I feel that I'm on a treadmill! On Friday night I'm exhausted and need the weekend to recharge myself. I feel guilty that I'm not with my children, but feel a great sense of satisfaction and fulfillment from my career. I never expected I'd feel so torn." Linda, an office manager, wrote, "Guilt is felt because I work and know my son would prefer it if I were home. Stress-filled situation in managing both roles."

Jean, an assistant director of nursing from California and the mother of two teenagers, clearly stated the mental gymnastics we go through.

> When the kids have a problem then I feel guilty—question if I should have a career. How much time should I spend on self? Is it okay to take a class and miss dinner hour? If my husband does one more thing, I feel too guilty. Do they (husband and kids) need me? Should I take a new job that would require even more energy away from husband and kids. Should I ask family to move thirty miles closer to a new job so it would be commutable for both of us? The kids would have to change schools for such a small difference. How do you weigh our needs against kids and/or husband?

Nancy, of Albuquerque, New Mexico, works in trust investments. She has an eighteen-month-old child. This is what she had to say about the conflicts she feels:

> I like my work and I love being a mother. I do feel guilty about the fact that I am not home with my son full-time. Sometimes, however, I question whether I would be happy at home all the time. And that makes me feel even guiltier. In a way I'm glad that question has been decided for me. I do not envy women who really can afford to be at home but choose to work. They must feel even guiltier than I do because they don't have an economic justification for work.
> Another source of conflict is the question of a second child. With two children, life becomes extremely complicated. It may not be worth it to work, and various work expenses (car, gas, clothes, lunch, etc.). . . . But can we really afford that? . . . But if we can't afford that, should I not have a second child at all?

The problems, the self-scrutiny seem universal. Across the country, Sue, the vice president of a North Carolina bank and mother of two young daughters, wrote, "There is *always* conflict. If I didn't work I could do more special things with my children; if I didn't have children I could spend more time at work. . . . I always worry that I'm not spending enough time with my subordinates and planning for the future direction of my department."

A divorced data processor expressed it this way: "I am afraid of personal burnout. Will I be sacrificing her later years because I am trying to do so much now? Will I expect her to drive, and succeed as her payback to me for my sacrifices? Am I asking too much of myself? Of [her]? Right now I am not planning for her education after high school—I feel she will have to plan on a scholarship. Others make me feel guilty about this. I hope she won't."

Another woman, a mother of five, wrote, "Getting married young, divorced, single parent, no money, not much job skills, no support from other people, parents and ex-husband. Bosses aren't helpful to single parents/kids. Good babysitters are hard to find. . . . I feel guilty about working long hours and low pay. Lots of problems raising family alone."

Add to these pressures the baby-sitter quitting, children with chicken pox, laundry to be done, dinner to be cooked, deadlines to be met. For working mothers the demands are real, the problems immediate; and few can be put on hold.

It's easy to understand why the words we use to describe ourselves are those of difficulty and dilemma: "juggling," "balancing," "swimming upstream," "on a treadmill," "martyred," "torn," "pulled," "feeling split in two."

With such extraordinary demands on us, we must have inordinate energy, clarity of purpose and sureness about ourselves in order to succeed. But, instead, a sense of apology pervades our attitudes and often our actions.

We may rail against the stereotypes, condemn the conventional thinking that women cannot or should not work and be mothers, and yet deep within us we accept that early prohibition that we should not do both, that we are in violation of some sacred code.

CHAPTER 14

The Girl Most Likely to Succeed

IN HIGH SCHOOL everyone liked Cindy Gold. President of the senior class, a cheerleader, a good athlete and a good student, Cindy was voted Girl Most Likely to Succeed in our graduating class.

We had worked together on school performances, distributed leaflets and spent hours sprawled on the floor painting oaktag posters for her campaign. We signed each other's yearbooks, vowed to keep in touch no matter what, yet failed to beyond our junior years in college.

It was her voice that I recognized first, a voice that hadn't changed in the intervening years—calm, lilting, familiar. I turned to see Cindy Gold talking to another woman outside a midtown office building. Suited, leather attaché case in hand, Cindy's appearance seemed to fulfill our classmates' prophecy. Only over lunch the following week did I learn of a gap between the appearance and reality.

After graduating from a large eastern university, Cindy worked briefly as a high school English teacher. She loved her job but quit when she married a medical student. After having two children, Cindy and her husband, Jack, moved to Boston, where he was doing a residency in radiology.

Staying at home with her toddlers, Cindy found herself drawn into the women's movement of the early 1970s. Through the reading and support groups and the bright-bannered demonstrations that came like waves of foam over those Cambridge cobblestones, Cindy "became conscious of being [her] own person." Urged on by this new awareness, she took the law boards as soon as the family returned to New York. The deal she made with herself: If I get a 650, I'll apply. Her score: 651, and the applications went out the next day.

"My first job after law school, the one that I just left, was with a lawyer who was going out on his own," Cindy told me. "He approached me and said that he was going to form a real estate investment company. It sounded ideal." But after almost two years, Cindy decided that it wasn't challenging enough. "I felt, though, that I couldn't look for another job while I was working for him; it made me feel too guilty." Cindy shook her head, as if she really didn't understand her reaction. "I feel that he gave me a job—now this is a woman's thing, playing out something that a man never feels. Why do I feel that I owe it to him to stay there? Why do I feel that I was betraying him?" she asked rhetorically.

The irony is that the partners she worked for did not share her misgivings. In fact, when she was leaving, one of them asked her why she didn't at least continue to come in and use the office. "Because I feel guilty if I make a phone call," she'd replied. The partner, a little hurt, had protested, "But I never made you feel that way, did I?"

"No," Cindy had answered, "you didn't, but the moment I'm on the phone I get a knot in my stomach." "I know that men don't feel this way," she said to me.

Cindy also had conflicts about asking for a salary increase. Feeling that she was not being paid adequately, she still couldn't bring herself to ask for more. "I knew that the company wasn't prospering. A man, I think, would have said, 'I need more money. I want more money, pay me more.' As a woman, knowing their financial situation, I felt much more connected and responsible . . . I didn't want to feel as though my salary was taking from their families."

As we sat talking, a picture flashed through my mind: Cindy Gold in our high school yearbook, high ponytail, Peter Pan–collared blouse, smiling out over the caption: Girl Most Likely to Succeed.

"Do you want to be successful?" I asked.

"Oh, yes. Definitely," she said immediately. "I do. I want to make a lot of money."

The disparity between Cindy's conscious wish to be successful (doing what you want in your work life and feeling good about it) and the way she is trying to achieve it are painfully clear. Like so many of us, Cindy puts a higher premium on relationships—on "being connected"—than on furthering or advancing herself. The psychological baggage that women bring to the workplace is packed with the need to be nice and to value relationships over everything else, according to Beth Milwid.[1] This need causes working mothers great anxiety.

When asked, "How do you feel when your mothering responsibilities prevent you from giving your all to your job," women characteristically answered in terms of relationships. They did *not* say things like "it means that I have to work harder the next day," or "I take extra work home"—both of which are most likely true. Their response always involved other people. A Detroit businesswoman "feels guilty toward her employers"; a barge dispatcher who is raising her child alone "feels guilty toward her co-workers"; a midwestern writer feels that she "has cheated her employers"; a California therapist and family counselor feels as though she has "let her clients down and destroyed some of their trust." And always there is the guilt; to employer, employee, co-workers, peers, subordinates.

Men, as Cindy noted, don't seem to indulge in this kind of self-chastisement. My doctor, for example, thinks nothing of letting his patients wait while he talks on the phone to the contractor who is renovating his co-op; a lawyer friend thinks nothing of using work time to talk to his stockbroker, but women feel "terrible guilt" if they have to use the office phone to check on a sick child.

Men take these distractions in stride. "It's part of my daily routine to check with my broker," one told me. Men do not feel that they are betraying anyone, violating a trust. Why *ever* do women?

In the late 1960s Martina Horner, who is now president of Radcliffe College, studied women's responses to success. Her work demonstrated that women have more difficulty with the idea of success than men do; they don't pursue professional advancement the way men do, and the entire notion of succeeding means something different to them. Since Horner's study, psychologists have devoted a lot of energy toward understanding the roots of this phenomenon. Most agree that it stems from the differing ways in which males and females identify with and separate from their mothers.[2]

As we have already discussed, for little boys, masculinity is defined through *separation* from their mothers. Little girls, however, are not encouraged toward separate strivings from their mothers. Rather, their femininity is defined by *attachment* to the mother. The implications of these crucial facts of our development are vast.

Harvard's Carol Gilligan writes, in *In a Different Voice,* "The male gender is threatened by intimacy, while the female gender is threatened by separation. . . . Males tend to have difficulties with relationships, while females have much greater need for ongoing attachment and have problems with individuation."[3] In her pioneering study Gilligan demonstrated that "men see danger more in close personal affiliation rather than in achievement, while women perceive danger or are threatened by impersonal achievement because it brings with it the danger of isolation, the fear that in being set apart by success, they will be left alone."

While these fears may exist to some extent in all women, they affect working mothers with particular force. As we have seen, today's working mother has dramatically separated from her own mother. She has struggled against identifying with that mother whom she loves, to whom she *needs* to feel attached, but whom she sees as inferior in some ways. The guilt over breaking away from the traditional role of her mother becomes reactivated when she herself is a mother and leaves her children to go to work. This makes her particularly vulnerable to fears about isolation, competition and personal achievement.

One doctor gave voice to these worries: "My own mother regards my work negatively—she thinks that I should put it off till my child is grown," adding, "on some occasions I feel that I'm being very narcissistic to think that I'd be a good doctor and to spend my time away from [my son] when he needs me. So, too, I sometimes feel that I'm being selfish when I spend time with him and not with colleagues discussing a case." And this is from a woman who divides *all* her time between her profession and her child and doesn't take a moment for herself. What is selfish about being a good, devoted mother? What is narcissistic about being a conscientious doctor? The "selfish feeling" is one that we have when we are pursuing our own goals rather than our mothers'. It makes us feel alone and isolated. It makes us feel guilty.

It is the terror and guilt over being disconnected that is actually behind the phenomenon of the fear of success, according to Dr.

Stiver. In her clinical experience, Stiver has seen "many women struggle [to separate], to defend against their identification with their mothers, whom they see as critical, devalued, and unhappy. Yet these same women fear betraying their mothers and experience considerable guilt if they move ahead and demonstrate 'differences' from [them]."[4]

"There's a lot of guilt about surpassing or doing something different from our mothers," New York psychoanalyst Joan Erdheim explained. If a woman had a mother who was a housewife, who was bogged down around the house, there is concern about having something different, something better. And it's a theme that fits for a lot of women, regardless of whether they are working for self-fulfillment or survival. A woman's feelings about her work may be more closely linked to her relationship with her mother than to other factors.

"My own mother was a housewife and I felt guilt for not being what *I* considered to be a proper mother (at home) and not being able to be home when the children were and I felt terrible about not being able to concentrate on my career," said a secretary from the Midwest. Another woman said that her mother "feels I'm cheating my children and selfish for working"; while another said her "mom makes it look like I'm looking down on her for *not* working." Still another complained that her mother "brags about always being home for her children. She's not interested in knowing about my work."

An executive from New Jersey clearly understood that "my limitations at work are from being a forty-year-old woman brought up in the fifties and early sixties." An executive with a Fortune 500 company and a mother of a three-and-a-half-year-old said that her greatest conflicts come from the fact that her own mother thinks that she should be at home, while a librarian from Arkansas wrote that her mother thinks she's a failure as a wife and a mother.

The guilt looms as large in the office as it does in the nursery and has the same destructive effects. "It makes me on edge at work and I am not as effective as I should be," wrote a counter manager for a cosmetics company in a large retail store. "Guilt . . . makes me feel rushed and agitated in my work—I do not make the best decisions during those times," wrote Nancy, a California CEO of a toy manufacturing company and the divorced mother of two. A nursery school teacher from Maryland complained, "When I feel guilty I don't do a good job"; and a woman who worked as a meat wrapper in Ohio said it made her "cross with customers."

Like these women, most of us can identify the superficial effects of our guilt. When I yell at my children as I'm rushing off to an interview, I feel an overwhelming sense of unhappiness, of unease. But what I haven't always been aware of is the insidious way my guilt feelings have affected my professional life. The guilt that we recognize is only the tip of the iceberg. The rest is buried in our unconscious, eroding our efforts to succeed.

While women may believe that they want to advance, "the mother's example may say to a woman on a subconscious level that having a career, rather than staying home with her children, is unnatural," according to Dr. Shelly Robin, a New York therapist. "Many women, who believe that they are really deeply committed to their careers, discover that the real reason that they are not advancing is not due to actual obstacles on the job, but to *hidden emotional blocks* [emphasis added]."[5] As Matina Horner's work has shown, internal conflict often thwarts a woman's strivings for achievement.

CHAPTER 15

Going Nowhere Fast

I FIRST MET Joyce at a children's birthday party, where among the balloons and brightly colored streamers, we instinctively drew together, both of us writers with young children who were plagued by doubts about our professional abilities. We talked with an openness more typical of years of friendship than minutes. By the time the high-pitched voices around us had sung "Happy Birthday," Joyce and I knew a lot about each other's professional foibles and follies. And of our hopes: mine, the publication of the mystery I had written, and hers, the possibility of a new job, one that would move her beyond her long-held position as copy chief at a New York publishing house.

The job had been offered, but now, as we sat weeks later in a café where the voice from the jukebox moaned a plaintive "Love Me Tender," Joyce's mood contrasted sharply with her enthusiasm at the party. "I always thought that when my youngest child was in kindergarten, I'd go back to work," she said. "And now here I was, offered this managerial job—the company is growing, they want more from me—it would be a corporate position. I really came close to taking it, but the problem was, I couldn't bear to leave my daughter, despite the fact that she would be in school all day, and I would only get home about one and a half hours later than she." Joyce took a sip of wine and sighed deeply.

"I'm losing a lot of things that I would have liked," she continued after a moment. "Like the big office. I would have been the publicity manager of six or eight people. Today there was a big party for the department heads, and I had to say to myself that this is one of the things that I have given up."

Joyce felt that during the weeks that she deliberated about the

job, she had learned something about herself. "I have trouble separating. You see," she said, "I have this problem with the idealized
fifties mother. She's always lurking near me—right away there is
this image which emerges every time. I'm standing in the kitchen
with an apron and I must be baking something because there is
flour all over the place and one kid is on either side and it's warm
and cozy and that's her. It's Donna Reed, Jane Wyman—I don't
know."

Measuring herself against this media image of perfection from
the world of our mothers, Joyce feels lacking, however good her
work actually is. "I don't have much [confidence] at all. I've written a couple of books and people tell me I'm wonderful," she said,
"but I don't feel wonderful."

Much of this feeling comes from her relationship with her
mother, who discouraged Joyce from taking the job. "When I told
my mother what I decided, she said, 'I guess we're just not ambitious women,' and it made me want to run out and do something
ambitious."

But Joyce did not do anything ambitious. Instead she held herself back. Like many working mothers, Joyce remained tied to a
standard of behavior that impeded her professional progress. This
pattern of turning down promotions and/or opting for less demanding jobs often begins right after a woman becomes a mother.
Meg Wheatley and Marcie Schorr Hirsch, the authors of *Managing Your Maternity Leave,* were surprised to discover just how
many women thought about changing to less demanding jobs
while they were on maternity leaves.[1] Similarly, in the book *The
Balancing Act,* five young women, all with very clearly defined
career goals, told how motherhood brought unforeseen consequences to their working lives. "Four of the five settled for a re-
duced version of their career aspirations." One of these four
explained that she was shocked at how quickly she felt pulled
back into a traditional role.[2]

In addition to the reidentification with our mothers, there are
many reasons the period after the delivery is not the best time to
make binding decisions about our professional lives. The combined effects of lack of sleep, hormonal changes, differences in
our daily routine and in our sense of self create an uncharacter-
istic emotional intensity. Some women find they become tearful,
others, irritable; just about all are exhausted. As Wheatley and

Hirsch point out, most women home with a young baby cannot imagine how anyone could ever manage to work at a pressured job and be a mother.[3] Women who already have one child cannot understand how anyone with two children can cope with the multiple roles. It's helpful to talk to women who have gone through this phase of mothering and have then returned to work. It's helpful, too, to realize that the first few months with a baby, whether it's your first or your second, are generally the hardest. Certainly they are the most demanding in terms of your physical energy. By the fourth or fifth month, most babies are on good sleeping and eating schedules, and you will find yourself more relaxed and rested.

Wheatley and Hirsch suggest that you use your maternity leave to think about your job situation in the context of your new responsibilities at home. This doesn't mean necessarily switching to a lower level job. On the contrary, high level positions are often the ones that will give you the kind of flexibility you now need. When you are analyzing your present job, these are some of the things you might want to keep in mind: Does your seniority allow you to make your own hours? Will you be able to work at home from time to time? Do you feel secure enough in your job to take a day off if the baby is sick? This sort of latitude can be of enormous help in juggling your many responsibilities.[4]

But if your job doesn't offer these benefits or if the day-to-day pressures you feel are too great, in spite of them, you might want to think about other job possibilities during your leave.

Try to hire a baby-sitter or a baby nurse for a few hours a day, and schedule some lunches with friends or with discreet business associates to help you explore other areas of employment. Even if you do decide on a new career, it's better not to make a switch immediately. It's easier to return to a familiar job when you are still getting adjusted to an infant. Wheatley and Hirsch suggest that you wait nine to twelve months before looking for a new position. A premature job search is not an "effective career or parenting strategy."[5]

Unfortunately, what starts out as a sound decision may become an excuse as women stay in low-level jobs too long, noted Marilyn Machlowitz. For whatever position you were in when your baby was born, in a few years time you are probably ready to take the next step forward. A delayed job search is not an effective career or parenting strategy either, as a woman I'll call Karen discovered. A social worker in the Department of Community Medicine at a large metropolitan hospital, Karen was twenty-nine years old when her son was born. Although her job as a caseworker had become somewhat repetitious in the five years she had held it before becoming a mother, Karen returned to it after her maternity leave. But now her son John is six years old. Karen is still in the same entry level position she was in before his birth. She no longer feels hopeful about making a change. "Several interesting positions actually did come along, one right here in this hospital as the director of liaison between the medical center and the community. But I never pursued any of these opportunities, and now they seem to have stopped coming my way," Karen said. "First I wanted to wait until John started nursery school, and then kindergarten," she explained. "I didn't want to take a high pressure job that would put me under more tension and give me less patience with him. But in a funny way it backfired. Now I feel very nervous about my professional future and I tend to take it out on John."

The remorse Karen feels is shared by other working mothers. In a random sample of three hundred women living in the Boston area, researchers Dr. Grace Baruch and Rosalind Barnett found that their most common regret was abandoning their education or not pursuing career goals more seriously so that they could devote more time to their children.[6]

In studying why women do not get as far in management as men, MIT economist Lester Thurow attributed the disparity to the slackening of a woman's professional commitment during the years between twenty-five and thirty-five. Those years, when a woman is cutting back on her career to be more available to her children, are crucial to professional advancement, according to Thurow.[7] Once a woman stays at one level too long, the pattern becomes established and she tends not to move out of it even if her personal circumstances have changed, as a thirty-seven-year-old bank executive, Gloria, found out.

"Eleven years ago, when my son was born, I made a decision to switch to part-time," she explained. "Now it's tough to handle, in that I put the lid on how far I could go professionally. It was my choice entirely," Gloria assured me, "but the fact is that I can't advance as far as I'd like to if I were working full-time."

"So why don't you switch back?" I asked, knowing that her children are now eleven and eight.

"I don't think I can ever catch up, but it's a good question," Gloria said with a faint smile, "and something that I've thought about a lot. I don't know. Even when I interview at another job, I ask for a part-time position, knowing that they aren't ready to go with it and that I'm defeating myself. It's strange," she said ruefully. "I'm such a planner, and yet I did this to my own career."

Now that Gloria's children are in school a whole day and away at camp for the summer, she ponders her job situation again and again. She says that she tells herself that the children still make demands. "But," she adds, "that may all be an excuse."

Being a writer gives a person lots of excuses—an excuse to wear faded blue jeans and a work shirt long after your contemporaries are sporting silk blouses; an excuse to work unconventional hours; an excuse to indulge in unconventional behavior. But it can also give you an excuse not to advance your own career.

In that way it is the perfect profession for me, for no one expects writers to be pushy or aggressive. We write for the pleasure of communicating, for those moments of clarity that come after days of work. So if my agent wanted to send out a piece, fine; if she chose not to, it was also fine. If my editor wanted to publicize my book, fine; if not, also fine.

But it wasn't so fine. Not really. Not in those inner reaches of the psyche where anxieties war with ambition. Why did my anxieties always win out? Why did I always urge my publishers to keep my traveling to the minimum? Or insist, if I was scheduled to tour four cities, that I be flown home after each one? When I was asked to do more, I immediately unfurled my banner of excuses: the children would miss me; I have no one to pick them up at the nursery school; there's no one to make dinner.

"When you get in touch with your own feelings, you can see that the obstacles are really of your own making," said Dr. Shelly Robin.[8] So, for me, the excuses about leaving my children were really my guilt over the distance I was traveling from my childhood ideal of the perfect mother. I did not understand it then, of course, although I now know the pattern to be quite common.

Eleanor Berman, author of *Re-Entering*, writes that every career counselor is familiar with the ploy women use of inventing road-blocks to their professional advancement so that they don't have to deal with the guilt of taking time and attention away from their families.[9] Obstacle-making is particularly frequent among those women raised by traditional mothers, according to Dr. Rhoda Green, who heads a New York–based management consulting firm. If a woman's own mother was at home, she is apt to be afraid to confront a situation that encourages her professional success, Green explained. "Women have difficulty moving out of the scene in which they were raised."

But that doesn't mean that we can't do it. If we wonder whether we are holding ourselves back professionally by staying at a low-level job too long or not pursuing advancement, there are a few ways of knowing for certain. One career counselor suggests that a working mother draw up a plan for herself so that she will know when to take the next job. Values and situations change over a period of time. "At one point family concerns might be a top priority, but as children get older and your husband becomes more invested in his work, maybe you'll be ready to take on more responsibility, work longer hours, or do some traveling."[10]

Another suggested asking yourself the following questions: Do I hate leaving for work in the morning? Am I in a dead-end position? Are others being given more stimulating work? Have I been bypassed for a promotion? For a salary increase? For new responsibilities?[11]

If you have answered yes to any of these questions, it is probably time to move on—a scary thought, perhaps, but scarier still to stay when you think of how miserable a bad job situation makes us. And management experts have some suggestions for diffusing the fear. Be discreet. If possible don't let anyone at your office know that you are looking for another job, and don't leave your job until you have found a new position. "You're more valuable and have more leverage if you have to be persuaded to accept a new position." Don't personalize. Many working mothers feel overly grateful to their bosses. "She taught me everything," or "She understood when I took off to be with my sick son," they say, and allow these feelings to stand in the way of leaving. Don't equate leaving your employer with betraying him or her (or your mother, which is really more to the point).[12] The best bosses encourage their employees to move on and take pride when they do. Remember, your success is a reflection of how well they trained you.

These pointers will help you know when it is time to move ahead and help you cope with the office departure. But how can you deal with your feelings about how increased work responsibilities will affect your home life? How can you deal with the guilt—the underlying reason that kept you at your old job too long? One way is to think back to Karen, the social worker, and the impact her job inertia ultimately had on her interactions with her son. As Eleanor Berman explains, working mothers can't really give up their goals without feeling serious resentment.[13] This resentment will harm the very relationships we are seeking to enhance.

Another way to get beyond the guilt is to communicate openly and honestly with your family about the expectations, reservations and concerns you *all* have about your new position. Reassure your children that your love and your attention to their important needs will continue even if you are not home as much or as early in the evening as you used to be. If your youngsters make you feel guilty, as mine often do, with pleas of "Oh Mommy, please stay home," give them the opportunity to express their feelings, *but* also tell them yours and why you are doing what you are with your life. And finally, "keep your perspective. Remember that change, even positive change, takes getting used to."[14]

CHAPTER 16

Children and Self-Sabotage

"WORKING MOTHERS OFTEN sabotage their achievements. They may do something self-destructive or question the 'real' meaning of their work at a time when they really need to do something productive," said therapist Joan Erdheim, who has observed this phenomenon countless times. And the problem is compounded because we are so busy outwardly striving to meet the multiple demands of our lives that we don't really see how we are inwardly hindering ourselves.

As soon as Jill joined the Chicago public relations firm, she was recognized as a real go-getter. Perceptive, conscientious and witty, she immediately won her senior partner's trust and her clients' confidence. By the time she was thirty she had two major accounts, one a chemical company and one a large manufacturing firm. "I was in danger of making my work my life and probably would have if I hadn't married Tom when I did."

While Tom Riley was as committed to his career as an advertising executive as Jill was to hers, their insistent desire to spend time together encouraged them both to keep their normally long work hours within reasonable bounds. The intensity with which they worked spilled over into other areas of their lives. "We worked hard, vacationed hard and played hard."

They bought a home, even thought about buying a horse, which Jill had wanted since girlhood days when she had stopped riding. Life was energetic, fast-paced. So, initially, it was hard to fathom the slow, sweet wish for a baby that crept in and out of her thoughts.

"Suddenly I began to notice pregnant women on the street, women whom I might not have even noticed before, and suddenly, strangely, they seemed part of a wonderful and compelling club that more than anything I yearned to join."

Slim and graceful, Jill couldn't wait until her pregnancy showed. "In fact," she said laughingly, "I started wearing those loose-fitting Laura Ashley dresses long before I needed to, hoping that someone would notice." When people at work did notice, there was mild curiosity, a little bit of old-fashioned concern about her climbing the stairs between the two floors of the firm, but that was it. They knew Jill, knew that she was fused to her work.

"I was thrilled to be pregnant and even more thrilled when Tanya was born. I looked at her and fell in love." Even so, Jill never considered staying home. "If I were home full-time, I'd go crazy. I'd get bored. That's all there is to it. Maybe I could take it for one day a week but that's it. I'm not a shopper, I hate going to the hairdresser," she said, giving her long blond hair a shake. "I guess that I just don't have much use for the kinds of things [our mothers did], so I don't really see what I'm giving up by working."

No apparent conflict there. No conflict, either, over child care—the best around. Jill described her baby-sitter as a kindly-grandma type who'd raised three boys of her own and was eager to take on the nurturing role again, especially of a little girl.

There were many projects to catch up on: some management changes at her client, the manufacturing firm; the prospect of getting another account; and some work to do for one of the partner's accounts. So Jill attributed her first "mistake" to trying to spread herself a little too thin. "More of an embarrassment, really, than anything else," she said. "I let a blueprint for an annual report go out with a mix-up between the columns for pounds and dollars," she admitted sheepishly. Fortunately the partner for whom Jill had been doing this report caught the error before it went to the printer.

The next time she wasn't so lucky. "Somehow, some way—I still can't understand how it happened," Jill reflected, shaking her head, "I missed the deadline for delivering the final approved blueprint of the annual report to the printer for my chemical account." Jill made no attempt to burden someone else with the error. "At the firm a large part of my job was to lay out, set a timetable and meet it in connection with the annual reports. This slip-up cost everyone a lot of money and effort. The chemical company had to pay for overtime at the printers in order to have the report printed, dried and delivered to be mailed with the proxy statement. It was a nightmare," Jill said.

The third mistake was even more serious. Jill put a tombstone (the official term for an ad in a financial paper) in on a secondary offering of stock for the manufacturing firm a day earlier than the completion of the public offering. The Securities and Exchange Commission gave the company a hard time over it, resulting in major efforts and expense in Washington, before it would approve the final offering prospectus.

It was a grievous error—ominous, almost symbolic. It was as if, unknowingly, Jill was erecting a tombstone to mark the end of her career. Not surprisingly, her firm lost the account with the manufacturing company, and also not surprisingly, Jill lost the opportunity to be made a partner.

Although Jill did not then appreciate why she had orchestrated her own failure, psychoanalytic theory provides some clues. When women return to work after having a baby, they miss the infant and may experience guilt that they are neglecting the baby, according to Harold Blum, a psychiatrist.[1] Since that unconscious guilt seeks a punishment, women may unwittingly become destructive of their careers. When they do encounter professional failure or setback, they become unhappy and frustrated, and this has repercussions in their interaction with their children. Jill reported, "I found myself taking little pleasure in Tanya."

Rona had been an executive with a company for ten years before becoming a mother. She consulted a psychologist when her baby was six months old because she no longer seemed able to motivate her staff. Those working under her complained that during the last half-year she had become distant and demanding, a sharp contrast to the way she had been before becoming a mother. The dissatisfaction among her subordinates was so great that Rona feared the company president would learn of the problems.

During the course of her psychotherapy, it became apparent that Rona had a lot of difficulty leaving her son in the care of a baby-sitter. She felt so guilty not being home to nurture him that she suppressed the empathetic qualities that had made her such a successful manager. It was as if on some level she was thinking, if my son isn't going to receive the benefit of my warmth and caring, then my business associates aren't either. Before she was able to analyze the roots of her guilt and attempt to cope with it, Rona allowed it to hurt her professional relationships.[2]

Another example of how a working mother's guilt over leaving a child can sabotage her career comes from Ellie, a California personnel manager. Ellie's boss was a stickler for punctuality, but Ellie never managed to get to work on time. As she explained it, "one thing or another always kept me behind schedule." One morning Ellie remained at the baby-sitter's home for an hour because her daughter Elizabeth was crying; another time Elizabeth took an "especially long time finishing her bottle"; on a third occasion the baby spilled milk all over herself and had to be bathed and redressed before Ellie would bring her to the sitter's home.

Of course Ellie might have tried to avoid these morning crises either by getting up earlier so they would have more time or by giving the sitter increased responsibilities, such as giving the bottle. But Ellie didn't try these alternatives, and a circuitous pattern became established. Her guilt first attached itself to leaving her baby, but in time she became guilty about getting in to work late. She began to rush Elizabeth in the morning, but that only led to more spilled bottles and other mishaps, more irritability on Ellie's part, more guilt and more lateness. The cycle ended unhappily with the loss of Ellie's job.

Dr. Brazelton, who has seen many such situations in his practice, commented that the "unconscious, often inexpressed feeling of cheating or guilt about any satisfaction in life beside the 'womanly role' of housekeeping and child care is the biggest danger for women and their children." It is dangerous for children because, as Brazelton points out, the unrecognized guilt interferes with the many opportunities for positive interaction with her child that the working mother has.[3] And it is dangerous for women because when we use our children to harm our careers, it hurts us personally as well as professionally. While our unconscious guilt may seek failure, on a conscious level we want to succeed. As Karen Horney asserts, our self-esteem is measured by our own and others' estimation of our success. When we see ourselves as failures, we also see ourselves as unworthy and devalued.[4] And, of course, when we take our unhappiness out on our children we feel guiltier still.

Kathleen, a district sales manager for a computer company, went to a national sales conference with her six-month-old in tow. Her mother-in-law was perfectly happy to have her grandson stay with her for a few days, but Kathleen felt better having her son with her. Her associates, however, did not enjoy having a crying, teething baby along, and it is doubtful that the baby enjoyed being carried from meeting to meeting.

Kathleen, as it turned out, didn't enjoy it either. "This was the kind of meeting where high visibility is important, and I had to spend so much of my time in the hotel room taking care of my baby that I missed out on most of the informal interactions that are absolutely vital to my work." Looking back on it, Kathleen said, "It really had a negative effect on my career in that company; it's two years later and I'm still berating myself for bringing him to that meeting."

Marlene Arthur Pinkstaff and Anna Bell Wilkinson, specialists in training and developing human resources, are concerned about the way in which guilt can undermine a working mother's success. They tell of a talented friend who worked herself up to be next in line for department head at one company, only to quit because she wanted to spend more time with her children. In three months she started up again with another company, and the same thing happened all over again. This is because she never resolved her conflict about combining work and motherhood, a conflict, say Pinkstaff and Wilkinson, "which transposes into a fear of success."[5]

Annette, from a steelworkers' town outside Pittsburgh, did not come to terms with her conflict about her two roles until after the self-defeating actions she described to me. Married by the age of twenty, Annette had two children before a separation from her husband threw her into the work force. Although she'd had no formal training, she had a flair for art and design and managed to get a job as an interior decorator with a furniture store. "I was very good at it," Annette recalled. "I had nice clientele, and although I was working for the store, people requested me to work for them privately. I had an opportunity to branch out as a full-time thing, not connected to the store."

But while this represented an exciting new possibility, it was laden with difficulty for Annette. "I clutched," she admitted. "I was brought up to be a mother, not a career woman. I realize now what I did. I actually put in so many failure factors that I failed myself."

"What kinds of things did you do?" I asked.

"Oh, like not getting things done on time, procrastinating. Not making sure that the customers got the furniture they ordered when they wanted it. Not researching things to find out what was available. I just kept putting everything off, spending more time with my daughters and less time at work."

In talking about why she felt she had been afraid to succeed, Annette, now forty-one, professionally secure and keenly introspective, looked back on her childhood and the lack of support she'd received from her mother's model. "It's always the woman who has to put herself behind what the man wants. My mother is very subservient to my stepfather, as she was to my father. I had a deep resentment about it. It was a conscious thing. I was never going to end up like my mother," she said emphatically.

Fortunately Annette was able to understand her self-defeating conflicts relatively early in her career.

"Most often the person affected is unaware she is doing herself in until she has quit a job just prior to promotion, disappointed her supervisors, overeaten defensively, delayed excessively or botched the project that could have made a difference in her professional career," noted Denver-based creative-stress consultant Dr. Betsy Morscher.[6]

The task ahead of us is to identify our self-sabotaging behavior before we have committed professional suicide. And doing so is neither easy nor painless. It will mean scrutinizing inner motives and defenses, seeing ourselves refracted through a lens that is neither familiar nor always comforting. For while we may say we truly believe that we feel guilty because we spend twenty minutes of our work day on the phone with our children or that we feel at fault for letting our colleagues down as we rush from the office to attend a Little League game, we are actually allowing these situations to "confirm" the feelings of culpability inherited from our pasts. These events merely rekindle the unconscious guilt that originates in our conflicts over separation.

Knowing and understanding this is an important step out of the emotional labyrinth in which we've been caught. But it is not all. While the truth may make us free, it will not necessarily change set modes of behavior. But working at them—chipping away at them like a sculptor at work—will. It may mean calling upon all our strengths and skills and perhaps those of others. For sometimes mentors or friends can discern patterns that we are unable to.

About two years ago my friend Jackie, a free-lance fashion illustrator, began to miss her deadlines for submitting sketches. When I asked her why she thought this was happening, she explained that she didn't have enough time to work, since she always stopped as soon as her children came home from school. Some days she had put in a good five hours before they got home, and she was ready to leave her studio at three. But on other days it took her longer to formulate her ideas, and stopping at an artificial point really affected her creativity.

Since I knew she had a full-time housekeeper who could easily watch the children a few afternoons a week, I wondered why she was being so rigid. It seemed particularly strange because what Jackie loved about working free-lance was the flexibility it afforded. When I cautiously suggested that she might be using her children as an excuse to avoid success, she slowly acknowledged that I was right, that there was no rational reason she had to leave her studio every afternoon at three o'clock. There were, however, *irrational* reasons: Jackie's work was becoming very popular. On some level she feared that the more successful she was, the less she would "be like a mother."

Once I pointed out what Jackie was doing, she began to change her self-defeating pattern. But even if we do not have others to call our attention to our self-sabotaging ways, we can monitor ourselves, according to Joan Erdheim. "It's possible to keep these concepts in your head and try to check yourself out when things are not going well. Others suggest minimizing the importance of the goal or task you want to achieve as a good way to reach it, or fantasizing that you are successful, so that you will feel comfortable with the idea.[7] Of the utmost importance is not to use your children as an excuse. It will hurt them, it will hurt you and it will inevitably hurt your career.

Some of us manage to achieve in spite of ourselves. In spite of our prohibitions and misgivings, we succeed. But rather than allowing ourselves to reap the psychological rewards of our work, we undermine our accomplishments, pass them off as nothing, deny ourselves pleasure.

She calls herself the prune face, but no one who has spoken to, or been in the presence of actress Maria Tucci would agree. With large, quiet brown eyes, it is easy to imagine her as the Shakespearean heroine she has played so often on the New York stage. A great favorite at the productions in Stratford, Connecticut, Maria has also appeared in the movie *Daniel* and has starred in several television shows. She is serene, sensitive and successful in a harsh world where few make it though many try.

Yet rather than feel elation, joy and pride in her accomplishments, she is haunted. "Somewhere deep inside my psyche is the idea that the perfect mother does not work." And at first, on becoming a mother, she did not work, taking long leaves after both her daughter Lizzie and son Nicky were born.

With each birth Maria, whose passion for acting is ingrained in her soul, felt as if she were one with her children. "I spent so much time with Nicky that I had no idea I was a separate human being. I did not know that I existed without him."

She stopped taking parts, and then they stopped coming her way. "Oh, Maria," people would say. "Yeah, she'd be great for it, but who can get her?"

Inevitably the lack of work depressed her, and her husband and friends urged her to resume her career. But when she did, she insisted on such a rigorous routine that she squeezed the pleasure from it. Doing a play in New Haven when Nicky was three, Maria worked a ten-hour day and drove home to Manhattan every night because she found it so difficult to be apart from him. Working on a television miniseries in Boston when Nicky was five, Maria flew home every morning on the 2:30 A.M. flight from Boston and took the 9:00 A.M. shuttle back so that she could be with her children one and a half hours a day.

Hardly sleeping, hardly eating, Maria readily admits that that kind of schedule was "not for them." Maria's husband, her parents, a baby-sitter, a housekeeper and lots of friends were all available to fill in for her. "No, it's for me. *I* have the need to be the perfect mommy, to make every moment magical."

It is 7:30 A.M. Maria sits close to Nicky, reading, hugging, his face still puffy from sleep, hers hiding well her nights of travel, which are visible only in indigo smears under her eyes. Although

Maria is considered a major actress, she doesn't feel comfortable with the part. "My friends can't believe how I put myself down," she said. There is much praise for her work and critical acclaim, but something keeps her from embracing her success. "Somewhere is the image that the good mommy is always there, and even though I know that it's not true, it is true. I can't seem to rid myself of it."

A woman I'll call Meg also denied herself pleasure in her achievements. The mother of two young daughters, Meg enrolled in her local community college. "I got through the first semester with a 4.0 [A average]. By the time the second semester began, I had my son. I couldn't find anyone to sit for him and there were no day-care facilities at the college." Undaunted by this, Meg came up with an idea. "I went to each one of my instructors and I said that I needed to bring my baby with me to class—I had gotten a baby seat for him," Meg told me in a telephone interview.

All of them agreed to this plan and told her that unless the baby started to cry, it would be fine. "For the most part I scheduled my classes around his nap times. It worked out well." So well that Meg finished the second semester with another 4.0 average.

The trouble started, when Meg realized that she had the potential to excel. "The third semester I took twenty-four credits to get done faster—twenty-four credits plus a job, plus a child, plus the two older girls. I wouldn't say no to anything. I was editor of the newspaper. I was in a couple of plays, I was on committees, I was active in the church." By overloading herself, Meg undermined her joy in her accomplishments.

"[Because of their guilt], many working mothers manage to sabotage the pleasure that their professional lives bring," Dr. Martin Cohen told me. Anecdotes abound. One therapist described a patient, a litigator, who had a fender bender each time she won a case. Another told me about a patient who used physical ailments—bad menstrual cramps, migraines—to prevent her from basking in the glory of her achievements.

When we recognize that we are doing this, it's easier to stop. As Meg said, "I keep these incidents in mind to remind myself not to overload; I *can* limit what I want to do." And she might have added, "I have the right to enjoy my achievements."

CHAPTER 17

Fraudulent Feelings

MY DEAR FRIEND Peggy tells me over and over again that she feels like a fraud. And yet in the fifteen years that we've been friends, I've never known her to be dishonest. She's straightforward, incredibly decent and open about her life. Why then does she feel this way?

"I keep waiting for someone at work to discover that I'm not really as good as they think I am. You know," she said, "I often feel as though I'm pulling the wool over their eyes." The strange thing about this is that Peggy knows more about computers than anyone else I know. After graduating from college in the late 1960s, she started "fooling around" with those strange machines at a time when PCs and DECs might have been confused with college fraternities.

A keen interest in math as well as high scores in mechanical ability on achievement tests indicated her direction. "I like to take things apart and see how they work," she told me, a trait her five-year-old son, who used to dismantle everything in the house, obviously had inherited.

While many of us were fighting for a place in the male-dominated corporate world, Peggy was there, capable and confident in her job. She took a short maternity leave when Zachery was born, tried part-time work for a while but found that she felt depressed and enervated at home. "I suddenly had all this time on my hands and I didn't know what to do with it. I was watching TV, eating much more than I wanted to. I was waiting for Mark [her husband] to get back from work. I felt that my mind was atrophying—that I needed the stimulation of other adults."

The project that she had been working on also seemed to need the stimulation of Peggy's mind—there were frequent calls from work, frequent entreaties to come back and, finally, she gave in. But once back at work, she felt strangely insecure. "I felt inadequate as a mother, and that made me feel like I was fooling the world because people didn't seem to guess that I shouldn't really be there. Men," Peggy added, "don't seem to have this. We are brought up to be . . . mothers, to take care of other people. . . . [It's] almost that we don't deserve it—this success."

The persistent feeling that she is deceiving others erodes her confidence and often her performance. "The other day I had to give a presentation to some of the vice presidents on recent developments in on-line communication between personal computers and mainframe hardware, and I was so nervous that my voice was shaking. I kept making mistakes. Afterward several people complimented me on my performance, but I think they were just being nice. I really feel that I blew it."

And so many of us share Peggy's pervasive self-doubt. "Women like these," said Dr. Irene Stiver, "characteristically . . . minimize their abilities and devalue their effectiveness despite their high achievements. When they do achieve a success, they feel that it was a fluke, that they are in over their heads and will be found out any minute."

" 'In over my head' is a good description," wrote a West Coast administrator and mother of three. "I'm afraid to take on some things that I should think of as challenges. I undervalue myself, I guess," she continued. " 'In over my head' hits about once a week," confessed a marketing manager from San Francisco. "I often feel like a fraud."

"Most people see me as better than I am," confided a divorced personnel manager for a law firm in Illinois. "When overcome by feelings of fraud," she "stands in the shower and cries to release the tension."

In Massachusetts a university professor who teaches a course called Career Development and Women in Management wrote, "I consider myself less competent than others do. . . ." An auditor-accountant from Tennessee and mother of two also rated herself as less competent than her associates ranked her, and she feels that she is "often credited for coming up with solutions which are just good luck, or guesses."

We are consistently giving ourselves low marks, denying our

abilities and underselling ourselves. A divorced mother from Houston who is director of Student Administration at a large university admitted that she is well thought of by her colleagues, but "I certainly *never* see myself that way," she emphasized. A librarian from Oregon and mother of a fifteen-year-old daughter said, "I look better than I really should because I'm the only person in my building doing what I do and the only one who knows what can be done that I'm not doing."

From all over the country voices of self-doubt combine in a chorus of inauthenticity. We're not really experts or professionals or competent to perform our jobs. We're impostors, fakes, tricksters. Unfortunately, these feelings reinforce themselves. We either mar our performance, as Peggy did, thereby "confirming" that we're not really so good, or we might do the reverse. Many of us become workaholics, because that way we can attribute our success to our extraordinary efforts. Without working harder than anyone else, we should be seen as failures.[1]

Working mothers seem to be particularly susceptible to these concerns. Psychologists who have studied the impostor phenomenon find it commonly affects those who are the first in their family to do something. Said clinical psychologist Dr. Joan Harvey of the University of Pennsylvania, "it can evoke deep anxieties in them about separation."[2] Unconsciously working mothers equate success with betraying their loyalties to their mothers, with separating from the ideal standard of mothering. As one psychoanalyst said, "What seems to be career anxieties are actually anxieties and guilt over her failure as a mother."[3]

We feel like impostors, then, because we don't feel a "rightness" about working. In describing their deepest feelings about their dual roles, women confessed: "It doesn't seem natural. I feel as though I'm breaking with tradition," said an East Coast banker; "I feel as though I were abandoning my natural responsibilities—very stressful," said a secretary from North Carolina; "I feel robbed of what should be our natural rights—both my children's and mine," said a sales and production coordinator from Arkansas.

No wonder we feel fraudulent. No wonder we feel this sharp sense of betrayal. No wonder when we don our business garb, we feel as though we're dressing up for some masquerade. Recognizing the irrational nature of these feelings is a powerful way of getting beyond them. So is sharing them, according to experts in the field. "When 'imposters' realize other people have these feelings too, and that in light of their actual accomplishments such feelings are just not realistic, it can be a terrific relief."[4]

CHAPTER 18

Working More and Enjoying It Less

"I'M THE GIRL who can't say no," Anna, an English professor at a large university, told me in a telephone interview. "In addition to my regular course load, I'm sponsoring eight master's degree students (three more than required); I have four students doing senior tutorials with me; I'm a faculty adviser, which consumes hours of my time each week; and I'm on the Appointments Committee, the Curriculum Committee and the Student Housing Committee. And I've agreed to organize a conference on the symbolism in Robert Lowell's poetry that the college is sponsoring next fall.

"The worst thing about this schedule," Anna continued, "is that work seems to beget more work. Last week, for example, the head of my department called me to ask if I could please fill in the next day on an oral doctoral exam for a colleague who was taken sick with the flu. When I suggested another professor who would be more familiar with the student's field, American romantic literature, he replied, 'I thought of her too, but I called her office and she already left for the day. I knew you'd still be working.' I agreed to do it," Anna said, "but I felt angry, having to leave my office quickly to rush the children off to bed so that I could read up on Walt Whitman and other romantic poets."

Like many working mothers, Anna is a workaholic—someone who is addicted to work. Marilyn Machlowitz, who wrote a book exploring this phenomenon, uses the term *workaholic* to describe someone "whose desire to work long and hard is intrinsic and whose work habits almost always exceed the prescriptions of the job they do and the expectations of the people with or for whom they work."[1]

Take, for example, Elizabeth Whelan, a mother, a scientist and a self-proclaimed workaholic. Her list of activities included the directorship of the American Council, its twenty employees and half-million-dollar budget; a teaching appointment at Harvard; writing numerous magazine articles and a newspaper column; periodic radio shows and daily appearances on Cable News Network. "I was rushed between the cable studio at the World Trade Center in lower Manhattan, Short Hills [her home], my New York office and Newark airport, from which I was whisked off at least eight times a month to far-off places," noted Ms. Whelan, who finally was becoming so emotionally and physically stressed that she had to cut back on some of her commitments.[2]

In talking to mothers who are workaholics, I was struck by how driven they were to work at such an extraordinary tempo. "I have to work this way. Two, three, maybe even four nights a week I have to stay at the office until ten, eleven o'clock," one business woman told me unhappily. Those who are addicted to work lack the free will to work less than they do, explained New York psychoanalyst Dr. Jay Rohrlich. Karen Horney labeled this feeling the "tyranny of the should."[3]

As Dr. Helen De Rosis, associate clinical professor of psychiatry at New York University School of Medicine, explained, "The workaholic can't say . . . 'Today I'll stay home because my child is sick.' She can't make that decision."[4] So drawn by her need to work, she lacks the freedom to decide not to work, even if the decision is not in her best interest or in her child's.

Because so many working mothers are faced with decisions similar to Dr. De Rosis's example, and because time is so valuable to them and so scarce for the workaholic, it's important to understand why mothers become addicted to work. Women can use work as a defense against anxiety, stated Dr. De Rosis.[5] We have already seen how working mothers who are anxious that they are really impostors may become workaholics. There are other reasons as well, which emphasize different emotions.

Another explanation focuses on the issue of control. Machlowitz found that one quality common to workaholics is the need to be in control, to take charge.[6] For all women, motherhood represents a dramatic loss of control. "My life is not my own," is a frequent way new mothers express this feeling. For the woman who has been working, the difference between her life before and after becoming a mother is enormous. However self-directed she is, the threat to her autonomy is very great upon becoming a mother, said Dr. Ethel Person, a psychoanalyst connected with Columbia University.[7] From the time she gives birth, a mother feels an overwhelming responsibility for another life. She is no longer in charge just of herself but also of someone who will be dependent on her for years to come. Unlike the homemaker, however, who raises her child herself, the woman who returns to work is relinquishing a great deal of that responsibility to a caregiver. Her perception of her loss of control is greater than that of the full-time mother. And although the children of mothers who work and those who are at home appear to have the same number of accidents, illnesses and unhappiness, as we have already discussed, the working mother blames herself for these mishaps. If I had been there, Billy would not have fallen off the swing, she thinks, and then becomes greatly concerned about her lack of control over her child's life. To make up for this feeling, she overcompensates by becoming a workaholic who takes charge of all projects and doesn't delegate any responsibility in her office.

Dr. Rohrlich suggested another dimension to the relationship between mothers and workaholics, one that centers on their guilt. Many people who feel guilty push themselves to work harder and harder, noted Dr. Rohrlich.[8] In an experiment to test the relationship between hard work and guilt, conducted by the General Electric Company, one group of hourly workers was continually led to feel that they were being overpaid for their labor. Their productivity was then compared with a control group, which believed that it was being fairly paid. "The results clearly indicated that the people who felt overpaid had high levels of guilt and that this guilt translated into harder work and higher productivity than the control group demonstrated."[9]

The guilt, of course, does not have to emanate from the work environment, as it did in the GE study. As Dr. Rohrlich demonstrates with numerous case studies of workaholics, the unconscious guilt generally originates from a sense of having wronged a family member or loved one.[10] We know that working mothers feel guilty about not being home with their children. These women are desperate to prove the necessity of their working. Like Anna, they attempt to make a monument out of their work, to create an institution of it so that their careers are substantial and unquestioned.

In order to show how important it is to be working instead of being home, workaholics try to maintain the myth that they are ir-
replaceable, indispensable, that only they can do the job. They
want to convince themselves and others that they have to work because they are vital to the organization.

The guilt that impels them to become workaholics, however,
like all guilt, seeks punishment. Said one hospital administrator,
"I'm perpetually tired and worn out. I have deep circles under my
eyes; I'm always losing weight. I feel tense and irritable. I'm afraid
of burn-out by the time I reach forty," this thirty-five-year-old admitted. As Dr. Rohrlich explained, when people work grueling
hours, don't take time off and don't vacation, they are repudiating
pleasure, and that "does a great deal towards salving their con-
sciences."[11]

Rosemary Jennings, the psychologist, finds herself taking on a
blistering work load at times. "I think there's a feeling that a lot
of us have that this is very selfish, being mothers and also working.
When I was around other mothers who didn't work, and . . .
when I observed them with their children, I would feel that they
were doing a better job. I felt then that I wasn't a good mother,"
said Rosemary, who is considered by all to be a splendid mother.

The guilt, however, that she experiences over this "failure"
makes itself felt. "For me, it's taking on more than I can handle.
I can't say no [to work]. I take on more and more, and I get totally
exhausted. . . . and then I don't enjoy anything."

There's additional unhappiness for the workaholic mother in
her feeling that she is not spending enough time with her children. "I feel terrible every night when I insist that my children
get to bed early so that I can work," said Anna. "I know that I'm
shortchanging them," another workaholic asserted, and Elizabeth
Whelan admitted that until she modified her routine, she hardly
saw three-year-old Christine. Workaholics typically stretch the time
they can devote to their jobs, but, as one explained, she could use
the early morning hours to do paperwork, but she could not very
well spend it with her son.[12]

Life is generally difficult for the offspring of workaholics, wrote
Machlowitz. Children do not have the opportunity to observe
their mothers working productively at an office but, rather, see
them at the end of the day when they are exhausted, irritable and
sometimes bored. Many children of mothers who are addicted to

work are convinced that their mothers would rather be reading the *Wall Street Journal* than playing with them. While mothers may forget how little time they spend with their children, the children do not, according to Machlowitz. However much a work-aholic mother may love and care about her child, the child may grow up not realizing the depth of these feelings.[13]

Studies done on the children of workaholics indicate that when they become adults, they either follow their parents' pattern and become intense and hard driving, or they become the exact oppo-site: "beach bums or the equivalent." Machlowitz found that few people addicted to work want their children to be like them, and few, also, I'm sure, would choose the other alternative. How can workaholic mothers break their addiction?[14]

The first way is to appreciate the damage that a constant sched-ule of work overload is inflicting on your emotional and physical health and on your children. Machlowitz suggests that you can improve your interaction with your youngsters by bringing them to your office periodically or by buying your children toys or books that relate to the kind of work you do so that they will feel more connected to you.[15] You can begin to do this immediately, while you are still figuring out how to taper off your hours, and slowly wind down your commitments.

Since workaholics commonly do far more than is necessary to complete a project—one doctor said it takes a workaholic twelve hours to do what others get done in eight—begin to limit the amount of time you spend on any one thing. This is especially important because bosses often view chronic overtime as a "sure signal that you or your workplace is disorganized, inefficient or out-of-control."[16] If it usually takes you five hours to complete a report, try doing it in three. You'll be surprised to see that the quality probably won't suffer; it may even improve. Michele Mattia, a management-development manager at the Research In-stitute of America, suggested "setting goals and priorities by an hourly schedule" (I'll get this done before lunch and that before the 3:00 meeting). Decide what work has to be done before so-cializing. Keep personal calls short. Make sure that you set up time in the day for concentration on your work and make it pub-lic, so that you have an opportunity to finish your assignments quickly and efficiently.[17]

Force yourself to work less by planning vacations, lunch breaks and shortened days, and enlist your family's help. One husband of a workaholic mother told me that he had his wife's secretary schedule two-hour lunch appointments for them every so often. "Then I take her to a wonderful restaurant where the only rule is No business."

Another way to cure your addiction to work is to remember that workaholics don't always excel professionally and aren't necessarily well thought of by their associates. Machlowitz admits to being startled by her finding that some workaholics are "among the world's worst workers."[18] They may unwittingly do great damage to the organizations to which they are so committed. They sometimes create a pressure-cooker environment, expecting others to work with the same intensity that they do. They are often seen as demanding and difficult to work with. And, since they tend not to delegate, they deprive their staff of opportunities to grow and learn, and this can be very demoralizing to their younger associates. Mothers who are workaholics also have to think about the model they are offering to female subordinates. If talented young women believe that the only way a mother can achieve professional success is to assume inordinate responsibility, they may be discouraged from attempting to combine the two roles.

Finally, when you have the freedom to decide how much time you want to spend working rather than being driven to put in long hours, you will *really* be in control of your life, and the benefits to your family, career and sense of self will be enormous.

CHAPTER 19

Separate but Equal?

"I HAVE AN ironclad rule: I *never* take off when the children are sick, but I leave work at five P.M. no matter what," said Susan, a mother of two and a senior editor at a New York publishing house.

"Work and family are two separate worlds for me," asserted Katherine, a computer programmer from Utah and mother of a three-year-old.

From all over I heard the same conflict. "If there's a school play that I'm missing, I go to work but feel guilty all day." "I'm not honest and feel guilty." "I tell the truth and feel guilty."

"I generally feel either (a) guilty about not getting work done or (b) guilty about not spending enough time with my kids, but usually (c) both."

The professional persona; the private persona. Two lives, two different sets of responsibility, two separate spheres lacking apparent confluence. The trouble is that they often exist in one person, causing constant tension and unhappiness. Even when routines are established and going smoothly, it takes inordinate energy to maintain the distinction. But when the unexpected happens, the dailiness, the familiarity, is ruptured—a late baby-sitter, a sick child, a school bake sale, a business trip—and women feel as though they are truly being ripped in two.

"It was Jessica's birthday party at school. I wasn't planning to go. I was closing on a piece," an editor of a weekly magazine told me. "It was an important article, one I had worked on, really coaxed from the author, no one else could take it over for me. But even though I was working like a fiend all day long, I kept thinking about Jessica and that I was missing her party. Finally, at ten minutes to one, I went tearing out of the office. To hell with this, I thought. The tears were streaming down my cheeks the whole cab ride to the school. I can't take it, I thought. I can't take being a hard-nosed professional one minute and a nurturing mother the next. I felt truly schizophrenic."

Few questions scratched the emotional surface as deeply or elicited as strong a response as those about specific conflicts between home and work: conflicts over time, energy, loyalty. Missing a Boy Scout picnic, leaving work early to be with a sick child, turning down a business trip—"makes me feel crazy," "I'm being pulled apart," was how women described the feelings.

While women actively strive for the distinction between personal goals and career goals, men don't see a problem and are constantly trading off between each set when conflict threatens the balance. To be sure, when men do take time off to be with their children, they do not feel or encounter the same difficulties that women do. At a seminar for working parents, a salesman for a sports magazine stood up and declared, "If our child is sick and my wife can't come home, I don't lie. I call up and tell the truth. My associates say, 'Oh, aren't you wonderful for doing that.' "[1]

Arnie, my husband, found the same thing. When my pregnancy with Andrew required that I remain flat on my back in bed for seven months, Arnie assumed a large share of our infant Alison's care, leaving work early to play with her, taking time off to take her to the doctor or just to the park. The time he spent parenting enhanced him in the eyes of his colleagues, while I, who was still teaching my seminars to students who were bussed to my home, felt diminished in the eyes of mine.

"You feel you have to prove you're not the stereotypical woman —the kind who says the career is terrific until the kids come and then gives it all up," said Jane O'Malley, a lawyer from Syracuse, New York. "We constantly have to prove that we're not going to let our home lives interfere with our jobs," agreed Ilana Knapp, a chief financial officer for a small Wall Street securities firm.[2]

In order to demonstrate that our families do not intrude on our work, we go out of our way to maintain a distinction. We keep separate lists of things we are responsible for in each setting; we keep different appointment books and calendars. We minimize the role our children play in our lives. One guidebook for working mothers urged keeping your children at a "low profile in the office." Following that advice, we discourage our children from calling us at work and refrain from discussing our families with our colleagues. Said Karen Gonçalves of the Cambridge consulting firm Arthur D. Little, "I didn't keep a picture of my daughter in the office; I would travel anywhere, no matter how hard it was for me."[3]

Ruth Adams, an executive saleswoman for a New Jersey firm, commented that there are "certain things that I just can't talk about at work." Adams related one incident when she couldn't stay late to meet with her boss because her baby-sitter was sick. He told her to do what she had to do, but not to tell him about it. Fair enough. Few bosses want to hear the desperate cry, "my baby-sitter didn't show up. . . ."[4] But many of us are going too far to maintain a separation between work and home. Women commonly phone in that they are ill when they are really staying home to be with their sick child. Then when they are sick, many feel no choice but to go to work. "The whole office thought I had pneumonia when my son was the one who actually had it," said Sara, a middle manager for a big insurance company. When Sara did come down with the disease, she struggled through and missed only two days of work.[5]

Although we feel that our survival depends on this strategy of separating home and work, it does not. Rather, our insistence on making a distinction between our two worlds and the absolute commitment we make to maintain that distinction stems from raw guilt.

"I feel guilty about not being able to always control and separate my work from my home life," wrote Melinda, a secretary and mother of three from Texas. "It is remorseless sense of guilt that makes women attempt the explicit separation," wrote Anne Jardim and Margaret Hennig.[6] It is the kind of guilt that "makes them feel that if they are good parents they cannot be good workers and if they are good workers they cannot be good parents," says Stephen Segal. It is our guilt that severs our sense of legitimacy and entitlement to do both.

"For years I was compartmentalizing myself," said a bank vice president. "I was Judy Fishman, worker, mother, wife—a woman cut in thirds. I was a different person in my different lives, and I wasn't even aware of how diffuse this lack of integration was making me feel. Then I began to notice things, like the days I'd come to work, I might forget to wear makeup. One day I forgot to put on a slip, and that was an indication to me that something wasn't working right. I felt a confusion about who I was," Judy recalls. "Another day I was on the phone and someone asked who I was and, you know, I had to stop and think who I was at that moment.

"Looking back on it, I think that the problem for me, and probably for lots of other women, is that we don't feel comfortable putting all the parts together. It's as if we're not convinced that we can do—should do—all the different parts."

Hennig and Jardim call this strategy of separation a "loss-lose strategy."[7] And they are right! We lose, our families lose, the organizations for which we work lose. The separation keeps us in a state of perpetual fragmentation and alienation from our lives, unable to feel comfortable about who we really are.

An investment broker and mother of two expressed it this way: "I never wanted my children to feel rejected so I consciously undermined how important my work was to me. But it backfired. They never took my job seriously, and now—even as teenagers—they aren't prepared to make the kinds of family concessions my schedule requires. Even worse, I feel that I've deprived them of knowing about a whole other exciting side of me."

As long as we lack a coherent personal vision, we will not be able to integrate the organization for which we work into a functioning whole; neither will we be able to accept conflict and ambiguities in our co-workers. And we cannot really expect others to accept these characteristics in us.

We complain that "men often have difficulty understanding that a woman can have a baby, be an executive and be family oriented all at the same time,"[8] but *they will never understand* unless we show them it can be done. We must show them, not by denying, hiding or apologizing about the other side of our lives, but by boldly accepting it. Only when we feel secure about being working mothers can we urge the concrete changes in the work environment that our identities demand.

We can begin by no longer being, in Judy Fishman's words, "men/women" who try our best to fit into a culture whose traditions, rules and implicit codes are derived from male experience. As Dr. Stiver points out, women generally are in work settings where men predominate and are in the most powerful positions. It is men, then, who set the climate for "professional behavior."

Women sometimes have difficulty conforming to what they believe are expectations for professional behavior when these expectations conflict with their own experiences, needs, inclinations and talents, wrote Dr. Stiver.[9]

Until recently, however, women felt that they had no choice but to adapt to these standards. Now, however, management consultants are finding that we can be successful without adhering to what Marilyn Machlowitz calls the management/business career myths. One of these myths is that you must have a mentor to succeed. Women have traditionally been considered to be at a disadvantage because they generally did not have mentors. In Machlowitz's study of sixty professionals, half men and half women, who achieved success at an early age, only two reported the aid of a mentor. A second myth Machlowitz debunks is that you have to be able to move when your company wants you to. With the increasing number of dual-career marriages, many businesses are changing their relocation requirements. Even IBM, which in the 1950s was said to stand for "I've Been Moved" because of the company's policies, has reported a decline in the relocation rate of its working population. A third fallacy is that being homebound for a period of time will automatically hold you back. Jobs don't disappear, said Machlowitz, especially if you've already proved your worth to your company. During the time that you are not working, however, stay in touch through phone calls and appearances at professional organizations.[10]

Machlowitz says it's also possible to turn some of the "liabilities" of being working mothers into assets. Instead of being apologetic that you can't stay late, emphasize that you can come in early. Instead of bemoaning the fact that you are out of the office with a sick child, make a point of making business calls from home. "No one," says Machlowitz, "needs to know where you're calling from." If your child gives it away by crying in the background, a simple statement that you are home is all that's needed. No apology; no lengthy explanation is called for. "Remember how much important work traditionally has gotten done when men are on the road. All work of value doesn't have to be done seated behind a desk," she explained.

Look at the case of Jane P. Metzroth. A stockbroker, she was confined to bed for six months with complications from pregnancy. Using a bit of ingenuity, Jane had a computer terminal installed in her home and had her office phone ring directly in the living room. She conducted multimillion-dollar deals flat on her back in her living room and no one knew the difference.[11] Dr. Rhoda Green, the management consultant, suggested that working mothers ask themselves, is the work getting done? Am I doing the job that I was hired for? If you've answered yes to both questions, that should be the bottom line.

Many women found that being a mother actually enhanced their performance at work. It broadened their understanding and insights; it seemed to unleash new energies and interests and brought out new talents.

"Since becoming a mother I have greater sensitivity to my staff," a group media supervisor from Chicago wrote. "I am more mature and have a wider range of experience," said a corporate consultant from Michigan "A greater consideration of others, I'm more understanding of others' needs," a trade show producer from California noted; "More perceptive," thought an actuary from Washington. "Having children has made me better organized at work and better able to give attention to details," reported an executive secretary from Missouri; "I have broader interests and skills now that I have children," explained a commercial banker from North Carolina; "Patience, insight, empathy," a realtor from Ohio believed; "I've gained the ability to juggle many projects, 'people skills,' compassion," wrote a director of public relations at a hospital in Florida. "I never realized I had so much patience. Helping my children has taught me a lot about developing the abilities of my staff," a New York systems analyst told me.

For many of us, the discomfort that we feel over our dual roles has prevented us from incorporating the qualities that we associate with mothering—nurturing, empathy, emotion—into our jobs. Instead we have separated them from our work life, minimized them, denied them; and in so doing we have not only hurt ourselves but we have deprived our careers as well. As Dr. Stiver explained, we believe that masculine characteristics at work are good and feminine ones are bad, so we attempt to model ourselves on the masculine example. But this is not necessarily in our best interest.[12]

Joann, a saleswoman for a computer company outside Chicago, tried to act like her male colleagues, she explained in a telephone interview. "I dressed in mannish suits and attempted to copy 'the boys.' " It wasn't until her boss advised her that some business associates found her intimidating and tough that Joann began to change her style. "It wasn't hard to make the transformation; it meant being myself," Joann told me. She began to dress differently, in mauves and yellows, and to allow her natural warmth, spontaneity and kindness to come through in her business dealings. "Of course I haven't gone so far as to tidy up the conference room, but I have displayed some traditional female qualities and it's helped my career."

Dr. Stiver suggested that women stop worrying about being "branded hysterical" if they exhibit some emotion at work. Often the importance of an issue is communicated by an emotionally expressive style of speaking, observed Stiver. By letting our associates know how strongly we feel about something, we often can win them over to our point of view. And Florence Skelly advised women to stop emphasizing the "no difference" between men and women in business situations. Skelly's surveys showed that people do perceive a difference, and in some ways that difference can be beneficial.[13]

Audre Wenzler, an executive with a major accounting firm, provided a good example of how being a mother gave her an advantage in dealing with her secretary. Audre's secretary had gotten off welfare, put herself through secretarial school and was quite capable. But soon after she started working with Audre, her daughter began to have major problems at school, causing her to miss work and to be preoccupied. Because she is a mother herself, Audre felt that she could "be much more sensitive to what this young woman was going through." She told her secretary that her daughter was probably feeling angry at her for going to work, and she encouraged her to bring the child to the office, which she did. Audre took her to a store and bought her a coloring book. "If she likes it here and sees that her mother does, she might not feel so threatened by the job or want to put it in jeopardy by acting so bad," Audre reasoned. When I questioned why she was willing to do this, she answered that she was happy to be helpful, and "really," explained Audre, "she'll do her job better than if she has her child on her mind." The secretary benefited, Audre benefited, the company benefited—a sure win-win strategy!

Judy Fishman, the banker, also works hard to make her business life and personal life mesh. She integrates her empathic side into her business life by being compassionate and caring toward her associates. Judy tries to "legitimatize" the role of children in a professional setting by talking about her youngsters and by asking her colleagues about theirs. Women executives like Judy appreciate the fullness that children bring to our lives. The task ahead is to incorporate this richness into our work.

Many young women are absorbed by questions about when to have children, if they can have them, and how motherhood will affect their jobs. As they explained, as long as they kept thinking that maybe next year they'd be pregnant and then out on leave, they were reluctant to take on lengthy projects, accounts or cases. Once they are mothers, however, the resolution to these issues brings forth new energy. Women feel as though they have settled one of life's major decisions, and it is freeing. They are able to concentrate on long-range career plans and to make the kinds of decisions that were previously difficult because of the uncertain timing of their childbearing.

There are also feelings of accomplishment and maturity associated with maternity. Whether they have babies at twenty-five or forty, women regard motherhood as the single most important rite of passage into the adult world. Women speak of a changed self-image and a greater sense of authority and competence. And well they should.

Among the many things they are gaining as mothers are the qualities traditionally associated with effective managing. Problem solving, decision making, coordinating different activities and projects, planning for the future, evaluating ideas and advice and developing the resources and talents of others are all skills that women acquire as they raise their children. As Robert B. Trempe, senior vice president at Provident National Bank in Philadelphia, said, "If you can handle a two year old, no depositor is going to rattle you."[14]

Learning how to deal with different kinds of behavior is certainly one skill most mothers develop. But equally important is that the experience of motherhood seems to stretch our capacity for concern and caring for others. "Being a mother has given me a higher regard for the human race," wrote Susan J. Brasch, a consultant from Nebraska. This enlarged understanding of others is an asset that mothers can integrate into their jobs. When we respect our co-workers and their priorities (even when we don't agree with them), when we use encouragement to motivate our staff, when we are sympathetic to personal difficulties and problems that may periodically mar a subordinate's performance, we will be helping to create a work environment that is life-enhancing for all.

PART FOUR

In Our Marriages

CHAPTER 20

Love and Work:
A Worthy Partnership

FREUD IDENTIFIED LOVE and work as the requisites of a fulfilled life. "The aim of treatment," Alvin Blaustein, a New York psychiatrist, told me, is for "the patient to be able to love and to work, not to be hampered by conflicts, inhibitions, self-doubts." Literature, also, has upheld love and work as twin goals.

Tolstoy wrote, "One can live magnificently in this world, if one knows how to work and how to love; to work for the person one loves, and to love one's work."[1] But this is not as easy as it sounds, for while both require a good attitude about oneself, they tap different psychological impulses. "Work has to do with ambitions, reaching potential, it is more an expression of aggressive energies, while love searches for contact," explained Blaustein.

Work seeks achievement; love seeks affiliation. They have different tempos, drives and needs. Blending the two into one well-functioning individual is a difficult enough task; blending the two into one well-functioning couple is even harder.

While love and work seem to be equally valuable today, this has not always been the case. Of the two, work has enjoyed a better press throughout our nation's history. In fact, few ideas are more deeply ingrained in the American psyche than the work ethic. As early as the colonial period, parents were required to train their children "in some honest calling, labour or employment that may be profitable for themselves or the Country." Indeed, this was so important that parents who were negligent were subject to fines.[2] Love, on the other hand, is not mentioned by our earliest forebears. What we know of it, we have to deduce from wills and other contracts in which husbands provided for their wives. It existed, of course, but it was not considered vital to the couple, both of whom were expected to work. The function of the couple was economic.

The ethos of work catapulted forward in our collective imaginations with industrialization. Compared to work, love became even less significant; it was considered part of "woman's domain."

Women, who in the colonial period had been contributing members of the economy, were, during the nineteenth century, bound to the home. A cult of true womanhood arose, which insisted that women were pure—in body and mind—submissive, pious and, above all, domestic. Love and nurturing became a woman's sphere; work and providing, a man's, and except for a brief interruption during World War II, this division persisted down through the 1950s.

Oh, how work was then exalted as ranks of gray-flannel-suited men marched from the new suburbias into the hallowed corporate world. Oh, how hard and fast were the traditional roles.

The go getting male ability was exhibited in the many material goods that he provided. But the visible signs of this new affluence—the cars, the televisions, the big house—the importance of work above all else caused nagging concerns among psychologists, social theorists and couples themselves that it was resulting in a withering of love, an attenuation of family ties.

In part a rebellion against the materialism and politics of the fifties, and in part sustained by the very prosperity it condemned, the sixties saw huge numbers of people moving out of the work culture and into the love culture. At no other time in our nation's history had work seemed so unimportant and love or lovemaking so important.

The values of the work world—discipline, logic, hierarchy, authority—did not seem to resolve the pressing problems of the era. Born out of hope, some madness and inspiration, the counterculture encouraged romantic faith in nature, in intuition, in spontaneity and in love.

Students went to universities to learn, not to work; many dropped out of established society completely. And if most Americans didn't flock to communes or leave their jobs, they became more relaxed about them. Many thought less about work and success and more about fun and about love or loving. Their language, clothing, hairstyles—all reflected the "hang loose" attitudes of the young.

Social historian William O'Neil found of the sixties that "the range of individual responses was great, but the overall effect was to promote sensuality and to diminish the . . . work ethic."[3] People wanted to live richly satisfying lives; they wanted—as they said—meaningful relationships. Men and women—couples—looked to one another for commitment, sharing, warmth, for shelter from the storm. The function of the couple had become love.

The seventies brought economic hard times and the women's movement. Few men had the luxury of not working, and women, if they had it, didn't want it. But if people were again thinking more about work, it was not fifties-style. Too much had happened since then; we had learned too much.

We had learned that men can be warm and nurturing, that women can be competent and achieving. We had learned that sex-stereotyped roles keep everyone prisoner. We had learned that work and love are equal values—for men, for women and for couples.

So husbands and wives went forward in the eighties with love and work in "exquisite equilibrium"—a cheerful duo rushing off to pressured jobs all day and then coming home to share housekeeping, child care and, most of all, each other.[4] But while this image still holds with an almost mystical power, the reality is something quite different.

The dual-career family is having more than a little trouble. Arguments over housework, money, competition over status, lack of time for communication and sexual intimacy are diminishing the happiness we hoped for.

While few of us would opt to return to the traditional roles of our parents' marriages, the endless decisions of our own are posing some unanticipated problems. Stories come pouring forth of expectations unmet, needs unsatisfied, contracts unfulfilled. So many areas for deliberation, so much room for disagreement. As one attorney told me, "My most challenging cases are those I make for my husband to prepare Annie's breakfast each morning."

There are other challenges as well: encouraging and facilitating the career of your spouse while pursuing your own work; sharing in the family responsibilities without compromising your autonomy; finding the time and energy to nourish family ties and still be effective at work.

These challenges are always with us. From the moment we arise and decide who is going to get to the office early and who is going to get the children dressed and wait for the sitter, we are engaged in constant dialogue, with each other and ourselves.

While the lines of conflict seem to be drawn over how professional and domestic responsibilities are meshed in a marriage, the underlying issues are infinitely more complicated: What makes us feel loved in a relationship? How much control are we really willing to relinquish to our partners? How ready are we to compromise on our aspirations and expectations? How comfortable are we really with an egalitarian relationship? What does it feel like to be going through life with a mate we expect to be much like ourselves: to love as we do, to work as we do, to be equally sharing, caring and providing? When our roles become blurred, do our identities as well? In what ways can we still feel womanly in today's marriage?

We are awhirl with questions, intimate and complex, which lurk beneath the surface of our most routine decisions. Working these through with our spouses is extraordinarily hard, but it is made even harder by our guilt, another party to the debate.

When we identify the insidious role guilt plays in our relationships with our husbands or boyfriends, we can begin to meet the exciting challenge of the dual-career family—the challenge of combining our individual quests for fulfillment, equality, achievement, love, respect and commitment with those of our mates. No mean feat, but one that promises a family life that is vital, stimulating and deeply satisfying for us and our children.

CHAPTER 21

Share and Share Alike

Nobody smiles doing housework
but those ladies you see on TV.
Because even if
the soap . . .
that you use
   is the very best one—
housework
   is just no fun.

Children,
   when you have a house of your own
   make sure, when there's housework to do,
   that you don't have to do it alone.
   Little boys, little girls,
   when you're big husbands and wives,
     if you want all the days of your lives
     to seem sunny as summer weather
     make sure, when there's housework to do,
     that you do it *together.* (emphasis added)[1]

SO THE FAMILIAR husky voice of Carol Channing told the millions of listeners to a popular children's record of the early seventies, *Free to Be You and Me,* that housework, like love, was best when it was shared. The children liked the music, the parents approved of the message. Surely when two adults live in a house together, both should be responsible for its upkeep, particularly if both are employed outside the home. The idea was equitable, sensible; so sensible that most of us went forth into the seventies and eighties with the conviction that dividing household chores was as simple as splitting the week's shopping in half. But a funny thing happened on the way to the supermarket—we found that we were stuck with the whole list.

At first we didn't notice that we were still doing the lion's share of caring for the lair, we were so wedded to it as our traditional job.

"A housewife is a woman; a housewife does housework . . . a man cannot be a housewife," writes sociologist Ann Oakley in her classic study *Woman's Work,* and as Oakley pointed out, it has been this way since industrialization. As one woman wrote, "our window on the world is looked through with our hands in the sink."[2] The image is vivid and bitter. Woman captive in the home, hands engaged in domestic tasks, eyes gazing futilely beyond.

And yet with few exceptions, members of both sexes accepted the role of housewife as appropriate for mature females until the early 1970s, when the women's movement focused on the inequities in the housewife's position.

Housework was not real work, for the housewife was not paid, received no benefits or insurance and could join no union, but anyone who had ever done housework knew that indeed it was work, and hard work at that. It was said to be the most exalted role that a woman could have, but it was tedious, menial and mundane—and regarded as such by most wives *and* their husbands. Housework was what all married women did, and yet there were few jobs more isolating and stultifying. It was supposedly a privilege to be able to stay home and "just do housework," but if it was so wonderful, why didn't men want to do it?

The search for explanations assumed an increasing urgency in the years after the feminist critique was popularized. And yet the more things changed, the more they seemed to stay the same. As the exodus from the home to paying jobs continued, radical changes in the division of household labor simply did not take place.

In their book *American Couples,* which was based on literally thousands of interviews, sociologists Pepper Schwartz and Philip Blumstein reached the sorry conclusion that housework of the eighties is by no means a joint endeavor. Even in households in which husband and wife both felt strongly that housework should be shared equally, "when they broke it down to time actually done, the idea of shared responsibility turned out to be a myth. Even when the husband was unemployed, he did much less housework than a wife who worked fulltime."[3] A recent issue of *Monthly Labor Review* reported a "very small increase in the hours of housework done by married men (still under 3 hours per week or one-sixth the time spent by working wives)."[4] Unshared housework is a major source of friction in families with both parents employed. Like a festering sore, it spreads feelings of resentment, of not being appreciated, respected or valued.

Because the unequal division of household tasks can jeopardize the health of the entire relationship, it is important to understand why it exists, so that it can be changed. That many husbands should cling to the traditional household roles is not at all surprising; that many of their wives do also, is.

"How satisfied are you with the division of household responsibilities," I asked working mothers throughout the country, and the answers came back loud and clear.

"Very dissatisfied"—a computer programmer from Michigan; "I do 90 percent, he does 10 percent, UNFAIR"—a marketing manager from Maine; "Not really satisfied"—a CPA from Maryland; *"Help!"*—an executive recruiter from New Jersey; "Bad situation, anger, resentment"—a secretary from Minnesota.

The vast majority of working mothers interviewed were dissatisfied with the amount of household-related work they did as compared to the amount done by their husbands. But while these women feel "put upon" and "taken advantage of," they also felt "uncomfortable" in asking for more help, either from their husbands or, if it was affordable, from outside agencies or hired housekeepers.

Cheryl is an engineer, married to a pastor in Montana. The couple have two young children and a lot of financial responsibilities. Going back to work six months after her second child was born was an economic necessity, but Cheryl nonetheless feels guilty: "I am failing as a wife and mother." To compensate for this guilt, she assumes 70 percent of the child care/homemaking, to her husband's 30 percent. "Even though we verbally support nontraditional roles in the home, I carry the major portion of child-care and homemaking responsibilities. Though at times of stress I feel somewhat resentful and that this is unfair, I accept this situation, not wanting to disappoint or inconvenience my husband because of my work."

The sense of apology Cheryl feels runs through the words of other women like a stream. Maryanne is a home economist from Kansas, the mother of two teenagers, married to an executive recruiter. She admitted that her husband was willing to help with the housekeeping, but she has a problem asking for assistance. "I [still] feel guilty having him do my chores. . . . I apologize for having to ask him when I know he's tired too. I feel torn between a clean orderly house and my need to get rest," she said. "In my case," wrote a California attorney, married to a chemist, "I feel that my house is not as neat as my mother's. I don't meet her standards."

So once again we pay homage to our image of the ideal mother, guiltily cleaning and scrubbing and polishing and baking at her shrine. "When the children first arrived, I tried to do in 64 hours what housewives do in 168 hours," revealed a property manager from Virginia. "I leave my office," wrote an executive secretary from South Carolina who is married to a self-employed contractor, and "when I arrive at home, I am a housewife, maid, cook, seamstress . . . as well as friend and mother."

We are still standing with our hands in the sink, but instead of gazing wistfully out the window, as did our mothers, our eyes are busily scanning a report due in the next day. And this we call progress!

When Judy Hampton's daughter Abbie was three months old she returned to her position as an executive with a Colorado advertising agency, explaining that she "missed the office atmosphere and intelligent conversation" that work offered. Abbie goes to a day-care mother only three blocks from the Hampton home, whom Judy describes as "wonderful. [She] loves children, is very well organized and leans toward the educational toys, etc., plays and talks *with* the children, not *at* them."

Judy's satisfaction with the caregiver is matched by her satisfaction with her job. Rating it a 9.5 on a scale of 1 to 10, she found it "just what I have wanted." With a good income, a company car and a husband who does equally well in his work, Judy seems to inhabit the best of all worlds.

Yet she is tormented by deep and persistent doubts about continuing to work. "I feel I'm missing out on those things that make a mother 'a mom,' " she wrote. "It is like I must prove every day that working does not interfere with the house and Abbie. And, of course, it does. It has to. So I work twice as hard and get half as much done. . . . And it doesn't help that I have always *hated* housework; this creates a lot of tension between my husband and [me]."

Like Judy, many women considered the unequal division of household chores to cause the "greatest amount of strain in the marriage." Indeed, some identified it as the cause of their separation or divorce.

I sat across the table in a large, friendly restaurant in a suburb of Detroit, talking to Laura Klinger, a speech pathologist who recently started her own practice. The mother of two sons, Laura has been divorced for many years, and at forty she says she is in better shape emotionally, physically and professionally than ever before. "I was married young and had my children while I was still young, while my husband was still in law school. I had been raised to believe that motherhood was natural, something that you loved doing, and, well—it didn't come naturally to me."

As soon as Laura's husband got a job, Laura applied to the University of Michigan and got a teaching assistantship in speech and audiology. "I loved teaching in a college, I loved the profession," she said emphatically. "I was working more than a forty-hour week, my children were one and three and I was still doing all the domestic work as well."

I asked her why.

"I knew what my husband's expectations were—we had an agreement. He did all the things that men are supposed to do—went to work every day, brought home a good living. For my part, the house was supposed to be clean, the children taken care of, shopping done, dinner was supposed to be cooked."

"But that agreement was made before you knew you would be employed outside the home. Why didn't you try to renegotiate it?" I protested.

Laura shook her head resolutely. "I felt that *I* had an obligation to do it. I felt a lot of self-blame, of guilt. He was keeping up his end; I had to keep up mine."

But her unspoken words of resentment eroded the good feelings that Laura worked so hard to maintain. "After a while I began to feel like a drudge, as though nothing I was doing outside the house was being understood or appreciated.

"But why should we feel guilty just because we don't live up to our mothers' expectations for us?" Laura asked rhetorically. "My mother [at 88] is so removed from me; it's not feasible to live her life. Why, after all these years, do I still feel that I have to?"

For so many of us raised on the slogan Neatness Counts, it's hard to believe that it doesn't—or that it doesn't count as much as other parts of our lives. But if you find that you are doing too much waxing, polishing, scrubbing and cooking, it's time to reassess your family situation. *Setting priorities* is such an overused phrase that it has almost lost its meaning. But if ever there was a place for it, it is in your weekly list of household chores. Many dual-career families are lowering their housekeeping standards. So if you are running low on time and energy, figure out the most important things to do and skip the rest.

Working mothers shared several time-saving methods with me: Many women make master shopping lists of the basic items they buy and photocopy these so that housekeepers, teenage children and husbands can shop without asking what is needed. All family members and housekeepers should be encouraged to keep running lists of things that they use up or special items that they want bought, so that these can be added to the larger list. Stockpiling staples, such as paper goods, canned foods, soups, cereal and the like, is another good idea. Having a good supply of frozen dinners can also be a comfort.

Buying groceries once a week rather than in dribs and drabs after work saves you time and energy, as does having things delivered. Many working mothers told me that they had meats, vegetables and dry cleaning delivered to their homes as often as possible.

Shopping for our children, another time-consuming chore, can also be made easier. Many women use catalogs for purchasing. I try to condense Alison's and Andrew's clothing shopping into two days: one in the fall, the other in the spring. Armed with my lists, I blitz the large department stores where I have the best chance of buying most of what I need. What I can't find on those two days, I try to pick up when I am doing other chores. I also stock up on holiday gifts and birthday presents for my children and their friends in two major shopping sprees at a large discount toy store. It's also a good idea to load up on wrapping paper, ribbon and even cards—items that you'll need during the year but can be a nuisance if you have to buy them one at a time.

Aside from shopping, cleaning is the other major household task facing us. Throwing out as you go along keeps clutter from accumulating into a major chore later on. Children, even those under six years old, can help with cleanup. Stepchildren who visit on week-ends should also be encouraged to help out. Begin with a few simple responsibilities, for Alison and Andrew it was putting their dirty clothes in the hamper and clearing their dishes off the table. When Laura, now off at college, was their age she used to set the dinner table on the week-ends she spent with us. As children get older, they can move on to other chores. Making their beds, putting away their toys and cleaning spills are reasonable responsibilities for kindergartners.

If the tasks are age appropriate and presented in a matter-of-fact way—"We all have to share in the housekeeping"—children are usually cooperative. Some mothers make games out of the work. One has her children "race" to see who cleans his room faster; another hides pennies under items to be put away. Her youngsters keep what they find.

I have the most success getting mine to pitch in when I give them a choice about what to do. Andrew, to our surprise, really liked using the vacuum cleaner. Alison decided on cooking. Ever since she was a toddler, she has loved to help out in the kitchen. Then her tasks were pouring and mixing whatever it was Arnie or I was preparing. But at seven years old she assists fully in dinner preparation, has a few cold dishes that she can make on her own and takes great pride in her abilities.

As far as cooking is concerned, I tell Andrew, "We do not have french toast on weekday mornings," and most working mothers with whom I spoke have similar mealtime guidelines. Breakfasts during the work week should be fast and nutritious. Cereal, melted cheese on English muffins, cottage cheese and fruit or yogurt with honey are all nourishing morning meals that you and/or your children can prepare quickly. For dinner, many women or their husbands make stews or casseroles over the weekend, which they freeze and then warm up after work. Others find simple broiled fish or meat easy end-of-the-day meals. Housekeepers, baby-sitters and older children can facilitate dinner by cutting vegetables and making salads and desserts in the late afternoon.

Many women, however, insist on preparing elaborate dinners or baking when they are really too tired. If you find that you are pushing yourself to do more cooking than you really want to, it may be that you are trying too hard to compensate for working away from the home by doing all the things a traditional mom does. Judy Fishman, the banker, realized this when she found herself spending endless Sundays in her country home making jellies and baking breads that she freezes so her sons will have "home-cooked foods, even on the nights I work late."

Psychologist Harriet Goldhor Lerner has found that the legacy from our mothers is a very strong influence on our need to do housework and our inability to ask for help. Although a woman may hold "liberated ideas about sharing parenting and housework, her deeper feelings [may] not entirely match her stated beliefs." And it is these feelings that make us wonder if our requests for help are legitimate.[5]

First we must confront these feelings and our reasons for keeping the work load to ourselves. Only then can we begin to bring about change. Dr. Lerner suggests a nonblaming approach. Telling your husband he is a male chauvinist pig isn't likely to get the dishes done. And be specific, she advises. Rather than saying something like, "I'd like you to be more considerate of my needs," say, "I could use some help with the laundry today." Another good piece of advice is, "Don't put your energy into trying to change another person who does not want to change. When help is not forthcoming, think hard and long about your own options for behaving differently."[6]

One woman I know became so frustrated about her husband's refusal to help with the dishes that she started serving on paper plates. Another woman, whose husband had earned two advanced degrees, told her that it wasn't that he *wouldn't* wash the kitchen floor, it was that he didn't know how. When he couldn't catch on even after she showed him, she simply stopped washing it herself. After three weeks of walking across a sticky floor, he suddenly saw the point and became very good at it.

Other women enlist their husbands' (and children's) help by holding family meetings to discuss and divide responsibilities. Most try to encourage "voluntarism" rather than recruitment. Some families give money, stars or presents to their children for jobs well done. Others save the money to hire a cleaning service once a month. Still others get housework done by assessing all the tasks that need doing on a daily, weekly and monthly basis, and then assigning them to family members. A woman from Virginia shared her method with me: The chores were divided into four blocks: cooking, housecleaning, kitchen, laundry and miscellaneous. Each block had a job description that would impress the CEO at a Fortune 500 company. The blocks were then assigned to the four members of her family and rotated each week. While this may sound too regimented to some, the underlying philosophy is unarguable: We all live in the house together; its upkeep is everyone's responsibility.

CHAPTER 22

Competition on the Home Front

> Husband: Boy did I have a rough day. You can't imagine how hard I worked.
> Wife: *You* can't imagine how hard *I* worked.
> Husband: I'm really beat.
> Wife: You're beat. What about me? I didn't even take a lunch break.

SOUND FAMILIAR? IT certainly does to me. Without even realizing it, evening conversation between Arnie and me had become verbal jostling matches. If he had an important project to get done, I had a more important one; if he was under pressure to finish a contract, I was under even more pressure with a deadline; if he was tired, I was exhausted. What was going on?

A competitive spirit may arise between partners when the male and female spheres are not strictly separated, and this can impair the relationship, according to psychoanalyst Karen Horney.[1] Unfortunately the working couple that puts a premium on shared roles and responsibilities is emerging as a prime candidate for rivalry and jealousy. The husband and wife generally have similar educational backgrounds and professional ambitions; both are striving for achievement, recognition and self-fulfillment. The likeness of their respective quests encourages comparisons between them. Who is earning more? Which one is more highly regarded professionally? Whose work is more valuable to society? To the family?

The couple's friends and parents frequently measure one spouse's accomplishments against the other's. So does the pair itself. "If he makes partner before I do, I'll feel just horrible," Suzanna, an accountant with a large firm, said about her lawyer husband. "I made a big fuss when my husband got promoted," said another woman, "but inside I felt jealous. Why wasn't it me? I'm as good at my job as he is at his."

When women first began pursuing professions, psychologists predicted that men would feel threatened and become competitive, especially if the wives were in fields similar to their husbands'. Recent research on dual-career couples, however, has revealed that rivalry is much more widespread than previously imagined. Psychologists such as David Rice of the University of Wisconsin Medical School found competition to be all but inevitable in the dual-career couple, regardless of the partners' fields. And, equally interesting, the wife is perhaps even more likely than the husband to be the competitive one in the relationship.[2]

In explaining why women may become competitive, some social scientists use the phrase "identity tension line": the stress aroused by departing from sex-socialized roles. Occupational advancement may make a working mother feel she is neglecting what she *perceives* as family responsibilities. The resulting tension leads to resentment and rivalry.[3]

My "identity tension line" developed after we had children. Before that Arnie and I had shared in each other's work—he the unofficial editor of my doctoral dissertation, I the unofficial arbitrator of his legal cases. We respected each other's careers, reveled in good luck and advancements and stuck together in setbacks. But we did not compete. Not only are we in different professions, but the outward signs of recognition and achievement in each are different. And we work differently. Arnie thrives on a pace that alternates between frantic and calm, while I do best when the pressure flows evenly.

So what had changed? Why was it now a matter of utmost importance for me to prove—on an almost daily basis—that I was working as hard and making as important a contribution to the family well-being? I still felt as I used to about Arnie's work, but now I was approaching my marriage with the competitive spirit of an Olympic gold medalist.

For me, as for so many other women, it was a way of justifying my professional life in order to mitigate my guilt over not being a full-time mother. If my job was as important, demanding, valuable as Arnie's, then I had reason to continue working without feeling culpable.

Because guilt is such an uncomfortable feeling, we try to avoid it, explained Dr. Willard Gaylin. This may result in childish behavior at times and probably leads to more domestic quarreling than any other emotion, Gaylin noted.[4]

Women try to minimize their guilt feelings in a variety of ways. As we have seen, some may become workaholics; others work at an average pace but become competitive; a few may be workaholics *and* competitive. Still others may allow career goals to slide for a while in favor of spending more time with their families. Cutting back on the work load may be entirely the mothers' decision, and they may well enjoy the rewards of being more available at home, but, cautions Dr. Rice, "for many career women, the sum total of gains and losses does not balance out fairly. When she assesses the professional sacrifices that she has made compared to her husband's, conflictual and competitive feelings and resentment may result."[5]

Sociologists Blumstein and Schwartz found that couples who are competitive are less happily married than those who are not, and it is easy to understand why this is so.[6] When communication and interaction are marked by one-upmanship, bickering and bad feelings must surely follow.

"I compete with my husband and it leads us into many arguments," confessed a marketing executive from North Carolina. A personnel director told me that she is always trying to prove that she knows more about computers than her husband, while a lawyer with a small midwestern firm acknowledged that she, not her husband, was the competitive one, and it caused them "many squabbles."

The majority of women who admitted that they competed with their husbands did so over work-related issues. Gloria, a manager with an automotive firm, who is married to a vocational rehabilitation counselor, confided that she competed with him "over who will spend time working in the evenings and weekends . . . whose job is more important." Carolyn, a college counselor married to a fast-food-restaurant supervisor, competes with her husband over whether her "career is more important than the personal happiness of the household." An executive secretary, married to a lead man for a manufacturing company in California argues with her husband over the position and status of her present employment; and a nurse competes with her college-professor husband over "whose job is more demanding, important, responsible, bigger."

Many of the women who vie with their husbands explained either in their questionnaires or during interviews that they have a hard time competing professionally. Competing at work is a complicated issue for some women. As we have seen, we tend to associate individual achievements and success with selfishness. Competing with our husbands does not bring about advancement. It does not win us any kudos, and it is really not intended to. Motivated by our guilt, it achieves the unhappy result of marital discord.

I watched this happen with my friends Ronnie and Steve. He is the manager of the municipal bond division of an investment banking firm, and she is a saleswoman for a blouse company. Whenever the four of us would go out to dinner and Steve mentioned an important upcoming business trip, Ronnie had an even more important one. If he was telling us about a successful negotiation, Ronnie interrupted to say that she had convinced the buyer of a chain store to place a large order for blouses. When Steve talked about an impending raise, Ronnie talked about her commissions. If he mentioned some outstanding work done by his staff, she talked about how well she had taught hers. And so it went through countless evenings together. Ronnie was intent on proving that her work was every bit as important as Steve's.

I might have thought that Ronnie was simply a competitive person if I hadn't known her to be totally modest in the days before motherhood made her uneasy about pursuing her career. Now, however, she was a fierce contender, and Steve responded in kind. Whether or not this kind of interaction carried over into other parts of their lives—like who was the best parent to their young daughter—I can't say. But I do know that the transformation of Ronnie and Steve from partners to adversaries was a sad thing to observe.

Sadder still was that Ronnie no longer took an interest in Steve's career. He had been passed over for partner two years in a row. He had one more chance. His whole professional future hung on his firm's decision. He knew it, we knew it, and so did Ronnie.

That's why it surprised me more than a little to find out that he had been made partner only at the end of a long telephone conversation with Ronnie. "Why didn't you tell me immediately?" I asked. "Aren't you excited?"

"Why should I be?" she said. "*I* wasn't the one made partner."

Unfortunately, Steve had overheard the comment, and his angry retort has become increasingly characteristic of the couple's interchanges.

Psychologists say that competitive feelings are sometimes expressed overtly, as Ronnie's were, and sometimes hidden, made manifest by bickering and anger that don't appear to relate to professional rivalry. Recognizing, however, that we do feel competitive, and understanding why we do is usually very helpful. My own insight into how guilt transformed me into self-appointed scorekeeper did a lot to break the pattern. So did discussing it with Arnie.

Psychologists advise working couples to talk about their competitive feelings openly with one another. Comparisons between them are natural and expectable. Angry competition and the unhappy feelings it arouses are not. Try not to view your boyfriend's or husband's professional gain as your loss.[7] If he can play a role in helping you be more successful, explore the possibilities with him. Perhaps he can be more encouraging, or take over some of your household or child-care responsibilities. However he can assist, being allies rather than adversaries will turn a threat to your relationship into an opportunity for growth.

CHAPTER 23

Money Matters

WHEN SHERRY, AN accounts manager for a graphic design firm, married Rick, a lawyer, she retained her own last name and her own checking and savings accounts. Although the couple pooled their funds for most purchases, Sherry felt she achieved more independence and control in the relationship by keeping her income separate. "I enjoyed the freedom to buy something for myself or for Rick whenever I wanted," she told me over lunch one day. But even more important was the enhanced self-image that came from taking an active role in the couple's fiscal affairs. "I felt good knowing that I was helping to raise our standard of living, both with my income and my ideas about how to spend it," Sherry explained.

When they were married for five years, the couple had a baby girl. Sherry returned to work after a four-month maternity leave. She still maintained her separate savings and checking accounts, but she noticed that more and more of her funds were going for expenses related to their daughter. "I also realized that I was limiting the shopping I did for myself to the absolute essentials. I weighed all my expenditures in terms of what that money could buy for my daughter." Rick, on the other hand, continued to shop for himself pretty much as he had before becoming a father, and now he was also using his income for large household purchases, vacations and investments. As this division of fiscal responsibilities persisted, Sherry felt that she was losing her say in the family finances.

"We just seemed to slip into a pattern," Sherry explained. "With parenthood we both became much busier; we had less time to talk over our purchases, and it just seemed natural that Rick should be in charge of the major ones. The problem was that when I did question him about what something cost, or why he had made a particular investment, he would accuse me of not trusting his fiscal management. I do have confidence in his judgment, but what I resent is being treated like a little girl."

Although annoyed and hurt about how their respective incomes were now divided, Sherry saw the split as inevitable. "I never realized how much it would cost me to go back to work after I had a child," she explained. "It seemed only right to use my money to pay these new expenses."

Sherry's story illustrates some of the ways motherhood can change a working woman's attitude about the money she brings into the family. Although working always incurs some costs—transportation, lunches out, business clothing—most childless couples come out ahead. Once they become parents, however, the new expenses cut deeply into their earnings. Child care, nursery school, extended day care programs, periodic housekeeping help—services that homemakers feel are optional—are just about vital when both partners hold jobs. When women total these expenditures, they may feel even more conflicted about returning to work. Added to the guilt about leaving their children is a new guilt about the money it is costing.

Ideally these additional expenses should be looked upon as a joint obligation rather than as the mother's exclusive responsibility. But this perspective is difficult for many of us. Most dual-career couples were raised by a father who was the sole wage earner and a mother who stayed home and did not earn any money. As Dr. David Rice explained, when such a couple has children, they may easily be pulled back into traditional sex-role behavior and expectations.[1] Our internalized norms, powerful and unknown to us, can make equitable preparenthood arrangements suddenly seem inappropriate. Rick no doubt now felt more comfortable in the provider role that he was assuming, while Sherry now felt that she had to "pay" for her right to work. She used her salary to give her daughter the services she unconsciously felt she should be supplying.

Like many other women, Sherry also tried to keep down her work-related costs. Bringing lunch to the office, walking instead of taking a bus or taxi to work and buying a minimum of business clothes are all methods common to working mothers. To some ex-

tent, cutting corners in this way is a realistic response to parenthood. Few of us can afford to enlarge our families without curtail-
ing our personal spending habits. All too frequently, however,
women underspend on themselves so that they can overspend on
their children—a guilt-ridden tactic that doesn't help anyone.

Another way women attempt to deal with their conflict over the
proper mothering role is to assume a more traditional position
with regard to family finances. Many professionally responsible
women told me that their husbands do all the family's financial
planning. "I sign my paycheck over to him and he gives me back
what I need," was a typical explanation. These women said they
had no idea of how much money the family had or how it was being spent. This ignorance may be the natural result of confining
your salary to pay for child care and the like, as it was for Sherry.
Or it may be a deliberate decision on your part; many women
simply feel more comfortable letting their husbands take over the
finances.

But, either way, it may represent an unconscious attempt to
"feel more like a mother," for, as one psychiatrist pointed out,
most of us were raised by women who did not participate in financial decisions or planning.

Underearning may also be an effort to assuage guilt about working. Some working mothers hold themselves back so that they will
not threaten their husband's earning power. "It seems to be the
one remaining taboo," management consultant Marilyn Machlowitz asserted, speaking about wives surpassing their mate's income. The women themselves feel uncomfortable about it. Many
wives do not want to earn more than their husbands.

I encountered this phenomenon similarly in professional and
nonprofessional couples, in women married to men they called
traditional as well as those married to "liberated" husbands. A
technical writer from Ohio would not earn more than her security
officer husband; neither would a project manager with an insurance company who was married to an attorney in Montana. A
clinical psychologist turned down clients when her income approached that of the Boston chemist with whom she lives. A free-
lance illustrator from the West Coast tried to keep her work load
and salary "just under" that of her husband, and a Sun Belt real
estate developer "could, but won't earn more than her husband."

Collen Reynolds is typical of many women I interviewed. She

is a thirty-eight-year-old mother of two girls, married to a dentist and living in Delaware. She works as a bookkeeper in a large investment firm. It is the work she has done since her marriage fifteen years ago and the work she plans to continue doing; a decision she feels compelled to stick by even though it causes her pain.

"People are always saying to me, 'Collen, what are you doing here? Why are you wasting your time? You know business, you could be out there earning a six-figure salary,' " she reported.

Yet Collen has repeatedly shied away from promotions and turned down opportunities for more lucrative and prestigious jobs.

Interviewing Collen in her small office, with her photograph of her daughters hugging their happy shaggy golden retriever, it is easy to identify with her colleagues' opinion of her abilities. Speaking precisely and thoughtfully, her whole manner conveys her intelligence.

"I know that I could earn more than I am now—earn more than my husband . . . but I know I never will," she said. For Collen the high-powered job and the big executive office will remain elusive fantasies. "I know the excitement of going into business, of going out there on my own. I can feel it, taste it, it's so real to me." She paused, momentarily studying the backs of her hands, and then in a slow, measured tone said, "But I'm too threatened by it. It would mean going through the transition of myself. It would mean taking away that mother-home feeling about myself, and that's a tough thing for any woman to go through."

But while women may try to expiate their guilt by underearning, they are not content with the decision. "I'm in great conflict over this," Collen admitted. "Probably I'll spend the rest of my life in conflict—I know I'll never feel whole."

For Collen, and for the other women with whom I spoke, the conflict churns within. It spews out in anger over powerlessness, over having to account for purchases, over stifled potential; and of course it leads to much bickering.

Marital counselors and psychologists have found that disagreements over money are a critical issue in relationships and a large source of arguments. There are several reasons for these disputes. For one thing, as sociologists Schwartz and Blumstein discovered, men and women contemplating a permanent relationship with one another seldom discuss finances. They are more likely to talk about their previous sex lives than their spending habits, the researchers noted. Then, too, few couples are prepared for the way parenthood may change their feelings about money and spending.[2]

Arguments over money have a particular intensity because income does impose a hierarchy on a relationship. While many of us reject the idea that money is power, a host of recent studies have shown that in the vast majority of cases, earning power translates into general power: the ability to influence decisions and to get one's way.[3]

Psychotherapist Carlfred B. Broderick noted that the second income has been called the "greatest democratizer of the family in recent years."[4] Women who make a contribution to their family's income have the potential of enjoying greater financial independence and autonomy. And many mothers feel a greater sense of self and of entitlement because of the money they bring in. But others, like Sherry and Collen, do not allow themselves the rewards of their efforts.

A woman who restricts her role in the family financial decisions to determining a baby-sitter's salary is not likely to have the same amount of control and self-esteem as one who participates fully. If you feel that fiscal responsibilities and decisions are unfairly split along traditional lines, there are a few ways to achieve an equitable balance. An essential first step should be an absolutely frank discussion with your partner about what earning money means to each of you. Early family associations about income, feelings about your allowance or childhood jobs may all be important.[5] Remember that your husband or boyfriend may be struggling as hard with traditional concepts as you are.

Next try to devise a way of sharing the financial burden so that neither one of you is responsible for all the costs relating to your children or for all the major purchases. Some couples draw up a list of their expenses and decide to contribute equally to pay them, with each keeping the balance of their funds in separate savings and checking accounts. Others pool their incomes completely and pay for everything jointly, keeping nothing separate. Still others pool their earnings except for a small set amount, which they put in separate accounts to spend as they wish.[6]

It also helps us to assume a more active role in fiscal management if we remember that it is really irresponsible for any mother to be financially ignorant or incompetent. Every one of us should contemplate the possibility that we might one day be solely in charge of our children's future. We should be as capable of taking over the family's finances as if that possibility were a reality. For those of us who feel insecure about managing money, a course at a nearby college or local Y or a consultation with a money manager might be in order.

And last, we will most likely stop underearning if we think for a moment about the financial pressure children put on us. There are increased expenses all around: food, clothing, medical, educational, recreational, rents, mortgages and untold miscellaneous items. Studies done in the 1970s (the most recent available) placed the cost of raising two children in a typical American family from birth through college at between $80,000 and $150,000. Present costs are no doubt substantially higher.[7]

By underearning, we are depriving the whole family: our husbands by unfairly burdening them with so much responsibility, our children by having less to give them and ourselves by putting an artificial limit on our professional and personal growth. Financial expert Tessa Warschaw asserts, "Holding back or stinting denies your partner his rightful benefit." As Dr. Warschaw points out, you're in it together. The more each of you is able to make, the better it is for the other.[8]

Fiscal management by conscious decision rather than by unconscious motivation may take you and your husband time and energy. But it is well worth the effort. Resolving financial tensions will go a long way toward diffusing other family tensions as well.

CHAPTER 24

Toward Intimacy

"I DON'T UNDERSTAND why you don't just go," Arnie would say to me time and time again, the impatience in his tone revealing that this was well-traveled terrain.

"Because I can't," I would retort. *"And* I don't see *why* you can't understand," I would say accusingly.

Where was it I wasn't going? It didn't matter. Out of town to visit my former college roommate, to an all-day seminar on family history, a ballet with a friend. Things I would have loved to have done.

My guilt, however, kept me immobilized and made me angry. I felt angry at myself for not feeling I could do these things, and angry at Arnie, too, because he couldn't appreciate my conflict.

Instead he would point to what he considered the certifiable signs of my good mothering. "The children are happy," "They have lots of friends," "You spend so much time with them."

Inevitably Arnie would become frustrated at his inability to convince me, inevitably I'd become angry that he was trying to, inevitably we would argue, inevitably I'd end up feeling guiltier still.

"My guilt and resentment are beyond my husband's understanding and are the basis of many disagreements," wrote a communications specialist from the South. "My husband doesn't understand my guilt, and I don't understand his lack of it," said a Denver financial expert.

However our guilt expresses itself—in intense flareups or long cool distances—it inevitably distorts communication and erodes closeness.

Of all the qualities in a marriage, intimacy is at once the most desired and the most difficult to achieve, reported Francine Klags-brun, author of *Married People*.[1] Intimacy needs the commitment of one partner to another and a willingness to sacrifice and compromise on each other's behalf. It means going beyond yourself to an appreciation of your mate's feelings and needs, and extending yourself to fulfill those wants. A mutuality of love and respect are crucial to intimacy, but the existence of those feelings alone does not ensure it. Social scientists who have studied relationships marked by enduring closeness have found that intimacy between a man and woman needs to be carefully nourished and grows over time.[2]

But while time is of the essence, it is often not available to the working mother. With very few exceptions, the women I interviewed regretted the lack of time they had with their boyfriends or husbands—cozy time, intimate time—to talk over events, ideas, each other. "Time," as one woman put it, "to get in touch with the person, not the parent or other worker I live with."

Asked how much time they had alone with their husbands or boyfriends during the weekdays, the overwhelming majority said none or practically none. Only a handful had an hour or more, and those either worked or commuted with their spouses. And the picture isn't much brighter on weekends.

It is easy to understand this scarcity of time. Many working couples become parents in their early thirties. In many ways this timing makes a lot of sense. The man and woman are well started in their respective careers. They have probably accumulated some money and have had the opportunity to enjoy recreational activities and vacations together. And they have developed the inner resources and maturity to enrich their children's lives.

But this timing of parenthood also means that they will be enduring the pressures of a young family and those of an upward career simultaneously. These couples will be dealing with the most time intensive stage of parenting when they are at crucial points in their respective professions. Decisions about such things as tenure, making partner and important promotions usually occur when people are in their early to middle thirties. While the crunch may be especially acute for those couples whose children and professional advancements arrive together, most working parents have little leisure time together.

One big obstacle is differing schedules. You have just finished

a major project requiring several late nights, and he is just starting one. He has just come back from a business trip, and you have
to leave for one. Even if you are home at the same time, the endless chores—cleaning, shopping, laundry, making arrangements for
your family—can be all-consuming. And when you are not engaged
in these tasks, you are most likely with your children.

Where Does the Time Go?, a comprehensive study of leisure in
America, reported that parents in dual-career households spend a
great deal more of their leisure time with their children than do
parents in a traditional home where just the father is employed.[3]
Working parents devise ways to maximize time spent with their
youngsters and their careers. They may, for example, alternate
nights staying at the office. Or if one of them has to work several
evenings in a row, the other may go into the office over the weekend. This way the children are benefiting from being with one of
their parents, but the couple is losing out on opportunities to be
together.

Considering the restrictions on working parents' time, it might
be expected that they would try to get away by themselves. And
yet a significant number of women I interviewed rarely vacationed
without their children. Even if they had available money and
baby-sitters, they didn't feel right doing it. "I feel guilty going off
without them," explained a successful businesswoman married to
a physics professor, whose children are eleven, fourteen and
twenty. "We don't take vacations without the children because I
would feel too guilty," wrote a teacher from North Dakota who is
married to a systems analyst. "I tried it once," said a journalist,
"but I felt so guilty I called home every day. My husband was
ready to kill me. We won't do it again."

Not deserving, not worthy, not entitled to fun. Guilt, the great
spoiler, can also explain why so many working mothers express
dissatisfaction with their sex lives.

With wit, pathos and piercing honesty, women explained how
being a working mother had led to diminished sexual desire,
affecting the romance and spontaneity of their relationships.

"Being a working mother has taken a heavy toll on my sex life,"
said one woman. "My sex life has never been so neglected," said
another, who quipped, "At this rate we'll never have to use birth
control." "I seldom have the urge to have sexual relations with

my husband." "My sex life is a fond memory relegated to my fantasy life."

The quality of our sex life is vital to the intimacy of a relationship. It affects how we feel about our partners and ourselves. Our sexual relations have the capacity to make us feel loved, accepted, attractive, powerful, giving, given to. Or they can make us feel the opposite—unloved, unwanted, rejected, unattractive, vulnerable. "All for love and the world well lost," said the scribe, but today's working parents seem to be losing love and embracing the world.

While endless jokes have been made about marriage ruining a good sex life, sociologists Blumstein and Schwartz found this not to be the case.[4] Instead the research showed the American couple to be enjoying a better sex life than previously imagined. But, if my survey of over 750 working mothers is any indication, our sex lives are dwindling. And Dr. Merle S. Kroop, associate director of the Human Sexuality Clinic at New York Hospital, corroborates this. Dr. Kroop believes that the lack of desire is more common in working mothers than in other women.

The women themselves explained it in terms of fatigue. "I'm too tired," "No energy left," "Drained." That working mothers are tired needs no explanation; that physical fatigue is the *main* reason they don't feel like making love does.

"Occasionally, fatigue, real physical exhaustion, does come into it, but if it's a long-standing complaint, we'd want to look into it," said psychotherapist Marcia Rabinowitz. Dr. Blaustein, who teaches at the Mount Sinai Hospital Human Sexuality Program, also questions accepting fatigue at face value. "Actually a lot of people use sex when they are tired, or tense and can't sleep," said Blaustein. "Many of my patients say it's better than Valium. Actually there is really not that much energy used for sex."

Dr. Sharon Nathan, of the Human Sexuality Clinic at New York Hospital, noted that many of us are too tired to have sex but not too tired to stay up until midnight to watch television. We have to understand where the fatigue comes from.

While the feelings of fatigue are quite genuine, Dr. Nathan and others suggest that they come from emotional sources even more than physical ones. Anger can certainly cause feelings of fatigue, said Nathan, who called anger the "flip side" of guilt. When women feel guilty, it often expresses itself in anger toward the husband and in self-directed anger, too. This, in turn, leads to feelings of exhaustion. "Clearly if women are feeling inadequate in the job that they are doing as mothers or homemakers or they are feeling guilty that they are not living up to the ideal they have from their early childhood, or maybe their husbands or mothers are making them feel guilty, they don't feel they deserve much sexual satisfaction. I think that it's especially valid for today's working mothers since they are the first generation to be doing this in this way," said Dr. Blaustein.

If a woman perceives her own mother as not having a good sex life or not having much pleasure in her life, she may have sexual difficulties, explained Dr. Kroop. "Absolutely one very common feature in lack of sexual fulfillment is the fear of surpassing their mothers," she asserted. On some unconscious level a working mother may feel, I have so much: my children, my profession, a man; how can I give myself the pleasure of a satisfying sexual relationship?

In discussing these points with a graduate school class in anthropology, most of whom were working mothers, one of the students joked, "You've heard of sex without guilt; what we have here is guilt without sex." And it's no wonder.

When we think about the guilt we feel toward our children and the anger and resentment we and our husband often feel toward one another over unequal domestic responsibilities, earnings and professional achievement, in addition to the physical overwork, it's no wonder our sex lives aren't better. It's no wonder women write, as one did, that being a working mother had led to a sense of "loneliness, a deep isolation from my husband."

But we do not have to stand by and watch our affectional ties wither and perhaps disappear. There are steps we can take toward intimacy. A crucial beginning, it seems, is to find time to be together, to give your marital relationship as high a priority as your children and your job. As Dr. David Rice points out, many working parents find time for everything except being together. Their sexual relationship becomes perfunctory and, of course, they become less emotionally intimate, explained the psychotherapist.[5]

But being alone with your husband means that neither of you will be with the children, and most of us find this terribly hard. One woman, who always included her children when she and her husband were together, learned not to feel guilty about spending time just with her husband. "After all, we're the ones who have to keep everything going, so we'd better keep going with each other!"[6] she explained. If we keep this thinking in mind, we might find it easier to take an occasional weekend trip or longer holiday without our young ones along. But even if we can't manage vacations alone, we can still make time for each other. A lunch together during the work week, a Sunday brunch, a romantic Saturday night dinner—all can be important.

One way to get more time is to carve it out of your regular schedule. When Arnie and I have to work late, we sometimes meet for a ten P.M. dinner or drink. Some spouses take off a Friday from work and make a long weekend by joining their partner at the end of a business trip or out-of-town convention. Other couples get a baby-sitter for an hour or so before a PTA meeting so that they can have dinner together first. Some of our friends have set appointments with one another. One has a standing Thursday-night "date" with her husband; another has started taking ballroom dancing classes with her spouse; a third began taking tennis lessons with her boyfriend—all to assure having some leisure time together.

Another strategy is to reevaluate how you are both using your time. Maybe you can cut back on some of your commitments; perhaps you don't have to go to every meeting or dinner to which you are invited. Try to weigh the advantages of your appearance at those functions with those of being alone with your husband. If, however, you really find that nothing you can do to alter your schedules is going to give you more leisure together—you have to be away for a week, he is closing on a deal—stay in touch by telephone; it will help you feel closer when you do see each other again.

"My husband and I tend to talk a lot . . . on the telephone," said Daisy Spier, vice president of research at Dancer Fitzgerald Sample, an advertising agency. Because her husband works in a different state, the couple cannot have lunch together, but "we've developed a phone relationship that we never had before," she said.[7]

There is one additional way of spending time with your partner that most of us overlook, and that is when you are home with your children. Obviously you won't have the same privacy as if you were alone—although some guidebooks for working parents do suggest locking the bedroom door and making love when the children are occupied elsewhere in the house. While this advice is controversial, child psychologists and marital counselors do agree that children should know that adults need uninterrupted time together. How long, of course, will depend on the age of the youngsters, but by the time they are in kindergarten (around age six), most children can be expected to play alone for at least a half-hour.

The best way to get some time with your spouse is to explain to your child that you need some privacy *before* he begins interrupting. You might say, "Daddy and I have some important things to discuss while we are having our coffee. Please don't bother us until we are through." If your child can tell time, you can give her an idea of when you might be finished by using the clock.

If your children protest that this is not fair, you can simply tell them that parents have things to talk about that don't concern them, or that children will not understand the discussion. This approach will not only help to reinforce the distinction between their world and that of grown-ups but will give you a chance to benefit from the distinction.

Having time together is important, but it will not necessarily make you closer. All the leisure in the world will not bring intimacy if it is not infused with trust, empathy, concern, respect and affection. Before we can begin to revitalize our relationships with these feelings, we have to be aware of two common pitfalls for working parents that can counteract the establishment of an emotional bond.

The first of these traps is having what one woman called a marriage by memo, so named because she and her husband were communicating with each other largely through little messages left on each other's bureaus. They had the opportunity to talk in person, but they felt more comfortable with this approach, she told me. Many of us are so accustomed to arranging every detail of our lives that we begin to organize our relationships, too. One woman found that she and her husband were planning for a precious day together by setting an agenda of things to do. Another said that the discussions she had with her boyfriend on whether they should marry were starting to resemble two principals considering a merger. Although it isn't possible or even desirable to be completely different people in our professional and personal lives, a detached business air is best left at the office.

Another potential difficulty for working parents is the tendency to use their children rather than each other to satisfy their cravings for emotional intimacy. Because of their guilt, women may be more apt than men to look to their children for affection and support, but psychologists have seen this phenomenon in both sexes.[8] Children are, of course, cute, lovable and perhaps even more responsive to attention than your spouse. But it goes without saying that if you are turning to your children to fulfill adult needs for emotional gratification, it will not only be damaging to your marriage but to your children as well by giving them the intolerable burden of being responsible for your happiness.

We can, however, guard against falling into these traps by working at recreating or strengthening our bonds with our spouse. Some couples don't like the idea of working at a relationship. They think it should flourish by itself. But social scientists report that the most enduring marriages are those that are carefully nurtured. And it makes sense. No one would expect his or her profession or children to thrive without careful attention; why should marriage be any different? In fact, dual-career couples may have to put even more energy into their relationships than do other couples, to resist being pulled back into the traditional patterns with which they were raised.

Some women told me that they make a particular effort to be sensitive to their husband's feelings. Nina, an accountant from Oregon, said that when she is tired or frustrated with the children, she turns to her husband and says, "I bet that you are tired," or "You must be really upset." "It's very easy for me to get wrapped up in all my pressures and concerns and forget about his. This is my way of putting myself in his position and finding out what's going on in his head," she explained. Nina achieves closeness with her husband by trying to understand and appreciate his feelings, and that makes him more responsive to hers.

Researchers have found that a key factor in successful marriages is the couple's knowledge of one another. In those that were the happiest, the husband's description of his wife—her appearance, likes, dislikes, insecurities, strengths and motivations—closely matched the description that she gave of herself, and vice versa.[9]

The better we know one another, the better able we will be to be mutually supportive. When our spouses complain or tell us about a problem, few of us actually say, "How can I help you?" But it's important to try to keep that question in mind. Sometimes there is something concrete we can do or suggest. Other times it's simply serving as a sounding board or confidante. But knowing that we can count on our mates for attention and, when we need it, assistance, is a powerful way of feeling closer.

To these ideas I would add another: Have fun together. Celebrate whenever you can—birthdays, anniversaries, promotions. We usually don't have much choice about the bad times, but we can make the most of the good. Bask in each other's successes and achievements, even the small ones. Buy or do something special. Sharing the joy is another step toward intimacy.

As couples find emotional nourishment in each other, their sexual relations will usually improve. But here again there is a special problem for working parents. We all tend to measure the quality of our sexual lives in terms of spontaneity, and spontaneous lovemaking is all but impossible for most of us. While the media and our own memories of prechildren days encourage this criterion, some experts believe that the importance of spontaneity is exaggerated. One of these is Frances Dincin of the Human Sexuality Program at Northwestern University Medical School. Sex doesn't always have to be spontaneous to be good, asserted Dincin, who advises her patients that some very sexually satisfied couples make appointments for sex, just as they have appointments to do other things they love, such as going to the ballet.[10]

Other counselors suggest that saying something like, "After the children get to sleep let's get into bed," is a far better way to have a good sex life than waiting for the unlikely time that you'll be home together without the children and nothing else to do.[11]

If your sex life doesn't improve as you become more emotionally intimate, you should discuss it with your spouse, as you should try to discuss other problems. A note of caution should be added here: Although communication with your mate will benefit from openness, there is such a thing as too much honesty. Some of the cruelest words have been known to follow the phrase "I want to be honest." Temper your truthfulness with sensitivity and kindness. Don't use honesty as an excuse for being hurtful.

It may be that you will want to consult with a sex therapist. If you decide on professional help, select a therapist with the same care you would use to choose any doctor. Your county medical society, your family physician, a friend whose judgment you trust are all good sources for names. Unfortunately, as in other fields, there are many frauds in this one. A physical examination may be part of the office visit, but under no circumstances should you agree to engage in lovemaking in front of or with the therapist.

You may want to find out about the different approaches to sex therapy before making your selection. Some counselors use behavior modification methods similar to those introduced by Masters and Johnson. These include learning certain techniques for touching and arousing your partner. Other therapists use psychotherapy; most use an amalgam of the two. Said Dr. Kroop, "People rarely come in who aren't helped in some way."

If you do have problems that require professional counseling, don't be discouraged or view it as a sign of failure. Sharing hard times and adversity are important steps toward growing together.

Remember that intimacy doesn't remain constant in a marriage. As the book *Married People* points out, sometimes you'll be more involved with your work or with your children than you are with your husband.[12] At times, too, the stresses of being a working parent will make you so tense and angry at your spouse that you'll wonder why you ever got married in the first place. But knowing that these are natural feelings, and knowing, too, how to get closer again will help you emerge from these painful periods with an even greater intimacy.

Life for working parents is at once hectic, pressured, enriching and exciting. It offers us the chance to help each other be all that we can be: an opportunity that is challenging, stimulating and inspiring.

CHAPTER 25

Stressful Roles/Successful Roles

1974. IT WAS September, and I was back at the Schlesinger Library at Radcliffe College to finish my doctoral research on the origins of American feminism. The air through the high open window was warm and fragrant as I read through bits of paper that were the private diaries and letters of nineteenth-century women. A piecing-together of lives, a montage of desperation and hope as sad as it was uplifting.

They were women for the most part unknown: the inarticulate, the unnoticed, the unremembered. And they were women who were known: writers, crusaders, reformers who are celebrated today. But even these famous women were unknown in the inner reaches of their being. Only in their diaries, hidden, private, or in their intimate letters to friends did they reveal their deepest fears, concerns and conflicts.

One of these was Harriet Beecher Stowe, author of *Uncle Tom's Cabin,* advocate of social justice and civil liberties. What child growing up in a New York City public school, as I did, hadn't heard of her? She was, indeed, one of the few women ever mentioned. And yet I didn't know—couldn't have imagined—the suffering, the pain, the anguish that preceded her literary work.

As a young woman, Harriet helped her sister, Catherine, open a school for young girls and would most likely have continued in this career had it not been interrupted by her marriage in 1836 to Calvin Stowe. Demanding, domineering and irascible, Stowe, a classics professor, expected complete obedience from his wife. Within their first years of married life, Harriet bore three children and consented to have Calvin's aged and complaining mother live with them. Then, suddenly, at the end of this decade, which

Harriet described as one filled with "pain, confusion and disappointment and suffering," when all she "proposed was met and crossed and in every way hedged up," her right side became totally and inexplicably paralyzed.[1]

Harriet went to a famous water-cure sanitarium in Brattleboro, Vermont, for therapy. There, as she described herself, "the shattered broken down invalid, just able to creep along by great care," began to reexamine her life. After a year away from the "constant discouragement [and] of hasty and irritated censure," Harriet felt the need to express her creative energies. Her family could no longer be "my chief main and portion," she realized, insisting that Calvin make certain concessions to her before she resumed cohabitation with him.[2]

Calvin took a teaching position in Bowdoin, Maine, and agreed not to inhibit her fledgling career as a writer. Harriet began to work on *Uncle Tom's Cabin* shortly after rejoining her family in Maine. Her ailments, not surprisingly, soon disappeared, and Harriet enjoyed good health and high productivity until her death in 1896, at the age of eighty-six.

I continued to read through piles of journals and letters, and what I read both saddened and surprised me: countless nineteenth-century women suffered as had Harriet Beecher Stowe with paralysis, numbness, tingling. Some recovered completely, as she had, but many had recurring symptoms throughout their lives.

Their contemporaries could find no explanation for this phenomenon, but modern psychology has. Called conversion reaction, this kind of ailment results from inner psychological conflicts that are expressed through symbolic bodily disturbances. Unrelieved guilt, unfulfilled emotional and physical needs and lack of self-esteem can all manifest themselves in profound psychological and related physical distress.[3] Nineteenth-century American women were actually being crippled by psychological conflicts.

That night I met with my friends at a nearby health food restaurant. Transplanted from other cities to do our research, we ate together each night and shared our work, our thoughts and ideas. Sobered by the despair of so many women before us, I was still full of hope for the future. I looked at all of us—young, intelligent and articulate—seated around the table. No problems would paralyze us; we were going to soar.

But ten years later I sat at my desk reading through a stack of questionnaires and wondered if I had been overly optimistic. "I have had neurological disarray for the last year. I suffered from paralysis, emotional and physical. One morning I woke up and my left side was paralyzed. No physical cause has been found."

At first I wanted to deny what I had read, assume its impossibility. Instead I reached for the telephone, got directory assistance and put in a call to the woman whose questionnaire it was.

Yes, it was true, she said. She'd been having spasms of numbness, of paralysis on and off for a year. They would come periodically and last about ten minutes. "Then one morning I woke up and my left side was [temporarily] paralyzed . . . I feel like it's an extension of my emotions," she said thoughtfully.

Did other working mothers experience such symptoms? They sure did. In the part of the questionnaire called "Yourself," they detailed a host of stress-related ailments. Well, of course we would feel stressed, I reasoned, considering the pressure-cooker demands of our lives.

But I had more than a little to learn about stress. I discovered that guilt itself causes emotional strain. It makes us much more likely to develop symptoms, and it also prevents us from taking the necessary steps to relieve them. Yet once we learn ways of getting beyond our guilt, we will be able to manage our different roles so as to optimize the benefits of each. Research done by Massachusetts sociologists Rosalind Barnett and Grace Baruch demonstrated that multiple roles can actually enhance a woman's well-being. In their study of four hundred women, the crucial issues to emerge were not how many roles a woman has but the way she feels about them, how she handles them and the supportive resources that she can draw upon.[4]

The mother who feels so apologetic about working that she overcompensates by cooking four-course dinners every night is going to experience greater role strain than one who is more secure about the choices she has made. Those who are comfortable with being both worker and mother actually find that one role can complement the other. Many women told me that they feel recharged playing with their children after work. "Doing something completely different, just getting down on the floor and being silly with my daughter, can be a tremendous relief after being at the hospital all day," a radiologist and mother of a three-year-old said. Others noted that each role helped keep the other in perspective. "If I weren't working, I'd be a lot more focused on everything my son did. I'd magnify all his minor difficulties and really obsess about them. My job keeps me more objective about my family," explained a corporate art consultant and mother of a seven-year-old. Another woman told me, "My disputes with my boss lose their intensity when my two-year-old cuddles up lovingly on my lap." Diane Cimine, an advertising executive, put it this way: "Whenever work becomes unbearable there is my son at home. And whenever he is giving me a very trying night, there is work to go back to. There's a sense of balance."[5]

Of course, there are times when things seem out of balance, when everything appears to be going wrong at once. But usually we can look to one part of our life to provide us with reinforcement and pleasure temporarily missing from another. As we become more comfortable with our dual roles, we will not only use one as a buffer against stress in the other but will readily call upon the resources for support that our different roles make available. We will be freer asking our husbands and children for help, and we will also utilize a major unnoticed resource: other working mothers.

While traditional wisdom has it that women are not helpful to one another on the job, many of us are finding sisterhood at the workplace. Research done by Wellesley College psychologist Anne Harlan found that when women get into a position of power, they tend to hire other women rather than men. Women bosses then work to develop the skills of their female staff and try to have them promoted. In another study, a nationwide survey conducted by *Parents Magazine,* the majority of respondents reported talking to other women at work both about personal and professional problems.[6]

As working mothers divest themselves of the strategy of separating home and work and begin to identify with one another, they will tap a rich source of support. In those companies where mothers are starting to seek one another out, they are finding mutual reinforcement. As Gay Kassan, an advertising executive, explained, "You cannot expect nonworking women to understand the demands you may feel, and most people at work without kids can't relate to your family pressures." But Gay reported that the working mothers within her agency provide each other with reassurance and, at times, sympathy. They also take real pride in one another's achievements. The news that a pregnant woman was promoted to supervisor was greeted with joy by the working mothers in her company.

Having multiple roles to coordinate can, of course, be stressful. But it is far more stressful to have to fit all our interests and talents into one acceptable role. As working mothers, we have the possibility of expressing our creative energies in a variety of ways. And as we find the deepest fulfillment in our different roles, we will also make the fullest contribution to each of them.

CHAPTER 26

Symptoms of Stress

BONNIE HELD OUT her hands for inspection. Her fingers were long and graceful, but the backs and sides of her hands were covered with scaly red patches. Anxiety eczema, the doctor had said. How long had she had it? She wasn't sure; certainly since she had returned to work after her son, Alex, was born. Actually it was her mother, a woman Bonnie described as "always doing everything perfectly," who, noticing her hands, had insisted that Bonnie see a doctor.

"Did your mother work while you were growing up?" I asked. Bonnie shook her head in an emphatic no. "She was an extremely bright woman who was accepted into law school but didn't go—a typical brilliant, well-bred *Feminine Mystique*–type housewife," Bonnie had called her. "I always had the feeling that she resented my career more than she admitted, particularly when I went back to work after Alex was born."

As for Bonnie, she had to deal with her own confusion about living a life different from the one she was raised to lead. "You see, I was brought up to believe that being feminine meant that you always had to be polite and smile," she said, her own impish grin playing cautiously on her face. "Even the household chores my brother and I were expected to do were divided along sex-linked lines."

Of course her brother was always encouraged to pursue a profession. But Bonnie was being trained for the role her mother had led: the wife of a professional, but surely not one herself.

But then Bonnie realized that she was interested in the law. "Even in high school all those Supreme Court cases fascinated me." She remembers rushing home full of energy and excitement to tell her mother that she wanted to become a lawyer. Her mother "roared with laughter" at the idea.

Her feelings of unease became worse, Bonnie recalled, after her son Alex was born. "I've accomplished something that she was unable to accomplish. I think that there was a long time when I felt that she resented me. . . . I think she resented the fact that I was able to do both."

Still Bonnie would be a mother and a lawyer. And she is a good lawyer. That is, when her conflicts don't prevent her from doing her best.

"I felt extremely guilty toward the partners," she said. "Like I was letting them down. I was leaving work every day at five o'clock, and this is a place that no one leaves before six-thirty or seven, and many people stay until two or three in the morning."

Still, she was working efficiently, taking work home when she needed to and certainly doing her share, until she began to develop aches and pains. "I had backaches, my nails were bitten to the quick. I had rashes . . . all over my hands. I was a walking bag of psychosomatic symptoms."

Morton Leibowitz, a Manhattan internist, told me that the majority of patients who come to him for stress-related illnesses (the most common reason otherwise healthy people consult a doctor) are *working mothers.*

"It might be stomach pains, chest pains, fatigue," but after ruling out physical causes, Leibowitz often finds these are stress-related syndromes. "When I say a stress-related syndrome, there is an underlying guilt that relates more to the mothering," Leibowitz explained. "I don't go beyond the clinical observation, but I sense it."

Many working mothers sense it also. "When my travel became so great last year, I worried about leaving home. Approximately an hour before departure each time, I came down with splitting headaches," said an accountant from Texas. Other women gave similar explanations for their symptoms: "Because like too many women I'm still trying to be Superwoman—perfect mother, perfect wife, perfect friend, perfect worker," wrote a woman from Colorado. A secretary from Minnesota expressed it this way: "Trying to please everyone (work, home, family) and not pleasing myself or caring enough about myself." And still another woman confessed, "I feel constant conflicts and guilt, things pile up and I feel that I must handle *everything* all the time. I get very tense tight feelings in the upper back shoulder area which results in headaches."

Dr. Georgia Witkin-Lanoil, author of *The Female Stress Syndrome,* became interested in the problem because of her own stress-related afflictions. "Like most working mothers, I was haunted by a long list of shoulds," many of which she was unable to do. Lanoil's conflicts kept her "stressed" and guilt-ridden," for, as she and other experts in the field point out, guilt is a "powerful hidden stressor."[1]

Of the three basic kinds of stressors—physical, social and psychological—the last, which includes guilt and anger, is considered to be the most damaging. Unlike physical stressors such as loud noises, which are transitory, or social ones—the death of a loved one, for example, which is a single external event—guilt and anger are internal and ongoing.[2]

Joyce Morrill, a designer of stress-management programs for corporations, said that the guilt that working mothers feel from operating in conflict with the traditional values of mothering, which "the majority still hold somewhere deep inside . . . is probably the most devastating source of stress."

"We have to think more about the effects of chronic guilt on the immune system," Dr. Martin Cohen told me. Guilt can produce such ailments as neuralgia, headaches, fatigue, numbness, cardiovascular and gastrointestinal symptoms, tinglings and even paralysis.

Beth-Ann and I were in graduate school together, both of us feverishly working on our dissertations. But in addition to being a student, she had already become a mother.

Just as she was finishing her dissertation, she began to complain of terrible stomach pains. Of course we immediately blamed the miserable coffee in the cafeteria. But even giving it up produced no improvement in her health.

Finally, when the pains became so severe that she literally could not work, she went to the doctor, who put her on a special diet. But still no change. Next came the battery of tests, X-rays, GI series. A lot of money and time were spent, but nothing was found. Tension, the doctor pronounced it, and told her to relax. Well, she tried to relax, to work less frantically, but the "tension"-

produced pains continued. For they were not due to her work but to the harsh clash of maternal ideals she carried with her.

Of course we didn't realize this then. Recently, through psychotherapy, Beth-Ann has begun to understand the relationship between her guilt and her symptoms.

It has only been in the past few years that doctors have begun to understand and acknowledge the role stress plays in everything from the common cold to cancer. Industrial leaders also have noticed the costs of stress-related illness, in terms of high absentee rates, company medical expenses and lower productivity. It's disconcerting but not surprising that an ulcer medication, a hypertension drug and a tranquillizer are the three largest selling drugs nationwide.

With its broad potential for harm, stress has become a ripe area for investigation. Doctors are trying to understand why two groups of individuals subjected to the same degree of tension will respond differently from one another. Why do some take the vicissitudes of life in their stride, while others fall apart?

According to social scientists, stress can be mitigated by a sense of control over life. Numerous studies have shown that workers who lack autonomy on their jobs are more prone to stress than are those in more influential positions. Similarly, stress seems to run higher among individuals who feel victimized by events than in those who can take charge of a situation. Social support and closeness of friends and family also diminish tension.[3] In one study conducted by Dr. Caroline Bedell Thomas of Johns Hopkins, "lack of closeness to parents" emerged as a major prognosticator of serious disease.

In general, those who have low self-esteem and who feel isolated and alone (whether they are in reality or not) are at higher risk.[4]

We have already seen how the absence of support from our own mothers can exacerbate our feelings of uncertainty. Nonworking mothers can also heighten our feelings of stress. "They make us feel guilty as hell," said one woman, while another commented, "I hear the putdowns a lot in their comments, like, 'Gee, I'm glad I get to go on the class trips, I really get to see how Jackie is adjusting to school. . . .'"

"Nonworking mothers seem to belong to an 'insiders' club. They form friendships. They know things I don't know, such as which after-school sports program is the best in town," said one "outsider" to the league.[5]

When I tell a group of mothers in the park that I usually work full-time," said an advertising executive, "it stops the conversation right there. There's a lot of hostility." And this feeling doesn't seem to be imaginary. When I asked some unemployed mothers at a private school meeting how they felt about those who worked, the response was fierce. "They're never around to help with the book sale but always tell us what books we should have," one mother said. "We're the ones stuck with keeping the school going," chimed in another. "They want to have it all!"

A sales manager who stopped working when her child was born told me, "I feel that the world is getting divided into two enemy camps—working mothers and nonworking mothers—and one day they might not be civil to one another."

And as another mother explained, "The nonworking mothers regard me with envy or anger. The working mothers I never get to see."

Our numbers are growing, but we spin in our individual orbits. When we cross one another's paths, it may be with the brief lop-sided smile of commiseration, but real communication? Who has the time?

To help reduce the strain, we must first appreciate that the collision of values is by itself stressful. Second, we must track the course of our stress. Take, for example, Judy, the banker. Her guilt, which made her feel a lack of personal integration, also drove her to bake nut bread and can peaches on weekends. She deprives herself of time with her husband and of time to relax, which is the whole point of going to her weekend home. And she certainly doesn't have time to accomplish any office work, all of which add to her guilt. Not surprisingly, she also finds herself clenching her teeth, a classic stress-related symptom.

Once you begin to see where the stress is coming from and how it is affecting you, it helps to realize that you are not alone. After reassuring his stressed patients that they are not suffering from a serious illness, Dr. Leibowitz tells them that "this is universal . . . that the woman across the hall, who they think is handling work and motherhood so well, is probably at her doctor's right now with the same complaints."

Dr. Leibowitz's analysis seemed so indisputably correct that I wanted to ring the doorbell of my working-mother-upstairs-neighbor and invite her in for a talk. Harried as we tend to be, with too few outlets for expression, our guilt inevitably turns back in on itself.

Whatever forums and networks are available to us should be used to reach other working mothers. Through our children, through our jobs, we should try to establish bridges for communication. Some women have started working mothers' associations within their organizations. Financial Mothers, a subgroup of New York Financial Women's Association, grew out of one stockbroker's problems finding a housekeeper for her son. The mothers' support group at the advertising agency Dancer Fitzgerald Sample had its beginnings when a vice president returned from a maternity leave and decided to contact the other women with babies. These groups have regular meetings at which problems are aired and strategies for coping with stress shared.

New research conducted by behavioral psychologists demonstrates that those who are able to confide their troubled feelings in others rather than bear their difficulties in silence are less vulnerable to illness. That is why just talking to those who have similar concerns can by itself help to reduce stress.[6]

Another benefit of communicating with other working mothers, in meetings or over coffee, is learning about their devices for dealing with tension. Joann, a staff manager with a New Jersey branch of AT & T, explained how she helped alleviate another woman's stress. "It was approaching summer vacation, and one of the other managers was concerned about finding appropriate supervision and activities for her children. Would her youngsters have enough to do? Did she trust her baby-sitters enough to watch her children in the town swimming pool? She worried. Joann was able to relieve her colleague's anxieties by telling her about the excellent summer day camp that her daughters had gone to. "Sometimes just pointing out an option that someone hasn't thought of can be very helpful," Joann explained.

Other women suggest minimizing tension by trying to avoid stressful situations whenever possible. For example, a project director at IBM told me that her daughter was in a day-care center that closed at six o'clock. Her boss, however, frequently started important meetings at four-thirty. "I'd sit in his office sneaking looks at my watch, all the while becoming more nervous. If I left in the middle of the meeting, my boss would be annoyed; if I didn't, the day-care workers and my child would be." She finally resolved this bind by finding a center that stayed open an hour later. She also realized that she could concentrate better in late meetings if she made clear to her boss before they started that she had to leave at a specific time.

Another woman said that she had learned to keep stress down by trying to organize her calendar so that potentially tension producing events didn't overlap. "I realized that I had to do this after I had allowed my daughter to have four friends sleep over the night before I was flying to the West Coast for an important meeting. No one got much sleep that night, and we were all irritable with each other the next day. I felt very stressed about leaving because I had been in such a bad mood with my daughter and because I was worried that my fatigue would mar my performance at the meeting."

Just as important as hearing about how others deal with stress is learning about yourself: identifying your personal stressors and trying to monitor them. One woman may feel stressed when she is tired, another when she is late for an appointment, a third when she has many things to accomplish in a short period of time. Knowing what is most likely to ruffle you and how to cope with it will reduce your day-to-day tension.

If being late makes you nervous, then make sure that you allow yourself extra time in getting to and from commitments, particularly if you are dependent upon public transportation. If you tend to get hassled if you have a lot to do and little time to do it in, experts suggest making a list with the time slots in which you can reasonably expect to complete each task. Then, instead of sitting at your desk feeling overwhelmed—I have to finish this report, speak with my secretary, leave early, take Tommy to the dentist, return the library books, shop for dinner—you will have mapped out a plan for yourself.

In general, writing things down seems to relieve stress. Several psychologists suggested that keeping a journal at times of acute stress (your daughter is failing at school, your husband is changing jobs, your father has been hospitalized) is a good way of ventilating painful emotions, particularly when we do not have others with whom to talk. Stephanie Miller of the Wall Street Counseling Service explained that making notes about a personal problem while you are at work can ease anxiety. Although you probably can't resolve much while sitting in your office, you are preoccupied with all the things you want to do when you leave. "Somehow making lists as these thoughts occur can be very reassuring and allow you to go back to concentrating on your work," she explained.[7]

Another device for easing tension is to remove yourself briefly from a stress-filled situation. If looking at the half-completed projects on your desk is making your anxiety level soar, then walk away from it; have a cup of coffee or chat with a colleague for a few minutes. If your children's constant arguing is getting on your nerves, try to find some quiet in your house. One psychologist suggested walking into a room and closing the door for a little privacy.

If you can't get away physically, try to do it mentally by letting your mind drift to an upcoming vacation or enjoyable event. Think about something pleasant and comforting. Better yet, try to *do* something comforting. Most of us have developed the inner resources to make ourselves feel better. It might be buying something for ourselves or for someone we love, or sitting down with a favorite book or record. Many find warm baths soothing; others treat themselves to a special food. "Instead of just getting a sandwich for lunch, I take myself to an Indian restaurant near work," explained Marie Ruddin, a psychiatrist and mother of a four-year-old.[8] However we do it, wellness consultants suggest a little self-pampering at stressful times.

It is also important to remember that during periods of acute stress, your energy levels are lower and you won't be able to get as much done as usual. Assess home and work responsibilities and try to eliminate all but the most essential commitments from the list. It is constructive, however, to try to stick to your altered schedule. Feelings of accomplishment are reinforcing to your sense of self and are a good balance to the demoralizing feelings of stress. Another *very* helpful piece of information is that most stress is self-limiting. However frazzled and overwhelmed you may feel at the moment, you will probably be calmer in a few days even if the source of stress hasn't been completely resolved.

When you have passed through a stressful period or event, try to analyze it so that you can learn from it. Was there some way of minimizing the upheaval? Some way of anticipating it? One major stress of working mothers is a sick or an unreliable baby-sitter. To prepare yourself for that possibility, it's a good idea to compile a list of alternative caregivers at a *nonpressured* time. You can then interview different people, explain the responsibilities in a leisurely fashion and tell them that you might need to contact them on the spur of the moment. If you know of several trustworthy people on whom you can call in an emergency, you won't feel so frantic the next time you get that I-can't-come-in-today 6:45 A.M. phone call.

You can apply this strategy to other areas of your life. One lawyer friend who does a lot of traveling, often with little advance notice, keeps an overnight case packed with a toothbrush, toothpaste, shampoo, underwear, stockings and a nightgown. She also makes sure that she has at least one suit fresh from the cleaners to take with her. Another woman I know has a job that calls for a lot of entertaining. She and her husband like to cook, so they usually entertain at home. "One time it turned into a real disaster," she recalled. "We were having an important dinner party and my son got sick the day before. I didn't get a chance to do the shopping or any of the preparation. I decided to order in from one of the local catering services, but the food was really awful. It was terribly embarrassing," she said. "Now I plan ahead. We've tried several different meals at the various gourmet take-out shops in our area, and I know which are the best. If we have a party planned and something at the last minute prevents me from doing the cooking, I know where I can have it done."

Because working mothers are so dependent upon the consistency of routines, it makes sense to have our backup systems in place before we need them. We will probably never be able to eliminate all the harmful stress from our lives, but by anticipating and knowing how to deal with it, we will be able to reduce our stress-related symptoms.

CHAPTER 27

Neglecting the "I"

"I FEEL GUILTY when I take time for a haircut and buy myself clothing," said Susan Rabiner, an editor at Oxford University Press. "I think that doing things for myself is the one thing I've decided to give up and at times I resent it. Butch manages to play squash, but I never get time to play tennis," reported Ellen Thomas, an attorney. Commenting on this phenomenon, Dr. Marilyn Machlowitz, a management consultant, said, "Most working mothers feel guilt about taking any transition time for themselves."

Betsy, an account executive with a large conglomerate, is typical of many women I interviewed: full-time worker, mother, wife, and full-time stressed. "I never realized how overloaded I was," she told me recently. "I guess I just always felt that if I wasn't working I should either be with the children or taking care of all the household chores. It never occurred to me to take any time for myself. Then I began to notice that I was tired all the time. I began to snap at the children and my husband, Jack, for no reason. And, even worse, I was starting to forget things at work or at home. I completely overlooked a birthday party my son was invited to. He was miserable that he missed it, and so was I.

"I began to feel completely snowed under," Betsy said. "I couldn't seem to get anything done, and that got me so worried that I had trouble sleeping. Finally Jack said, 'If you can't handle it, stop working.' But that only got me more upset. I didn't want to stop working. But I was feeling so inadequate. Why couldn't I handle it, I wondered."

Betsy finally spoke to one of the counselors in her company's Employee Assistance Program, who suggested that she keep a log of everything she did for the following week. At her next appointment Betsy showed the counselor her journal. "No wonder you feel stressed," Betsy reported the counselor as saying. "Look at all you're doing. It's enough for two people." With some guidance Betsy was able to feel comfortable taking some time for herself, but most of us are still unable to.

I was surrounded by working mothers who are financial experts; we were lunching on a dazzling spread. But the pace was anxious, hurried. These are women who live and work under extraordinary pressure.

Yet they told me they long to relax, to go shopping with a friend, to visit a museum, to do nothing at all. But they ignore these yearnings, as they would nothing else in their lives. When asked why they are reluctant to take a few hours for themselves, why their own time has become "an expendable luxury" of their hectic lives, they answer as in one voice—"guilt." Working mothers are too guilty to take any time for themselves.

An insurance agent from Georgia explained, "Our mothers taught us that you are a failure as a woman if the house isn't neat, an elaborate meal cooked, before you take one minute for yourself." A communications manager from Memphis expressed it this way: "We still feel that we should be home full-time, and if we aren't with our family in on-work hours, we are not good mothers—we are shirking our duty." A technical manager for a Massachusetts software company finds "that guilt is excessive for personal time."

Numerous studies confirm that "relaxation is essential to health and continued renewal."[1] It is also essential to the health of our family life. When we are constantly overworked, most of us find, as Betsy did, that our interactions with our families suffer. We may become short-tempered, impatient, depressed, apathetic. But, in spite of how bad we feel when we act this way, we don't seem to be able to find time to relax. *And not because we don't want to.* We hunger for physical and emotional respite from the dizzying demands of our lives, but we don't seem able to ease up.

First of all, the reality is that there is always something to do. If it's not our jobs or the children, it's the house. There is nothing like an automatic pilot for the working mother. Nothing flies by itself. Unlike the traditional husband who could count on his wife to keep things going smoothly while he was off at work all day, most women still have most of the domestic responsibilities. If we did laundry Monday, on Thursday there's a heap of dirty towels. If we helped our daughter finish a big report last night, our son has a list of spelling words that we have to quiz him on tonight. And so it goes. The majority of us have a hard enough time finding an hour to be alone with our husbands or boyfriends. It is almost impossible for us to make time for ourselves.

Then, of course, there is our guilt, which exacerbates our feelings of stress. To relieve these we would have to feel that we are entitled to do something for ourselves—a pottery class, a day alone—which, of course, we feel too guilty to do.

"We feel guilt about not being with the family, the social stigma of being selfish and wanting something only for yourself," said a legal assistant from Oregon. "We feel that we have to be self-sacrificing to justify doing something we really want to do," claimed a California retirement plan administrator.

"The guilt leads to not servicing the 'I.' It is the 'I' that gets lost," said Dr. Leibowitz. "One of the main appeals of the various stress management techniques is that they give women the license to do something for themselves," he explained. "These techniques give their guilt a rationalization; 'I'm not taking time for myself, I'm treating my stress symptoms.' " Leibowitz, who specializes in cardiology, "commends aerobics such as dancing or running." Others suggest deep breathing exercises and stretching, which can be done at your desk.

Some companies have instituted fitness programs for their employees, and for working mothers the advantages are immeasurable. Debbie Jackson, of Abt Associates, a social science research firm in Massachusetts, swims laps in the company pool during an office break. As Debbie said, "The professional life is very competitive these days, the hours long and hard. It makes a world of difference if you can run out and exercise between nine and six. Especially for the working mother, like myself. I feel guilty taking the time for myself at home, but if I exercise at work, I'm not depriving the kids. It means less guilt for me, and shows the company cares."[2]

Leibowitz has also found that it helps a working mother "to take an hour a day for an exercise class, a piano lesson, a walk in the park [if he tells them] you should not feel guilty about it—you will be a more effective mother because of it." He has, of course, tapped into an absolute truth about us: to do for someone else is acceptable; to do for ourselves is not.

When I first started running about four years ago, I justified my morning sprint by saying that it gave me so much more patience with the children. Not that I loved the time alone, not that I hungered for those empty cool mornings when I could watch the sun ignite the chrome and steel towers. No. Only that it made me a better mother. "I'm so patient with the children after a jog." Or that it made me a better writer. "I get some of my best ideas while running." I even wrote a book with running as the theme. Was I writing a book to justify my running? Or was I running to gain material for the book? I don't recall which came first, but I do know that my running became part of "work," my life again divided between career and children.

When I look back on all this, the force of this self-deception is astonishing. While running, I feel whole. But I wasn't lying, or deliberately deceitful; it was that I hadn't allowed myself to know the joy of those sensations. I, too, was having plenty of trouble servicing the "I."

This became dramatically clear to me when I ran my first race. Because races figured heavily in the book that I was writing, I felt I had to do at least one, reluctant competitor though I was. The course was relatively short, just four miles through Central Park, a route I had done many times. Yet it was tough: winding, steep, over Manhattan's version of Boston's Heartbreak Hill.

It was one of those damp summer days, mist clinging to the buildings, the paving stones near the park still wet with an early rain, as my family and I made our way toward Engineer's Gate, the entrance to Central Park adopted by runners as their turf. Passing through, you feel as though you are entering a special world with language, rites and rhythms all its own. Words—*10 ks, Nikes, shin splints*—are exchanged as bodies sleek and slender, and some with just a hint of bulge, pull and bend and prepare.

Over the loudspeaker came the notice to assemble, and I felt full of delicious excitement. "Remember to drink," the voice intoned; the sun, peering through the fog, promised a hot day. I found a place behind a woman with a feathery jewel hanging from one ear and a patch of purple in her hair. The gun sounded, and I took off after her, fascinated as I was by her appearance.

I took the first mile and a half easily enough, but the next part was harder. My starting pace had been too quick; the long, slow ascent conspired with the now-evident sun to do its damage. But still I kept going. "Come on. You can do it," the feathered one urged over her shoulder. I smiled at this generous bit of encouragement and pushed myself onward. Together we now ran, the asphalt under our feet a hot licorice road, but we had less than a mile to go, and around the curve I could make out the large Road Runners' Clock. Squinting, I saw that my time was far better than I had ever imagined it could be.

Up ahead, on the right side of the road, I saw Arnie and the children waving energetically. I saw them and I saw the finish line. And without thought or understanding, I stopped. "I can't finish," I said apologetically to my running mate as I took myself off the course.

"What's the matter?" Arnie asked incredulously.

"I don't know." And I didn't. "I just feel too tired."

"Go on," "Go back in," other bystanders urged. "You can walk in from here and still do it in good time," Arnie urged. "Oh Mommy, please finish," the children chorused.

And after a few minutes I did. But not with any conviction or feeling. And for a long time afterward I wondered why I had denied myself the glory of a true finish.

"Guilt diminishes the quality of the working mother's life," said Dr. Leibowitz. "Rather than enjoying their families, they are miserable, rather than enjoying their jobs, they are miserable." "We are made to feel that we are here for everybody else's benefit." "Perhaps we don't believe that we are worthy of a good time ourselves," one woman hypothesized, while another was more definite. "We're always convinced that others matter more, because of how we've been raised. Somehow myself always does come last," she added sadly.

Guilt extracts a great toll. It affects our interactions with our children—how we discipline them, how much we buy for them, the pressure we put on them to excel, how we relate to those who care for them. It mars our relationships with our husbands by making us competitive, unable to ask for help, unable to share fiscal responsibilities and unable to take time for each other. And it makes us feel emotionally and physically stressed.

To break these guilty patterns, we can start by being nicer to ourselves. One woman told me that she began to take dancing lessons twice a week as a way of being a little kinder to herself. "A secondary result," she reported, "was that I ended up being a little kinder to everyone else as well."

If you have difficulty being good to yourself, you are probably suffering from the self-sacrificing syndrome of most working mothers. There are, however, ways to conquer it. You can record all that you are doing in a journal, as Betsy did, to convince yourself that you need to slack off every so often. And once you do take some time off, you'll probably discover that nothing at work or at home suffers because of it. Most women reported that after a break they felt a renewed sense of enthusiasm and well-being.

Another strategy is to streamline the family chores so that you'll have more free time. Most working mothers advised others that they should hire as much help as they could afford: use cleaning services, have the tailor sew on buttons or hem skirts, let the laundry iron shirts, order in meals from time to time. While some of us might feel uneasy about these expenditures, they may actually be saving us doctors' bills for stress-related symptoms in the future.

Some women make sure they have leisure by scheduling it. One has an "unbreakable" dinner date with a few friends every other Wednesday night, another sets her alarm for an hour earlier than she has to be up so that she can read undisturbed, and a third who loves opera treats herself to season tickets. This kind of deliberate planning makes sense when we think about how easily time seems to disappear. It's a lot harder to let an opera ticket go to waste than to skip going for a walk by yourself.

Exercise—biking, dancing, jogging—are all good for stress management, and they have the added advantage of keeping you in shape. Some women join gyms near either their homes or offices. They enjoy being able to work out during lunch hour or on the way home. Often they go with friends or business associates. Others purchase a few pieces of home exercise equipment from the many available at affordable prices. These include stationary bicycles, weights, rowing machines and even jump ropes. The benefit of a "home gym" is that you can use the equipment in off hours or when the children are about. If, however, you are exercising or, for that matter, doing anything for yourself when your children are at home, you should make sure to tell them that this is time you are taking for yourself. Many children, particularly those five years and older, like to play by themselves. From time to time they will close the door and ask you to stay out. You can explain to your children that just as they like privacy, so do you. Letting your family know that you require your own time and space encourages them to have respect for your needs and interests. It's good for them and good for you.

Psychologist Suzanne Ouellette Kobasa, co-author of *The Hardy Executive: Health Under Stress,* told me that "commitment to self, to figuring out who you are, what your life goals are, is crucial for stress resistance." According to Kobasa, this commitment to your own priorities, along with a sense of control and an ability to see change as an opportunity for growth, will go a long way to keeping working mothers healthy. The benefits will be abundant when working mothers stop neglecting the "I."

Epilogue   *The Possible Woman*

TO BE A working mother is deeply enriching, often perplexing and always pressing. It is a world intensely alive with possibility, exhilarating, beckoning. But for our guilt. "I lost *me* and it's hard to recapture much either *of* me or *for* me," wrote one woman. Estranged from the elemental aspects of our being, we are emerging with a curiously fragmented self-image. We working mothers who have done so much so well, whose days are studies of strength and achievement, remain deeply ambivalent about our lives. Guilt and authenticity contend agonizingly within us.

"Guilt is like tearing apart our internal structure," explained Dr. Willard Gaylin, "that is why it is so painful to endure." To begin the transformation of ourselves and work toward self-integration and wholeness, we must reexamine the origins of our guilt.

It is true that we are mothering our children very differently from the ways we were mothered. We are women to whom the suggestion of similarity to our mothers' lives becomes a cause for deep anxiety and often rage. But that fierce rejection of our mothers' lives, for which we have suffered such guilt, has not been complete, however much we may think and feel that it has. We have rejected only our mothers' culture and the ways in which it molded them. It is hard, even to this day, to see our mothers as distinct from the social context in which they mothered.

In her autobiographical novel *Daughters of Earth*, foreign correspondent and social activist Agnes Smedley writes of her efforts to disengage her sense of her mother as an individual woman from the society that degraded women. For years she and her mother "gazed across a gulf of hostility." Smedley recalls resenting everything, "hating myself most of all for having been born a woman."[1]

But when her father, whom she had greatly admired, abandoned the family, leaving them in desperate poverty, she began to appreciate the oppressive circumstances of her mother's life. Reconciliation and friendship came late, as her mother was dying.

"Then the daily housework and worry of our little house bore heavily upon me," wrote Smedley, "and I thought ceaselessly of my mother. . . . To think of years and years of living like this as she had done!"[2]

The daughter in this book knew that she had to leave or be doomed to repeat her mother's existence. We, too, have left our mothers' lives behind us, in a guilt-ridden separation from which we have emerged divided, alienated, feeling an amputation of valuable parts of self.

But we have not lost these parts. They are present in our mothering. They were there in every woman I interviewed: a caring, an empathy, a fiery love for her children, an astonishing source of commitment and nurture. These qualities we have taken from our mothers and made part of ourselves. For, as Jung once stated, "every mother contains her daughter in herself and every daughter her mother."[3] In our urgent need to be different, we have necessarily denied that there is any bit of resemblance to the women who raised us. But the life-enhancing characteristics of our mothers are within us all—so much a part of us, in fact, that they are unnoticed.

We must strive to give voice to the more empathetic parts that are our mothers' and also our own. It will be difficult and sometimes painful to do this. Old ways of acting and thinking become set, immobilizing, automatic. To change them requires work, energy and conviction.

A few years ago I was asked to write an article on new concepts in hospitalization for a major newspaper; an opportunity I'd always hoped for but never dared to believe would happen. The piece involved extensive traveling to do on-site interviews with patients and personnel at different facilities. Although I'm usually apprehensive about being away from the children, I was so thrilled with the assignment that for once I was able to put my worries aside. And I felt comforted by the arrangements I'd made for them. Vilna, our regular baby-sitter, would work the whole week; my mother would fill in between four-thirty when Vilna left and six-thirty when Arnie got home. I'd discussed the trip and the article with the children and had made them notes on brightly colored paper, one for each day I'd be gone. I'd set up playdates for them and had enjoyed Arnie's enthusiastic planning of their meals. I felt full of excitement and expectation. But two days before the trip Andrew began to complain that his stomach and head hurt him. No real cause for concern, I told myself, a virus at age four is nothing to worry about. But the next day when a fever and the unmistakable blisters of chicken pox appeared, I was plenty worried. Neither Vilna nor my mother had ever had chicken pox. And, although my mother, knowing how important the trip was, offered to come anyway, I wouldn't let her. I could probably get a baby-sitter from an agency, but I really didn't want to leave Andrew with someone neither of us knew, especially when he was sick and uncomfortable.

The conflict welled inside me. What could I do? I had to be on the plane at eight the next morning. But I also had to be home with my sick son. My mind groped for some resolution, but it found none. I could not fulfill both these divergent needs. The timing of the trip had been carefully planned around the already-full schedules of doctors, administrators and patients at three hospitals in different cities. Coordinating interviews, meetings and flights had been so difficult that I feared rescheduling would be impossible.

I felt frustrated, torn, wretched. In other circumstances I might have stuck with my plans. But chicken pox? A new baby-sitter? This time I felt I had no choice. I walked into my bedroom and began to unpack the suitcase.

"What are you doing?" Andrew asked, rambling in.

"I'm not going," I said miserably.

"Why?"

"Because you're sick and I don't want to leave you," I said with more emotion than I'd intended.

Andrew looked at me for what seemed a long time, nodded wisely and left.

When I finished unpacking I was faced with the unpleasant task of telling the newspaper I was canceling the trip. The senior editor on the piece was a man I knew only slightly: formal, impersonal, a little intimidating. I'd lie, of course, tell him that I was sick, down with a bad flu. But the thought of lying was deeply troubling. I wasn't so much afraid of discovery. What bothered me was what I was lying about: that I was a mother who wanted to care for her sick child. Why couldn't I admit it? Why did I feel compelled to deny it? Was I so uncertain of my own realities?

I picked up the phone and reluctantly started to punch out the numbers. The secretary put me on hold as Andrew reappeared, eyes and face blurry with fever. "I'm sorry you have to stay home because of me," he said and put his head down on my knee.

There was within me a sense of bitter disappointment and shame, the first at not going and the second at making Andrew feel a responsibility that was rightly mine. But what about my responsibility for the life I'd chosen? For the choices, sacrifices, pains and joys?

The editor was now on the line, and Andrew was resting softly on my lap. Never before had the demands and rewards of my two roles seemed so vivid, dramatic, conflicting. My profession—my mothering—and I was in the middle, being torn in two by them. But I was also connecting one to the other. For an uncertain moment I sat mute, transfixed by this understanding. Then from deep within there came a sense of confluence, calm and centeredness. Yes, I felt real loss about canceling the trip and all that it might mean, but I had children, who, like all children, get sick from time to time. That was real, human. I would not wish myself without them, as I would not wish myself without my work.

"Hello, hello?" the editor said impatiently.

"I'm sorry, I'll have to postpone my trip," I responded. "My son is down with the chicken pox." I felt sad and happy, yet deeply at peace.

We all must find our own ways to affirm the human qualities we associate with our mothers as we go about our business lives, our community activities, our struggles for legislation responsive to our needs. We must do this deliberately, consciously, by analyzing our actions and behavior in the context of our newfound awareness. For only then will we be able to understand our separation from our mothers for what it really is: a rejection, to be sure, of all that was excessive, subordinate, menial; but a glorious preservation of what was nourishing, warm, human. When we know this—truly know it—when we work to integrate those values that we have taken from our mothers into those we have taken since we left her, we will know that we have neither repudiated nor failed to meet the *best* of our ideal standard of mothering. *And we will no longer feel guilty.*

With this understanding we will experience a release of spontaneity and energy. And, at last, we will feel whole and autonomous, and this will affect every aspect of our lives. We will be able to enjoy our children without apology. No longer haunted by the need to overcompensate for our working with excessive toys, clothes or activities, we will feel comfortable encouraging appropriate behavior and responsibilities. Once we are freed of guilt, our interactions will become more natural, balanced and pleasurable. The delight we take in our children will be matched by our pride in our model to them.

Our belief in the rightness of combining both roles will bring benefits at work. The old anxieties over fraudulence will be replaced by a new sense of authenticity, enabling us to embrace success energetically and enthusiastically. We will find, too, a growing intimacy with our husbands or boyfriends as the conflicts over household tasks, finances and professional achievement are displaced by open communication and sharing.

And we will feel a changed sense of self. Governed no longer by guilt's punitive demands, we will be in greater control of our lives: secure, confident and complete. We will be women who see beyond the problems of our two roles to their richest possibilities.

At last we will feel free to experience our own identities as working mothers positively and with assurance, and to strive to obtain better child care and benefits for us all. At last we can begin to change our guilt-edged world into one that is truly gilt-edged.

NOTES

Chapter 1

1. Sylvia Ann Hewlett, "Child Carelessness," *Harper's,* Nov. 1983, p. 21.
2. "How Long Till Equality?" *Time,* July 12, 1982, p. 26.
3. Ibid.
4. Robert Pear, "Wage Lag Is Found for White Women," *New York Times,* Jan. 16, 1984, p. 1.
5. "How Long Till Equality?" *Time,* p. 24.
6. Anita Shreve, "Careers and the Lure of Motherhood," *The New York Times Magazine,* Nov. 21, 1982, p. 56.
7. *New York Times,* Dec. 8, 1984, p. 41.
8. D. Susan Barron, "The Reviving Rituals of the Debutante," *The New York Times Magazine,* Jan. 15, 1984, p. 28.
9. Sylvia Ann Hewlett, "Working Mothers: Effects on Children," *New York Times,* July 27, 1983, p. 15.
10. Robert Coughlan, "Changing Roles in Modern Marriage," *Life,* Dec. 24, 1956, p. 110.
11. Shreve, "Careers and Motherhood," p. 41.

Chapter 2

1. Arnold Hutschnecker, "Do You Feel Guilty?" *Vogue,* July 1972, p. 160.
2. Sigmund Freud, *New Introductory Lectures on Psychoanalysis* (New York: W. W. Norton, 1964), p. 63.
3. Elizabeth Stone, "Mothers and Daughters," *The New York Times Magazine,* May 13, 1979, p. 17.
4. Ibid. For a more complete description of the psychological process of separation, see Margaret S. Mahler, Fred Pine, and Anni Bergman, *The Psychological Birth of the Human Infant* (New York: Basic Books, 1975).
5. Margaret Mahler, quoted in Stone, "Mothers and Daughters," p. 62.
6. Stone, "Mothers and Daughters," p. 91.
7. Quoted in Elizabeth Nickles, *The Coming Matriarchy* (New York: Seaview Books, 1981), p. 144.
8. Quoted in Willard Gaylin, *Feelings* (New York: Ballantine Books, 1979).
9. Hutschnecker, "Do You Feel Guilty," p. 160.
10. Quoted in Stone, "Mothers and Daughters," p. 91.

Chapter 3

1. Robert Coughlin, "Changing Roles in Modern Marriage," *Life,* Dec. 24, 1956, pp. 110, 112.
2. Julie Harris, "I Was Afraid to Have a Baby," *McCall's,* June 1956, p. 23.
3. Carol Hymowitz and Michaele Weissman, *A History of Women in America* (New York: Bantam, 1978), p. 312.
4. Ibid., p. 314.
5. See Mary P. Ryan, *Womanhood in America* (New York: New Viewpoints, 1975), p. 334.
6. Hymowitz and Weissman, *History of Women in America,* p. 326.
7. Ferdinand Lundberg and Marynia Farnham, *Modern Women: The Lost Sex* (New York: W. W. Norton, 1947), p. 256.
8. Hymowitz and Weissman, *History of Women,* p. 327.
9. Helene Deutsch, *The Psychology of Women,* vol. II (New York: W. W. Norton, 1945), p. 292.
10. Benjamin Spock, *Baby and Child Care* (New York: Pocket Books, 1970), p. 3.
11. Betty Friedan, *The Feminine Mystique* (New York: Dell 1963), p. 180; Paula J. Caplan and Ian Hall-McCorquodale, "The Scapegoating of Mothers: A Call to Change," *American Journal of Orthopsychiatry* (Oct. 1985), pp. 610–614.
12. John R. Seeley, R. Alexander Simm, and Elizabeth Loosley, *Crestwood Heights: A Study of the Culture of Suburban Life* (New York: Harper and Row, 1956), p. 174.
13. Helene Z. Lopata, *Occupation: Housewife* (New York: Oxford University Press, 1971), p. 210.
14. Quoted in Friedan, *Feminine Mystique,* pp. 52–53.
15. Quoted in Ryan, *Womanhood in America,* p. 344.
16. Hymowitz and Weissman, *History of Women,* p. 327.
17. Friedan, *Feminine Mystique,* p. 206.
18. Ibid., p. 207.
19. Hymowitz and Weissman, *History of Women,* p. 327.
20. Ibid., p. 335.
21. Friedan, *Feminine Mystique,* p. 23.
22. Lopata, *Occupation: Housewife,* p. 192.
23. Friedan, *Feminine Mystique,* p. 17.
24. Lopata, *Occupation: Housewife,* p. 51.
25. Quoted in Elizabeth Stone, "Mothers and Daughters," *The New York Times Magazine,* May 13, 1979, p. 76.
26. Ibid., p. 91.
27. Janel Bladow, "Where Are They Now?" *Working Woman* (July 1981), p. 58.
28. Gabrielle Burton, "I'm Running Away From Home," *Ms,* Feb. 1973, p. 73.
29. Pauline B. Bart, "Depression in Middle-Aged Women," in *Woman in*

Sexist Society, edited by Vivian Gornick and Barbara K. Moran (New York: Mentor, 1971), p. 163.

30. Esther Menaker, "Some Inner Conflicts of Woman in a Changing Society," in *Career and Motherhood,* edited by Alan Roland and Barbara Harris (New York: Human Sciences Press, 1979), p. 89.

31. Ibid.

Chapter 4

1. Elizabeth Stone, "Mothers and Daughters," *The New York Times Magazine,* May 13, 1979, p. 90.
2. Esther Menaker, "Some Inner Conflicts of Woman in a Changing Society," in *Career and Motherhood,* edited by Alan Roland and Barbara Harris (New York: Human Sciences Press, 1979), p. 92.
3. Ibid.
4. Doris Bernstein, "Female Identity Synthesis," in *Career and Motherhood,* edited by Roland and Harris, p. 114.
5. Menaker, "Some Inner Conflicts," p. 93.
6. Quoted in Stone, "Mothers and Daughters," p. 90.

Chapter 5

1. Quoted in Sylvia Rabiner, "How the Superwoman Myth Puts Women Down," *The Village Voice,* May 24, 1976, p. 11.
2. *Working Woman,* Oct. 1982, p. 59.
3. Madelon Bedell, "We Are Never Tired . . ." *Ms,* May 1973, p. 82.
4. Alice Rossi, "Equality Between the Sexes," in *The Other Half,* edited by Cynthia Fuchs Epstein and William J. Goode (New Jersey: Prentice-Hall, 1971), p. 180.
5. Caroline Bird, *Born Female: The High Cost of Keeping Women Down* (New York: David McKay Co., 1968), p. 181.
6. Roslyn Willett, "Working in 'A Man's World,' " in *Woman in Sexist Society,* edited by Vivian Gornick and Barbara K. Moran (New York: Meatar, 1971), p. 530.
7. Betty Friedan, "Feminism Takes a New Turn," *The New York Times Magazine,* Nov. 18, 1979, p. 94.
8. Lois Wyse, "So Long, Supermom," *Good Housekeeping,* June 1981, p. 106.
9. Gloria Norris and JoAnn Miller, *The Working Mother's Handbook* (New York: E. P. Dutton, 1979), p. 77.
10. Francine Hall and Douglas Hall, *The Two-Career Couple* (Philippines: Addison-Wesley, 1979), p. 104.
11. Friedan, "Feminism," p. 94.
12. Elizabeth Whelan, "Confessions of a Superwoman," *Working Woman,* July 1981, pp. 61–64.
13. Wyse, "So Long, Supermom," p. 106.
14. Judith Coburn, "Do Superwomen Really Exist," *Mademoiselle,* Dec. 1981, p. 8.

15. Jessie Bernard, *The Future of Motherhood* (New York: Penguin Books, 1974), p. 165.

Chapter 6

1. Judith Ballou, *The Psychology of Pregnancy* (Lexington, Mass.: D. C. Heath, 1978), p. 31.
2. Ballou, *Psychology of Pregnancy*, p. 33.
3. Quoted in Christine Doudna, "The New Madonnas," *Savvy*, June 1982, p. 37.
4. "Infant Day Care and Infant Care Leaves," *American Psychologist* (Jan. 1983), p. 92.
5. Ibid.
6. Quoted in Gloria Norris and JoAnn Miller, *The Working Mother's Handbook* (New York: E. P. Dutton, 1979), p. 17.
7. Mary Howell, "The Best Kind of Mother," *Working Mother*, Oct. 1983, p. 124.
8. "Frankly Speaking," *Seventeen*, Dec. 1981, p. 92.
9. Terri Minsky, "Advice and Comfort for the Working Mother," *Esquire*, June 1984, p. 157.
10. Laurel Sorensen, "A Woman's Unwritten Code for Success," *American Bar Association Journal*, Oct. 1983, p. 1418.
11. Ibid.
12. Quoted in Minsky, "Advice and Comfort," p. 153.

Chapter 7

1. Beatrice Marden Glickman and Nesha Bass Springer, *Who Cares for the Baby?* (New York: Schocken Books, 1978), p. 116.
2. Ibid., p. 115.
3. "Day Care in New York: A Growing Need," *New York Times*, July 20, 1983, p. C8.
4. Ibid.
5. Dana Friedman, "Encouraging Employer Support to Working Parents," A Report for the Carnegie Corporation of New York (1983), p. 93; "Child Care Finds a Champion in the Corporation," *New York Times*, August 4, 1985, p. 86.
6. Friedman, "Encouraging Employer Support," p. 18.
7. Friedman, "Encouraging Employer Support," p. 53; "Child Care Finds a Champion," p. 1; "More Corporations Are Offering Child Care," *New York Times*, June 21, 1985, p. A18.
8. Friedman, "Encouraging Employer Support," pp. 100–101.

Chapter 8

1. Quoted in Anita Shreve, "Careers and the Lure of Motherhood," *The New York Times Magazine*, Nov. 21, 1982, p. 58.

2. Ibid.
3. Quoted in Beatrice Marden Glickman and Nesha Bass Springer, *Who Cares for the Baby* (New York: Schocken Books, 1978), p. 178.
4. Quoted in Gloria Norris and JoAnn Miller, *The Working Mother's Handbook* (New York: E. P. Dutton, 1979), p. 26.

Chapter 9

1. T. Berry Brazelton, *Toddlers and Parents* (New York: Delta, 1974), p. 2.
2. Susan Muenchow, "The Truth About Quality Time," *Parents Magazine,* May 1983, p. 60.
3. "Real Quality Time," *Working Mother,* May 1985, p. 40.
4. Gloria Norris and JoAnn Miller, *The Working Mother's Handbook* (New York: E. P. Dutton, 1979), p. 135.
5. Sally Wendkos Olds, *The Working Parents Survival Guide* (New York: Bantam, 1983), p. 252.
6. Jeanne Bodin and Bonnie Mitelman, *Mothers Who Work* (New York: Ballantine Books, 1983), p. 75.
7. Burton L. White, *The First Three Years of Life* (New York: Avon, 1975), p. 180.

Chapter 10

1. *Working Mother,* "Letters to the Editor," March 1984, p. 123.
2. Mary Howell, "Gift-Swamped Kids," *Working Mother,* Dec. 1983, p. 50.
3. Howell, "Gift-Swamped," p. 51.
4. Ibid.
5. Ibid.
6. Lois Hoffman's work is discussed in Elizabeth Douvan, "Employment and the Adolescent," in *The Employed Mother in America,* edited by F. Ivan Nye and Lois Wladis Hoffman (Chicago: Rand McNally, 1963), p. 148.
7. Karen Horney, *The Neurotic Personality in Our Time* (New York: W. W. Norton, 1937), p. 95.
8. Douvan, "Employment and the Adolescent," p. 148.
9. Caroline Zinsser, "How to Get Kids to *Really* Help," *Working Mother,* Mar. 1984, pp. 42–46.
10. Ibid.
11. Anne Russell and Patricia Fitzgibbons, *Career & Conflict* (New Jersey: Prentice-Hall, 1982), p. 175.
12. Ibid.
13. Adele Faber and Elaine Mazlish, *Liberated Parents, Liberated Children* (New York: Avon, 1974), p. 141.
14. Ibid., p. 162.
15. Ibid., p. 164.
16. Ibid., p. 165.

Chapter 11

1. T. Berry Brazelton, *Toddlers and Parents* (New York: Delta, 1974), p. 45.
2. Ibid.
3. Caroline Zinsser, "The Discipline Debate," *Working Mother,* July 1983, pp. 61–82; James Q. Wilson, "Raising Kids," *The Atlantic Monthly,* Oct. 1983, pp. 45–56; "The Secret to Raising Healthy Happy Children," *U.S. News & World Report,* June 1981, p. 46; Julius Segal and Herbert Yahraes, "Bringing Up Mother," *Psychology Today,* Nov. 1978, pp. 90–96; "Handling a Difficult Child," *New York Times,* Jan. 9, 1984, p. B6; James Dobson, *Dare to Discipline* (New York: Bantam, 1970).
4. Richard Bush, *When a Child Needs Help* (New York: Dell, 1980); Glenn Collins, "Children and Stress: A Search for Causes," *New York Times,* Oct. 3, 1983, p. 18.

Chapter 12

1. Quoted in Linda Wolfe, "Growing Up Absorbed," *New York,* Oct. 4, 1982, p. 33.
2. Marie Winn, *Children Without Childhood* (New York: Pantheon, 1983).
3. Glenn Collins, "Does Early Teaching of Infants Have Merit?" *New York Times,* Mar. 3, 1982, pp. C1, C12.
4. Ibid.
5. David Elkind, *The Hurried Child* (Reading, Mass.: Addison-Wesley Co., 1981), pp. 33–35.
6. Mary Howell, "Superbabies: Why Mothers Want Them," *Working Mother,* Jan. 1985, pp. 71–72.
7. Elkind, *Hurried Child,* p. 37.
8. "Growing Up Absorbed," *New York,* p. 30.
9. Elizabeth Bailey, "Bringing Up Baby, 1984," *Savvy,* Mar. 1984, p. 87.
10. Martin Seligman, *Helplessness* (San Francisco: W. H. Freeman & Co., 1975), pp. 156–59.
11. Elkind, *Hurried Child,* pp. 177–79.
12. Ibid., p. 185.
13. Marie Winn, "The Loss of Childhood," *New York Times Magazine,* May 8, 1983, p. 21.
14. Margot Slade, "When Tots Join Adults Uninvited," *New York Times,* April 6, 1984, p. B6.

Chapter 13

1. "Why Women Aren't Getting to the Top," *Fortune,* Apr. 16, 1984, p. 40.
2. Ibid.; Tamar Lewin, "Women in the Board Rooms Are Still the Exception," *New York Times,* May 15, 1984, pp. C1, C8.
3. *Fortune,* "Why Women Aren't Getting to the Top," p. 40.
4. Louise Bernikow, "We're Dancing As Fast As We Can," *Savvy,* Apr. 1984, pp. 40–43.

5. Enid Nemy, "Role of Mentor for Women in Academia," *New York Times*, Dec. 26, 1983, p. 17.
6. *Fortune*, "Why Women Aren't Getting to the Top," p. 40.
7. Ibid., p. 41.
8. Bernikow, "We're Dancing," p. 42.
9. Barbara Basler, "Study Finds Stereotypes Affect Voters at Polls," *New York Times*, Feb. 12, 1984, p. 7.
10. *Fortune*, "Why Women Aren't Getting to the Top," p. 44.
11. Ibid.
12. Andrew Hacker, "Why Women Still Earn Less Than Men," *Working Mother*, Oct. 1983, pp. 25–32; Leslie Bennetts, "The Equal Pay Issue," *New York Times*, Oct. 26, 1979, p. A20; Andrew Hacker, *USA: A Statistical Portrait* (New York: Penguin, 1983); *Fortune*, "Why Women Aren't Getting to the Top," pp. 44–45.
13. Peggy L. Kerr, "Kerr Looks Back on Skadden, Arps Partnership Quest," *Legal Times of New York*, Oct. 17, 1983, pp. A1, 24.

Chapter 14

1. Louise Bernikow, "We're Dancing As Fast As We Can," *Savvy*, Apr. 1984, p. 42.
2. Matina S. Horner, "Toward an Understanding of Achievement-Related Conflicts in Women," *Journal of Special Issues* 28 (1972): 157–75. For a full discussion of the relationship between separation and success anxiety, see Carol Gilligan, *In a Different Voice* (Cambridge, Mass.: Harvard University Press, 1982), pp. 1–105.
3. Gilligan, *Different Voice*, p. 8.
4. Irene P. Stiver, "Work Inhibitions in Women" (Wellesley, Mass.: Stone Center for Developmental Services and Studies, 1983), p. 6.
5. Quoted in Eleanor Berman, "What Women Tell Their Therapists," *Working Mother*, Mar. 1984, p. 29.

Chapter 15

1. Meg Wheatley and Marcie Schorr Hirsch, *Managing Your Maternity Leave* (Boston: Houghton Mifflin Co., 1983), pp. 94–103.
2. Quoted in Nancy Lee, *Targeting the Top* (New York: Ballantine Books, 1980), p. 72.
3. Wheatley and Hirsch, *Managing Your Maternity Leave*, pp. 94–100.
4. Ibid.
5. Ibid.
6. Grace K. Baruch and Rosalind C. Barnett, "Role Quality, Multiple Involvement and Psychological Well-Being in Midlife Women," Working Paper No. 149 (Wellesley College, 1985); Grace K. Baruch and Rosalind C. Barnett, "Saved by the Job," *Working Woman*, Aug. 1984, p. 30.
7. Sally Wendkos Olds, *The Working Parents Survival Guide* (New York: Bantam, 1983), p. 29.

8. Eleanor Berman, "What Women Tell Their Therapists," *Working Mother,* Mar. 1984, p. 31.
9. Eleanor Berman, *Re-Entering* (New York: PEI, 1980), p. 142.
10. Linda Lee Small, "Nowhere Fast," *Working Mother,* May 1984, p. 25; Marie Moneysmith, "Dead-End Dilemma," *Savvy,* Jan. 1985, pp. 32–34.
11. Ibid., p. 26.
12. Ibid., pp. 29–30.
13. Berman, *Re-Entering,* p. 147.
14. Ibid., p. 143.

Chapter 16

1. Quoted in Erica Abeel, "Dark Secrets," *Esquire,* June 1984, p. 265.
2. Taken from a case study discussed by Irene Stiver, in "Work Inhibitions in Women," p. 7.
3. T. Berry Brazelton, *Toddlers and Parents* (New York: Delta, 1974), p. 33.
4. Karen Horney, *The Neurotic Personality in Our Time* (New York: W. W. Norton, 1937), pp. 244–47.
5. Marlene Arthur Pinkstaff and Anna Bell Wilkinson, *Women at Work* (Reading, Mass.: Addison-Wesley, 1979), p. 84.
6. Betsy Morscher, "Achievement Anxiety: Career Sabotage," *Harper's Bazaar,* Mar. 1984, p. 218.
7. Ibid., p. 174.

Chapter 17

1. Daniel Goleman, "Therapists Find Many Achievers Feel They're Fakes," *New York Times,* September 11, 1984, pp. C1, C12; Susan Seliger, "The Secret Fear of Being Found Wanting," *Working Mother,* March 1985, pp. 108–110.
2. Goleman, p. C12.
3. Erica Abeel, "Dark Secrets," *Esquire,* June 1984, p. 265.
4. Quoted in Goleman, "Therapists," p. C12.

Chapter 18

1. Marilyn Machlowitz, *Workaholics* (Reading, Mass.: Addison-Wesley Co., 1980), p. 11.
2. Elizabeth Whelan, "Confessions of a Superwoman," *Working Woman,* July 1981, p. 63; Machlowitz, *Workaholics,* p. 108.
3. Jay B. Rohrlich, *Work & Love: The Crucial Balance* (New York: Harmony Books) pp. 165–85.
4. Quoted in Machlowitz, *Workaholics,* p. 14.
5. Ibid., p. 15.
6. Ibid., pp. 44–45.
7. Quoted in Erica Abeel, "Dark Secrets," *Esquire,* June 1984, p. 262.
8. Rohrlich, *Work & Love,* pp. 182–85.

9. Ibid., p. 182.
10. Ibid., pp. 183–86.
11. Ibid., p. 182.
12. Whelan, "Confessions," pp. 61–64; Machlowitz, *Workaholics*, p. 82.
13. Machlowitz, *Workaholics*, pp. 85–86.
14. Ibid., p. 82.
15. Ibid., p. 127.
16. Jean Grasso Fitzpatrick, "Time," *Working Woman*, Oct. 1983, p. 72.
17. Ibid.; James M. Jenks and John M. Kelly, *Don't Do. Delegate!* (New York: Bantam, 1985).
18. Machlowitz, *Workaholics*, pp. 47–63.

Chapter 19

1. Anecdote told to me by Ellen Galensky, director of Family and Work Project at Bank Street College of Education on November 6, 1983.
2. Naomi Barko, "Corporate Etiquette," *Working Mother*, May 1984, p. 56.
3. Gloria Norris and JoAnn Miller, *The Working Mother's Handbook* (New York: E. P. Dutton, 1979), p. 159; quoted in *Fortune*, "Why Women Aren't Getting to the Top" (Apr. 16, 1984), p. 43.
4. Barko, "Corporate Etiquette," p. 56.
5. Norris and Miller, *Working Mother's Handbook*, p. 157.
6. Margaret Hennig and Anne Jardim, *The Managerial Woman* (New York: Anchor Press, 1977), p. 17.
7. Ibid., p. 182.
8. Barko, "Corporate Etiquette," p. 56.
9. Stiver, p. 4.
10. Marilyn Machlowitz, "Management/Business Advice Career Myth," *Working Woman*, June 1983, pp. 22–23.
11. See *Savvy* (September 1983).
12. Stiver, "Work Inhibitions in Women," p. 4.
13. Stiver, "Work Inhibitions in Women," p. 4; "Stock Talk," *Savvy*, May 1985, p. 18.
14. "When Mothers Are Managers," *Business Week*, Apr. 18, 1977, p. 155.

Chapter 20

1. Quoted in Linda Wolfe, "How to Succeed," *New York*, Feb. 16, 1981, p. 29.
2. John Demos, *A Little Commonwealth* (New York: Oxford University Press, 1970), p. 10.
3. William O'Neill, *Coming Apart* (New York: Quadrangle Books, 1979), pp. 266–67, 270.
4. Wolfe, "How to Succeed," p. 29; Maureen Dowd, "Women Equate Values of Job & Family," *New York Times*, Dec. 4, 1983, pp. 1, 66.

Chapter 21

1. Sheldon Harnick, "Housework," *Free to Be . . . You and Me* (New York: McGraw Hill, 1974), p. 54.
2. Ann Oakley, *Woman's Work* (New York: Vintage House, 1974), p. 1.
3. Philip Blumstein and Pepper Schwartz, *American Couples* (New York: William Morrow & Co., 1983), pp. 144–45.
4. "Working Wives and Mothers," *Monthly Labor Review*, Sept. 1981, p. 27.
5. Harriet Goldhor Lerner, "I Don't Need Anything From Anybody," *Working Mother*, Nov. 1984, p. 146; "Canned Corn Strains Abilities," *The Wall Street Journal*, July 25, 1985, p. 24.
6. Goldhor Lerner, "I Don't Need Anything," p. 148.

Chapter 22

1. Karen Horney, *The Neurotic Personality in Our Time* (New York: W. W. Norton, 1937), p. 168.
2. David G. Rice, *Dual-Career Marriage* (New York: Free Press, 1979), pp. 75–76.
3. Marjorie Shaevitz and Morton Shaevitz, *Making It Together As a Two-Career Couple* (Boston: Houghton Mifflin, 1980), pp. 24, 211.
4. Willard Gaylin, *Feelings* (New York: Ballantine Books, 1979), p. 51.
5. Rice, *Dual-Career Marriage*, p. 76.
6. Philip Blumstein and Pepper Schwartz, *American Couples* (New York: William Morrow, 1983), pp. 240–45, 251–53.
7. Marilyn Machlowitz, "Corporate Husbands," *Working Woman*, April 1983, p. 32.

Chapter 23

1. David G. Rice, *Dual-Career Marriage* (New York: Free Press, 1979), p. 49.
2. Philip Blumstein and Pepper Schwartz, *American Couples* (New York: William Morrow, 1983), pp. 52–56.
3. Ibid., pp. 53–56.
4. Carlfred B. Broderick, "Whose Money?" *Working Mother*, Feb. 1984, p. 125.
5. Elizabeth Ames, "Love & Money," *Savvy*, Feb. 1984, p. 81; Tessa Warschaw, "Men, Women & Money," *Savvy*, Feb. 1984, pp. 60–63.
6. Marjorie Shaevitz and Morton Shaevitz, *Making It Together As a Two-Career Couple* (Boston: Houghton Mifflin, 1980), pp. 144–50.
7. Quoted from Barbara J. Berg, *Nothing to Cry About* (New York: Seaview Books, 1981), p. 9.
8. Warschaw, "Men, Women & Money," p. 63.

Chapter 24

1. Francine Klagsburn, "Secrets and Pleasures of Long-Lasting Marriage," *Ms*, June 1985, p. 43; Jeannette Lauer and Robert Lauer, "Why Marriages Last," *Psychology Today*, June 1985, pp. 22–26.
2. Klagsburn, pp. 42–44.
3. "Where Does the Time Go?" Report by Research & Forecasts, Inc., for United Media Enterprises, New York: 1982, pp. 71–81.
4. Philip Blumstein and Pepper Schwartz, *American Couples* (New York: William Morrow, 1983), pp. 194–95.
5. "Motherhood in an Advertising Agency," *Working Mother*, July 1985,
6. Quoted in Hilary Ryglewicz and Pat Koch Thaler, *Working Couples* (New York: Sovereign, 1980), p. 138.
7. Quoted in "Motherhood in an Advertising Agency," *Working Mother*, July 1985, p. 65.
8. Rice, pp. 57–59.
9. Klagsburn, p. 44.
10. Francine Hall and Douglas Hall, *The Two-Career Couple* (Philippines: Addison-Wesley, 1979), p. 152.
11. Ibid.
12. Klagsburn, "Secrets and Pleasures," p. 43.

Chapter 25

1. See Barbara J. Berg, *The Remembered Gate* (New York: Oxford University Press, 1978), pp. 118–20.
2. Ibid., p. 119.
3. For a discussion of these symptoms, see O. Spurgeon English and Gerald H. Pearson, *Emotional Problems of Living* (New York: W. W. Norton, 1963), pp. 508–12.
4. Grace K. Baruch and Rosalind C. Barnett, "Saved by the Job," *Working Woman*, Aug. 1984, p. 23.
5. "Motherhood in An Advertising Agency," *Working Mother*, July 1985, p. 44.
6. See Lori Andrews, "Sisterhood on the Job," *Parents Magazine*, May 1983, pp. 27–28.

Chapter 26

1. Georgia Witkin-Lanoil, "The Female Stress Syndrome," *Working Mother*, Nov. 1984, p. 152.
2. Donald Morse and M. Lawrence Furst, *Women Under Stress* (New York: Van Nostrand Reinhold Co., 1982), p. 44.
3. "Stress: Can We Cope?" *Time*, June 6, 1983, p. 50; Jane E. Brody, "Emotions Found to Influence Every Ailment," *New York Times*, May 24, 1983, pp. C1, C2.
4. "Stress," *Time*, p. 50.

5. Andrea Thompson, "Darling I'd Go On the Class Trip, . . ." *Working Mother,* Sept. 1984, p. 78.
6. Daniel Goleman, "Confiding in Others Improves Health," *New York Times,* Sept. 18, 1984, pp. C1, C2.
7. "Personal Problems at Work," *Working Mother,* May 1984, p. 65.
8. Quoted in "Take Care of Yourself," *Working Mother,* June 1984, p. 56.

Chapter 27

1. Barbara Lau, "Necessary Breaks," *Working Woman,* July 1983, p. 60.
2. Quoted in Rob Goldberg, "Working Out at Work," *Savvy,* Dec. 1983, p. 59.

Epilogue

1. Agnes Smedley, *Daughter of Earth* (New York: The Feminist Press, 1973), p. 12.
2. Ibid., pp. 132–33.
3. Carl Jung, "Psychological Aspects of the Kore," in *Essay on a Science of Mythology* (Princeton: Princeton University Press, 1969), as quoted in Judith Arcana, *Our Mothers' Daughters* (Berkeley: Shameless Hussy Press, 1977), p. 171.

Bibliography

Books

Aldous, Joan, ed. *Two Paychecks*. Beverley Hills, California: Sage Publications, 1982.

Arcana, Judith. *Our Mothers' Daughters*. Berkeley, Calif.: Shameless Hussy Press, 1979.

Ballou, Judith. *The Psychology of Pregnancy*. Lexington, Mass.: D. C. Heath and Co., 1978.

Beauvoir, Simone de. *The Second Sex*. New York: Bantam, 1961.

Berman, Eleanor. *Re-Entering*. New York: PEI, 1980.

Bernard, Jessie. *The Future of Motherhood*. New York: Penguin Books, 1974.

Bird, Caroline. *Born Female*. New York: David McKay Co., 1968.

Blumstein, Philip, and Schwartz, Pepper. *American Couples*. New York: William Morrow and Co., 1983.

Badin, Jeanne, and Mitelman, Bonnie. *Mothers Who Work*. New York: Ballantine Books, 1983.

Brazelton, Berry T. *Infants and Mothers*. New York: Delta, 1969.

———. *Toddlers and Parents*. New York: Delta, 1974.

Bush, Richard. *When a Child Needs Help*. New York: Dell, 1980.

Caplan, Frank. *The First Twelve Months of Life*. New York: Bantam, 1971.

———. *The Parenting Advisor*. New York: Anchor Press, 1977.

Dobson, James. *Dare to Discipline*. New York: Bantam, 1970.

Elkind, David. *The Hurried Child*. Reading, Mass.: Addison-Wesley Co., 1981.

Employer Supported Child Care. An Idea Whose Time Has Come. San Francisco: Far West Laboratories, 1980.

Epstein, Cynthia Fuchs. *Woman's Place*. Berkeley: University of California Press, 1971.

Erikson, Erik H. *Identity, Youth and Crisis*. New York: W. W. Norton, 1968.

Faber, Adel, and Mazlish, Elaine. *Liberated Parents, Liberated Children*. New York: Avon, 1974.

Freud, Anna. *Normality and Pathology in Childhood*. New York: International Universities Press, 1965.

———. *The Ego and the Mechanisms of Defense*. New York: International Universities Press, 1966.

Freud, Sigmund. *Civilization and Its Discontents*. New York: W. W. Norton, 1961.

———. *New Introductory Lectures on Psychoanalysis*. New York: W. W. Norton, 1964.

Friedan, Betty. *The Feminine Mystique*. New York: Dell, 1963.

Friedman, Dana E. *Encouraging Employer Support to Working Parents*. New York: Center for Public Advocacy Research, 1983.

Friedman, Martha. *Overcoming the Fear of Success*. New York: Warner, 1979.

Fromm, Erich. *The Art of Loving*. New York: Harper and Row, 1956.

Gaylin, Willard. *Feelings*. New York: Ballantine, 1979.

Gilligan, Carol. *In a Different Voice*. Cambridge, Mass.: Harvard University Press, 1983.

Glickman, Beatrice Marden, and Springer, Nesha Bass. *Who Cares for the Baby*. New York: Schocken Books, 1979.

Gutman, Herbert G. *Work, Culture and Society*. New York: Vintage Books, 1967.

Hall, Francine S., and Hall, Douglas. *The Two-Career Couple*. Philippines: Addison-Wesley Co., 1979.

Hennig, Margaret, and Jardim, Anne. *The Managerial Woman*. New York: Anchor Press, 1977.

Hoffman, Lois, and Nye, F. Evan. *The Employed Mother in America*. Chicago: Rand McNally & Co., 1963.

———. *Working Mothers*. San Francisco: Jossey-Bass, 1972.

Horney, Karen. *The Neurotic Personality in Our Time*. New York: W. W. Norton, 1937.

———. *Feminine Psychology*. New York: W. W. Norton, 1967.

———. *Neurosis and Human Growth*. New York: W. W. Norton, 1950.

Hymowitz, Carol, and Weissman, Michaele. *A History of Women in America*. New York: Bantam, 1978.

Kaplan, Louise J. *Oneness & Separateness: From Infant to Individual*. New York: Touchstone Books, 1978.

Kaufman, Sherwin. *Sexual Sabotage*. New York: Macmillan Co., 1981.

Larwood, Laurie, and Wood, Marion. *Women in Management*. Lexington, Mass.: Lexington Books, 1977.

Lasch, Christopher. *The Culture of Narcissism*. New York: Warner Books, 1979.

Lee, Nancy. *Targeting the Top*. New York: Ballantine, 1980.

Lopata, Helena. *Occupation: Housewife*. New York: Oxford University Press, 1971.

Machlowitz, Marilyn. *Workaholics*. Reading, Mass.: Addison-Wesley Co., 1980.

Mahler, Margaret; Pine, Fred; and Bergman, Anni. *The Psychological Birth of the Human Infant*. New York: Basic Books, 1975.

Miller, Alice. *Prisoners of Chidhood*. New York: Basic Books, 1981.

Miller, JoAnn, and Norris, Gloria. *The Working Mother's Complete Handbook*. New York: E. P. Dutton, 1979.

Morse, Donald, and Furst, M. Lawrence. *Women under Stress*. New York: Van Nostrand Reinhold Co., 1982.

Oakley, Ann. *Woman's Work.* New York: Vintage House, 1979.

Olds, Sally Wendkos. *The Working Parents Survival Guide.* New York: Bantam, 1983.

Rice, David G. *Dual-Career Marriage.* New York: Free Press, 1979.

Robbins, Jhan, and Robbins, June. *An Analysis of Human Sexual Inadequacy.* New York: Signet, 1970.

Roland, Alan, and Harris, Barbara, eds. *Career and Motherhood.* New York: Human Sciences Press, 1979.

Rogalin, Wilman, and Pell, Arthur R. *Women's Guide to Management Positions.* New York: Simon and Schuster, 1975.

Rohrlich, Jay B. *Work and Love: The Crucial Balance.* New York: Harmony Books, 1980.

Ryan, Mary. *Womanhood in America.* New York: New Viewpoints, 1975.

Ryglewicz, Hilary, and Thaler, Pat Koch. *Working Couples.* New York: Sovereign Books, 1980.

Salk, Lee. *Preparing for Parenthood.* New York: David McKay Co., 1974.

Schenkel, Susan. *Giving Away Success.* New York: McGraw Hill, 1984.

Seligman, Martin. *Helplessness.* San Francisco: W. H. Freeman and Co., 1981.

Shaevitz, Marjorie, and Shaevitz, Morton. *Making It Together.* Boston: Houghton Mifflin, 1980.

Shainess, Natalie. *Sweet Suffering. Woman as Victim.* New York: The Bobbs-Merrill Co., 1984.

Sloane, Howard. *The Good Kid Book.* New York: The New American Library, 1976.

Stewart, Nathaniel. *The Effective Woman Manager.* New York: John Wiley & Sons, 1978.

Wheatley, Meg, and Hirsch, Marcie Schorr. *Managing Your Maternity Leave.* Boston: Houghton Mifflin Co., 1983.

Where Does the Time Go? New York: United Media Enterprises, 1982.

White, Burton L. *The First Three Years of Life.* New York: Avon, 1975.

Wilkinson, Anna, and Pinkstaff, Marlene. *Women at Work.* Philippines: Addison-Wesley Co., 1979.

Winn, Marie. *Children Without Childhood.* New York: Pantheon, 1983.

Articles

Abeel, Erica. "Dark Success." *Esquire,* June 1984, pp. 258–66.

Andrews, Lori B. "Sisterhood on the Job." *Parents Magazine,* May 1983, pp. 27–33.

Bailey, Elizabeth. "Bringing Up Baby, 1984." *Savvy,* March 1984, pp. 86–88.

Barron, D. Susan. "Reviving the Rituals of the Debutante." *New York Times Magazine,* Jan. 15, 1984, pp. 26–34.

Baruch, Grace; Barnett, Rosalind; and Rivers, Caryl. "Saved by the Job." *Working Mother,* Aug. 1984, pp. 23–30.

Bart, Pauline B. "Depression in Middle-Aged Women." In *Woman in Sexist Society,* edited by Vivian Gornick and Barbara K. Moran. New York: Basic Books, 1971.

Bedell, Madelon. "We Are Never Tired . . ." *Ms,* May 1973, pp. 82–88.

Bernard, Jessie. "The Family." *Radcliffe Quarterly,* June 1979, pp. 3–6.

Bernikow, Louise. "We're Dancing As Fast As We Can." *Savvy,* Apr. 1984, pp. 40–43.

Birm, Orville, Jr., and Dustan, Jane. "Translating Research into Policy for Children." *American Psychologist* (Jan. 1983): 85–90.

Brody, Jane E. "Emotions Found to Influence Nearly Every Human Ailment." *New York Times,* May 24, 1983, pp. C1, C8.

Brozan, Nadine. "Day Care in New York: A Growing Need." *New York Times,* June 20, 1983, pp. C1, C8.

———. "Number of Women with Two Jobs Doubles in Decade." *Chicago Tribune,* July 1980, p. 10.

Burtman, Andrea. "The New Latchkey Kids." *Working Mother,* February 1984, pp. 78–83.

Cadden, Vivian. "Infant Care, What Money Can Buy." *Working Mother,* July 1983, pp. 57–75.

Caldwell, Bettye M. "Real Quality Time." *Working Mother,* May 1985, pp. 39–45.

Chodorow, Nancy. "Being and Doing: A Cross-Cultural Examination of the Socialization of Males and Females." In *Woman in Sexist Society,* edited by Vivian Gornick and Barbara K. Moran. New York: Basic Books, 1971.

Coburn, Judith. "Do Superwomen Really Exist?" *Mademoiselle,* Dec. 1981, p. 34.

Collins, Glenn. "Children and Stress; A Search for Causes." *New York Times,* Oct. 3, 1983, p. C1.

———. "Does Early Teaching Have Merit?" *New York Times,* Nov. 3, 1982, p. C8.

Cook, Mary F. "Is the Mentor Relationship Primarily a Male Experience?" *The Personnel Administrator* 24 (1979): 82–84.

Coughlan, Robert. "Modern Marriage." *Look Magazine,* Dec. 24, 1956, pp. 109–112.

Davis, Isabel Kaplan. "Success v. Femininity." *Second Century Radcliffe News,* Apr. 1984, p. 9.

Dalsimer, Katherine. "Fear of Academic Success in Adolescent Girls." *Journal of Child Psychiatry* 14, No. 4 (Autumn, 1975), pp. 346–352.

Dullea, Georgia. "Conference Discusses Parental Job Leaves." *New York Times,* Mar. 11, 1985, p. C11.

Doudna, Christine. "The New Madonnas." *Savvy,* June 1982, pp. 33–38.

Fitzpatrick, Jean Grasso. "Stop Working Late." *Working Woman,* Oct. 1983, pp. 71–72.

"Frankly Speaking." *Seventeen,* Dec. 1981, p. 71.

Glenn, Norval D. "The Contribution of Marriage to the Psychological Well-Being of Males and Females." *Journal of Marriage and the Family* (Aug., 1975), 1321–1329.

Glick, Paul C. "Updating the Life Cycle of the Family." *Journal of Marriage and the Family* 39 (1977): 3–15.

"Going for the Win." *Savvy,* May 1985, p. 17.

Goldberg, Rob. "Working Out at Work." *Savvy*, Dec. 1983, pp. 54–60.

Goleman, Daniel. "Boss Seen as Best Buffer Against Stress." *New York Times,* Jan. 31, 1984, pp. C1, C10.

———. "Confiding in Others Improves Health." *New York Times,* Sept. 18, 1984, pp. C1, C2.

———. "Chronic Arguing Between Parents Found Harmful to Some Children." *New York Times,* June 25, 1985, p. C3.

———. "Therapists Find Many Achievers Feel They're Fakes." *New York Times,* Sept. 11, 1984, pp. C1, C12.

Goodman, Ellen. "Prospects for the Future." *Radcliffe Quarterly,* June 1979, pp. 1–2.

Gould, Carole. "Sitting in for Jane P. Metzroth." *Savvy,* Sept. 1983, pp. 22–27.

Hammer, Singe. "When Women Have Power Over Women." *Ms,* Sept. 1978, pp. 49–52.

Hewlett, Sylvia Ann. "Child Carelessness." *Harpers,* Nov. 1983, pp. 20–25.

Horner, Matina. "The Motive to Avoid Success and Changing Aspirations of College Women." In *Readings in the Psychology of Women,* edited by Judith Bardwick. New York: Harper and Row, 1972, pp. 62–67.

"How Long Till Equality?" *Time,* Jul. 12, 1982, pp. 20–29.

Howell, Mary. "The Best Kind of Mother, Does She Have a Job or Stay Home?" *Working Mother,* Oct. 1983, pp. 124–27.

———. "To Spank or Not to Spank." *Working Mother,* Mar. 1985, p. 102.

———. "Superbabies: Why Mothers Want Them." *Working Mother,* Jan. 1985, pp. 71–72.

Hutschnecker, Arnold. "Do You Feel Guilty?" *Vogue,* July 1972, pp. 109–110.

"It Ain't Necessarily So." *Savvy,* Jan. 1985, pp. 43–47.

Johnson, F. A., and Johnson, C. L. "Role Strain in High Commitment Career Women." *Journal of the American Academy of Psychoanalysis* 4 (1976): 88–92.

Kamerman, Sheila. "The Child-Care Debate." *Working Woman,* Nov. 1983, pp. 131–35.

Klagsbrun, Francine. "Secrets and Pleasures of Long-Lasting Marriage." *Ms,* June 1985, p. 41.

Klemesrud, Judy. "Americans Assess 15 Years of Feminism." *New York Times,* Dec. 19, 1983, p. B16.

Kobasa, Suzanne Ouelette. "How Much Stress Can You Survive?" *American Health* (Sept. 1984): 64–77.

Lau, Barbara. "Necessary Breaks." *Working Woman,* July 1983, pp. 59–64.

Lenney, Ellen. "Women's Self-Confidence in Achievement Settings." *Psychological Bulletin* 84 (January, 1977), pp. 30–33.

Letters: "What a Career Means." *New York Times,* Feb. 9, 1983, p. C11.

Letters: "Working Mothers Effects on Children." *New York Times,* July 27, 1983, p. A 33.

Machlowitz, Marilyn. "Career Myths." *Working Woman,* June 1983, pp. 22–23.

Marshall, Christy. "When the Answer Is No." *Savvy,* Nov. 1983, pp. 32–33.

McMahon, I. D. "Relationships Between Causal Attributions and Expectancy of Success." *Journal of Personality and Social Psychology* 28 (1973): 108–114.

Minsky, Terri. "Advice and Comfort for the Working Mother." *Esquire,* June 1984, pp. 153–57.

Moneysmith, Marie. "The Dead-End Dilemma." *Savvy,* Jan. 1985, pp. 32–34.

"Motherhood in an Advertising Agency." *Working Mother,* July 1985, p. 43.

Monson, Karen. "Dual Career Families." *Radcliffe Centennial News,* July 1979, pp. 4–5.

Morscher, Betsy. "Achievement Anxiety: Career Sabotage." *Harper's Bazaar,* Mar. 1984, p. 274.

Moulton, Ruth. "Women with Double Lives." *Journal of Contemporary Psychoanalysis* 13 (Jan. 1977): 64.

Muenchow, Susan. "The Truth About Quality Time." *Parents Magazine,* May 1983, pp. 59–64.

Nordberg, Olivia Schieffelin. "Do You Have the Guts to Take a Risk." *Working Mother,* Mar. 1985, pp. 32–35.

Penney, Alexandra. "Is It Possible to Have (Good) Sex with the Same Person for 20 Years?" *Ms,* June 1985, pp. 52–53, 94.

Pogrebin, Letty, "Working Mothers." *Ladies' Home Journal,* Jan. 1974, p. 56.

Porter, Sylvia. "Last-In, First Out Job Myth Shattered." *Chicago Sun-Times,* Dec. 3, 1980, p. 81.

Rabiner, Sylvia. "How the Superwoman Myth Puts Women Down." *The Village Voice,* May 24, 1976, pp. 11–12.

"Recharging." *Ms,* May 1983, p. 66.

Renshaw, Domeena C. "Sex and the Female Psyche." *Comprehensive Therapy* 4 (1978): 17–21.

Robertson, Nan. "Job vs. Baby: A Dilemma Persists." *New York Times,* Nov. 18, 1982, pp. C1, C10.

Rose, Phyllis. "Hers." *The New York Times,* Apr. 19, 1984, p. C2.

Segal, Julius, and Yahraes, Herbert. "Bringing Up Mother." *Psychology Today,* Nov. 1978, pp. 90–96.

Seliger, Susan. "The Secret Fear of Being Found Wanting." *Working Mother,* Mar. 1985, pp. 108–110.

Shreve, Anita. "Careers and the Lure of Motherhood." *New York Times Magazine,* Nov. 21, 1982, pp. 39–56.

Siedenberg, Robert. "Is Anatomy Destiny?" In *Psychoanalysis and Women,* edited by Jean Baker Miller. Baltimore: Penguin Books, 1973, p. 306.

Simon, Jane. "Love: Addictions on Road to Self-Realization?" *The American Journal of Psychoanalysis* 35 (1975): 359–64.

Small, Linda Lee. "Nowhere Fast." *Working Mother,* May 1984, pp. 25–30.

"Sports Health." *Ms,* May 1983, p. 69.

"Stress: Can We Cope?" *Time,* June 6, 1983, pp. 48–54.

Stautberg, Susan Schiffer. "The Rat Race Isn't for Tots." *New York Times,* Aug. 27, 1984, p. A23.

Stone, Elizabeth. "Mothers and Daughters." *New York Times Magazine,* May 13, 1979, p. 16.

Symonds, Alexandra. "Neurotic Dependency in Successful Women." *Journal of the American Academy of Psychoanalysis* (Apr. 1976): 95–103.

"The Secret to Raising Healthy Happy Children." *U.S. News & World Report,* Sept. 1981, p. 46.

Thompson, Andrea. "Darling, I'd Go on the Class Trip . . ." *Working Mother,* Sept. 1984, pp. 76–78.

Thurow, Lester C. "Sixty-Two Cents to the Dollar." *Working Mother,* Oct. 1984, pp. 42–44.

Tifft, Susan, and Wachtel, Eric. "Exceptions to the Rules." *Savvy,* Nov. 1983, pp. 37–43.

Weisstein, Naomi. "Psychology Constructs the Female." In *Woman in Sexist Society,* edited by Vivian Gornick and Barbara K. Moran. New York: Basic Books, 1971.

Wernimont, Paul F., and Fitzpatrick, Susan. "The Meaning of Money." *Psychiatry* 41 (Feb., 1978), pp. 421–430.

Whelan, Elizabeth. "Confessions of a Superwoman." *Working Woman,* July 1981, pp. 61–64.

Willett, Roslyn S. "Working in 'A Man's World,' The Woman Executive." In *Woman in Sexist Society,* edited by Vivian Gornick and Barbara K. Moran. New York: Basic Books, 1971.

Wilson, James Q. "Raising Kids." *The Atlantic Monthly,* Oct. 1983, pp. 45–56.

Winn, Marie. "The Loss of Childhood." *The New York Times Magazine,* May 8, 1983, pp. 18–27.

Witkin-Lanoil, Georgia. "The Female Stress Syndrome." *Working Mother,* Nov. 1984, pp. 152–62.

Wolfe, Linda. "The New York Mother." *New York,* Sept. 10, 1984, pp. 32–39.

Wyse, Lois. "So Long, Supermom." *Good Housekeeping,* Jan. 1981, pp. 105–106.

Zigler, Edward. "Infant Day Care and Infant Care Leaves." *American Psychologist* (Jan. 1983): 91–94.

Zinsser, Caroline, "The Discipline Debate." *Working Mother,* July 1983, pp. 61, 86–88.

Index

achievement:
    men vs. women on, 117
    work and, 157
    see also success
Adams, Ruth, 148
advertisements, superwoman myth
    and, 49
alienation, home/work separation
    and, 148-49
Allen, David, 89
Allen, Jeffrey, 89
Allen, Jill, 89
American Couples (Schwartz and
    Blumstein), 162
American Psychologist, 19, 59
anxiety, *see* stress, stressful roles
anxiety eczema, 198–99
attachment:
    to babysitters, 70–73
    femininity and, 117
    as provocative term, 58–59
autonomy, discipline and, 96
Axtman, Annette, 65

baby boom, 30
baby-sitters, 70–75, 129, 130
    as assistants, 73
    communicating with, 73–74
    firing of, 71–72, 74–75
    housework and, 167
    late arrival of, 11–14
    as mother, 72
    sick, 148, 206
    traits sought in, 72, 75, 128
Bailey, Elizabeth, 102
Ball, Lucille, 30

Ballou, Judith, 57
Barnett, Rosalind, 123, 195
Bart, Pauline, 37
Baruch, Grace, 123, 195
Beauvoir, Simone de, 22
Bedell, Madelon, 46
behaviorists, child rearing as
    viewed by, 31
behavior modification, 96, 190
Bell, Amanda, 47
Berman, Eleanor, 124–25, 126
Bernard, Jessie, 53
Bernstein, Doris, 37, 41, 44
Bird, Caroline, 48
birth rate, in 1950s, 30
biting problems, 94–95
Blake, Terry, 38, 39
Blanck, Gertrude, 26
Blaustein, Alvin, 157, 184, 185
Blum, Harold, 129
Blumstein, Philip, 162–63, 172,
    178–79, 184
bonding, as provocative term, 58–59
Born Female (Bird), 48
bosses, 125–26, 148, 196
Bradt, Peggy, 100–101
Brasch, Susan J., 153
Brazelton, T. Berry, 60, 61, 78, 92–
    93, 130
breast-feeding, 31
Broderick, Carlfred B., 179
business calls, from home, 150
business trips, 110, 215–17
    explanation of, 104–5
    guilt about, 90, 104
    stress and, 206
buying, as overcompensation, 84–87

with, *see* mother-daughter
  relationship
Daughters of Earth (Smedley),
  214–15
Davis, Susan, 45
day care, *see* child care
Demonstration Nursery Center, 67–68
deodorants, advertisements for, 49
depression, 37
  buying patterns and, 85–86
De Rosis, Helen, 141
designer clothing, 103–4
Detroit Edison, 30
Deutsch, Helene, 30
developmental approach to child
  rearing, 31
Dincin, Frances, 189
discipline, 92–97
discrimination:
  job, 29–30
  wage, 17–18
domesticity, cult of, 29–34
Douglas, Helen Gahagan, 29
Dwyer, Elaine, 81

Eden, Alvin, 53, 59, 78
education, 100–103
  marriage vs., 31, 39
  nursery schools and, 101
educational programs, overuse of,
  102–3
Eeyore's, 99
ego-ideal, 27, 41
Elkind, David, 100, 102, 103, 105
emotion:
  fatigue and, 184–85
  at work, 152
Employee Assistance Program, 207–8
"Equality of the Sexes" (Rossi), 48
ERBs (Educational Records Bureau
  examination), 101
Erdheim, Joan, 118, 127, 133
Etaugh, Claire, 19
Etzioni, Amitai, 19
executives, women as, 109–10
exercise, 209–12
extracurricular activities, overuse of,
  102–3

Fabrick, Stephen D., 105
family:
  democratization of, 179

romance of, 29–34
family meetings, 168
Farnham, Marynia, 30
Father and Child (Ross), 58
fathers:
  absent of guilt in, 25
  absent, 32
  lack of role conflict in, 25
  quality time and, 82–83
fatigue, emotional vs. physical
  sources of, 184–85
Fay, Madeline, 23
Female Stress Syndrome, The
  (Witkin-Lanoil), 200
Feminine Mystique, The (Friedan),
  35
femininity:
  attachment and, 117
  work and, 151–52
Financial Mothers, 203
firing:
  of baby-sitters, 71–72, 74–75
  fear of, 104
Fishman, Judy, 148–49, 152–53, 168
Flavell, John H., 100
Foshay, Ella, 43
fragmentation, home/work separation and, 148–49
Frailberg, Selma, 58
fraudulent feelings, 136–39
Free to Be You and Me, 161
Freud, Anna, 78
Freud, Sigmund, 26, 32, 157
Friedan, Betty, 49, 50
Friedman, Dana, 68–69

Galenson, Eleanor, 72–73
Galinsky, Ellen, 85, 96
Garonzik, Anne, 21
Gaylin, Willard, 172, 214
General Electric Company, 142
Gesell, Arnold, 31
gift-giving, as overcompensation,
  84–87
Gilligan, Carol, 117
Ginott, Haim G., 91
Glickman, Beatrice Marden, 65
goals, personal vs. career, 147
Gold, Cindy, 114–16
Gonçalves, Karen, 148
Good Housekeeping, 51
Graham, Katharine, 109